BRING IT ON

The
Complete
Story of the Cheerleading
Movie That Changed,
Like, Everything
(No, Seriously)

KASE WICKMAN

CHICAGO
REVIEW
PRESS

Published by Chicago Review Press Incorporated
814 North Franklin Street
Chicago, Illinois 60610
ISBN 978-1-64160-708-7

Select interview quotes have previously appeared in the author's article "'Bring It On':
The Complete Oral History," MTV News, August 6, 2015, http://www.mtv.com
/news/2224189/bring-it-on-complete-oral-history/.

MTV's "MTV News" used with permission by MTV.
© 2015 Viacom Media Networks. All Right Reserved. MTV, all related titles,
characters and logos are trademarks owned by Viacom Media Networks, a
division of Viacom International Inc.

Library of Congress Control Number: 2022945027

Interior design: Sarah Olson
Original line art: Damien Scogin

Printed in the United States of America
5 4 3 2 1

C O N T

ENTS

Part II

TAKE A BIG
WHIFF:
The Legacy

Page 159

INTRODUCTION

GET FIRED UP!

Ready? OK!

Let's just say it, loud, right into the megaphone for the folks in the back: *Bring It On* deserves a place in the cinematic canon and recognition as an Important Film.

It's the quintessential underdog story—I'm talking not about the Clovers or the Toros or members of either squad but about the film itself. Screenwriter Jessica Bendinger pitched the movie twenty-seven times before she got the go-ahead to put the film into development with Beacon Pictures, devoting years to research, writing, and pitching before getting the nod. And that nod? One producer recalls literally begging on her knees to get her boss to say yes to making the movie. That doesn't even account for what it took to get Universal Studios to agree to front the money for the production and distribution of the movie. (Even Mr. Tom Hanks,

1

never where you expect him to be, was involved at one point, supposedly eyeing the script and eventually landing the soundtrack on his Playtone record label imprint.) Even once the cameras started rolling, filmmakers felt that the movie's distributor met their rah-rah with a shrug.

A thousand butterflies had to flap a thousand wings before a single pom-pom was picked up on set.

Studio executives seemed to have a million excuses why *Bring It On* wouldn't work: There wasn't a star attached. Women don't watch movies. Men don't watch movies about women. Cheerleaders are dumb. Everyone hates cheerleaders; no one's going to see a movie about them. Actually, everyone loves cheerleaders, so they're boring. Women won't watch sports movies, and men won't watch sports movies about women, and, excuse me, who even said that cheerleading is a *sport*? One director was attached, and then not; another teen cheerleading movie was set to eclipse *Bring It On*, and then not; a star was interested, and then not; and on and on. The saying goes that you only need one yes, but if I've learned anything in reporting the complete story of the greatest cheerleading film that was almost never made, it's that in filmmaking, you actually need a multitude of yeses, over and over and over again. Yes to the pitch, the director, the cast, the soundtrack, every single day, a veritable relay race of yeses to get to August 25, 2000, *Bring It On*'s opening day in theaters—the butterfly effect, but imagine a pair of rah-rahing pom-poms where those wings would be.

The rest is pop culture history, affecting careers, language, cheerleading, popular racial literacy, and the future of filmmaking itself.

As for me, in August 2000 I was a freshly minted twelve-year-old in Eugene, Oregon, a volleyball player and budding musical theater dork who almost exclusively wore oversized T-shirts, soccer shorts, and flip-flops, the whole look really chef's-kissed with the oval wire-rimmed glasses we found out I needed after I read the Baby-Sitters Club Little Sisters book where Karen can't read the chalkboard and gets an eye test. If it sounds like I might not be the target demo for *Bring It On*, the anti-cool girl, *ha*, how wrong you are. I was flashing my own spirit fingers around Monroe Middle School and could (still can) recite every word to the opening cheer of the movie, as could all of my mall goth tween pals. In fact, a few years ago, going through boxes in my childhood bedroom, I found a one-sheet poster for the movie, probably ripped out of *Teen* magazine, perfectly preserved. If you've ever wondered whether you've always been the person you are, well, there's Exhibit A for you.

However, I was no more or less a *Bring It On* superfan than the next person (I firmly believe that the magnetic pull of Kirsten Dunst and Gabrielle Union combined is more than any human can withstand and absolutely dare you to find an American born after 1979-ish who doesn't immediately chirp "I love that movie!" when you mention *Bring It On*), until 2015, when I took up the mantle as unofficial historian for the movie by writing an oral history for MTV News in honor of the film's fifteenth anniversary. It was then that I uncovered the untold stories from all those years ago, from the (alleged!) arrests in Mexico to the tubes and tubes of Bengay the cast relied upon while they trained at cheer camp for the film. And now, more than two decades after the movie's release, there's even more to be told. While working on this book, I had the pleasure of talking on the phone and video chatting with more than seventy people for endless hours, and went into my seventh year (seriously) of reading daily Google Alerts for the phrase "bring it on," as I reported on the making and cultural impact of one of the greatest sports movies of our time.

The classic teen movie is kind of weird when you think about it (which, as you might imagine, I've done a lot): the experience of being a teenager is both universal and deeply specific, all at once. Every adult, after all, had to be fourteen for *an entire year*. Harsh, right? But the experiences are so personal, depending on your family, the year, the geography, all these other factors. Movies about being a teenager are even more complicated, since 99 percent of the time they're art made by people who aren't living those experiences anymore, starring people who aren't living those experiences anymore, *for* people living them now. No wonder we all have reputations for being so surly as adolescents; there's no way to escape being talked *at*. This book is the story of *Bring It On* and its legacy told through my eyes. I wasn't there when it was made (shocking, I know), I was busy scheming about how I could earn enough money from chores to order an American Girl doll over the phone. These stories are shaded not only by the decades that have passed and the memories of those telling them but also by those peoples' experiences talking about those memories and thinking about them. They're influenced by my own personal experiences—of life, of the movie, of connecting with all of these people and spending hours talking to them about how they made it and what they meant, and then how it was experienced. There will be quibbles and fact-checks and feelings, I'm sure. There always are. It's been a long time, and everyone is their own sharp-focus main character. This is, to the best of my ability and effort, the story of *Bring It On*, as told by me, Kase Wickman.

If you've ever waggled a spirit finger; wondered what the hell a front handspring step out, roundoff back handspring step out, roundoff back handspring full twisting layout is; or even vaguely thought, "Huh, I didn't realize the guy from *Ant-Man* somehow got his start directing a movie about high school cheerleaders and cultural appropriation"—and why we're still talking about it today, so many years later—this book is for you.

Like totally freak me out? I mean, right on. Grab your spankies, warm up those spirit fingers, and pass the spirit stick. A cheerleading movie that changed everything? I say: bring it on.

PART I

BLOOD, SWEAT, AND CHEERS

Making Bring It On

"The words 'big' and 'britches' come to mind."

—Darcy

"It's a mixed feeling: at first we think it's ridiculous, but you have to admire the difficulty and the audible-gasp-inducing risk." That's from page 1 of Jessica Bendinger's original treatment for *Cheer Fever*, dated August 26, 1996.

In the beginning, there was Jessica Bendinger. If you really want to *get* this movie, to understand how *Bring It On* transcended the label of teen cheerleading comedy and became the cultural touchstone that it is now, more than two decades later, then it's important to get to know a little about Bendinger, the film's screenwriter and mythical mother.

Before a single rah could be rahed or spirit stick could clatter to the ground with deafening metaphorical meaning, Jessica Bendinger was just a gymnastics-obsessed kid in Connecticut. Born in 1966, she had the same long, straight blonde hair back in her tweenage days that she has today, though now her screenwriting savvy is just as much a signature as her blunt-cut bangs.

"I was a very serious gymnast up until I had a growth spurt between, I guess, sixth and seventh grade or seventh and eighth grade," she told me in 2015. "I grew and I lost that sort of gravity and I couldn't do it anymore." She had been coached by Don Peters, who was later the record-breaking head coach of the US women's gymnastics team at the 1984 Summer Olympics (Mary Lou Retton brought home the gold from Los Angeles for the individual all-around, and the team took silver in the all-around competition, marking a new era in the Team USA program), and still later, in 2011, was stripped of his place in the USA Gymnastics Hall of Fame and banned from the sport for life after he was accused of sexually abusing three of his gymnasts, at least one of whom was seventeen at the time.

The seeds of hard-core athleticism and a healthy dose of Lycra were established at a young age, as was a natural gift for a turn of phrase inherited from a dad who worked in the ad business, along with a love for language that led her to major in English when she enrolled in Columbia University's class of 1988. Her professional jazz trombonist mother provided the showbiz gene. She was well versed in adapting to different situations, having spent significant time with both her mother in Connecticut and her father in Chicago. Oh, and there was also a healthy dash of glam: Jessica modeled in her teenage and young adult years. One of the first things I was told about her, before we ever even spoke, was that she posed for the cover of one of the Sweet Valley High books. (This is true—it's called *Questions of Love*.) She is five eleven without heels, according to her website, and for obvious reasons was bestowed the nickname "Tall-Ass Jessica" while in a friend group with multiple Jessicas. ("Short-Ass Jessica" was also accounted for.)

When Bendinger moved to New York City for college in the late '80s, she fell in love with hip-hop, the final ingredient in the primordial teen-movie stew that would, years later, evolve and become the idea for *Bring It On*.

"I know it was destined," she told me.

Maybe the true birthplace of *Bring It On* is the block of 116th Street between Broadway and Amsterdam Avenue in Morningside Heights, Columbia's Low Memorial Library. The hundred-plus-year-old building is a National Historic Landmark, and instead of containing the 1.5 million books it was designed for back in the late nineteenth century, it turns out it actually sucks at being a usable library (the best even the National Park Service can offer by explanation is that it "never really worked as a library reading room") and houses the university's administrative offices instead. This granite behemoth, however, is just a backdrop for the main event: the Steps.

The site of many speeches, Columbia's annual commencement, and many a hungover Friday-morning student meetup over coffee and bagels, the Steps are iconic, inseparable from the school's identity. It's also where an undergrad Bendinger got her first taste of step, a synchronized dance style historically performed by Black groups that audiences would eventually see mirrored on-screen in the Clovers' choreography style.

"There was a stepping competition on the steps of Low Library, and I had never seen step," she explained. "There was a Black fraternity that had done a demonstration, and it was fabulous, I was completely taken. One of the steps, which I've been credited for writing and I did not, [was] 'Brr, it's cold in here.' And I saw these very powerful, very passionate groups of Black step squads. I wrote it down, and I remembered it, as many people do, because it is such a catchy, memorable phrase."

At the same time, fish-out-of-water Bendinger, with her blend of an East Coast and a Midwestern upbringing, was finding her stream in New York. She worked as a fit model and a bartender, attended classes, did that uniquely New York thing where you make new friends and they are somehow Somebody and know even more Somebodies. Like how her friend Jessica Rosenblum worked the door at the now-defunct downtown music club Nell's, which Bendinger frequented because she could always get in. Which meant that she was in the room when Eric B. & Rakim personally handed the twelve-inch for "I Know You Got Soul" to the DJ to play. Which meant she met Def Jam cofounder Russell Simmons. Which meant she met the up-and-coming Beastie Boys and became "part of the Mike D posse" and danced onstage in Chicago at one of their concerts (she was asked to swap the Nikes she was wearing for Adidas before the show). Which meant that while she was chatting at a party about wanting to write, Bob Guccione Jr., son of *Penthouse* founder Bob Guccione and founder of music magazine *Spin*, overheard and took her on for an internship. And on and on and on.

"I had this crazy senior year of modeling and working at *Spin*, and knowing the Beastie Boys and playing Jay McInerney's message to me on my answering machine for people on my floor at school, going to the Grammys. I was in the front row of the Grammys, I think there's a shot of me I found somewhere, sitting in front of U2 at the Grammys," she told me. "Like, I was having the fucking time of my life. I was having a really good time, and I had no fucks to give. It was the late '80s in New York. There was no Internet. I was a hustler. And I was hustling for fun, and because I didn't know what the fuck I was gonna do with my life and I knew I had to maximize every possible opportunity at once, as only a person with anxiety knows how to do."

This go-go-go kept go-go-going. After graduation, Bendinger landed a permalance gig at MTV News, writing on-air copy for Kurt Loder. Went to L.A. for a string of pet-sitting and house-sitting gigs for a bit. She directed music videos, including for Queen Latifah's "Fly Girl," got nominated for a few Billboard Awards. She moved to France for a minute and wrote for TV there. All the while, she couldn't help but remember a press kit that had crossed her desk at *Spin*, for the 1989 movie *Say Anything*. When she read in writer-director Cameron Crowe's bio that he'd been a *Rolling Stone* journalist (as made, well, famous in fictionalized form in *Almost Famous*) before convincing John Cusack to hold up a boombox, Bendinger said, "It was like, oh my god, suddenly there was a path, I could go from writing about people creating to *creating*. . . . Really, it sounds so dumb now to say, but I needed somebody to say that I had permission to go from writing about music and movies and television to writing it myself. I didn't feel like I had the authority to do that."

So Bendinger, Tall-Ass Jessica, ended up in L.A., where she'd wanted to go all along. In the way that she always seemed to, she made friends, future boldfacers. She'd met Jeff and Marla Garlin in

France, kept the connection in California. Slept on the couch of a friend who ended up as director David Fincher's assistant. Fell in with the in crowd at the legendary alt-comedy show UnCabaret, which is still putting up its weekly shows to this day, on Zoom through the COVID-19 pandemic, and became friends with Richard Kind and Kathy Griffin. I think she was born under a friendly sign; Bendinger just says she's "super extroverted."

Broke and couch surfing, Bendinger straddled a dual reality where she was hustling but also had experiences like seeing Gwyneth Paltrow and Brad Pitt, then at the height of their extremely blond coupledom, at a house party with Fincher, about to break big for directing *Se7en*. "David used to call me Jessica Rabbit," Bendinger told me. Overhearing her fretting over her career, her (lack of) money, the usual twentysomething stuff, Fincher "turns around and says, 'You can write, Rabbit. Why are you fucking even dealing with any of us? You can write, you idiot.' And Mark says something like 'Yeah, you can write, like what are you worried about, just write!' . . . I didn't go to film school and the Fincher of it all and then the Cameron Crowe, right, and then I'm like, 'Oh, I have to write. Shit.' And in that moment it all came together in its own clunky way. And I wrote."

That "Mark," by the way, is *Mean Girls* director Mark Waters, another friendship forged through Bendinger's incredible feats of extroversion and right-time-right-place, who would end up being a lifelong friend and ally, along with his brother, *Heathers* screenwriter Daniel Waters.

Imagine you're throwing yourself a low-key birthday party at a bowling alley. So low key, in fact, that one of your guests might inform you that it kind of sucks and that you all should go to his *other* friend's birthday party. Imagine one of your guests is a pre-fame Kathy Griffin, and imagine that she uncomfortably agrees before you all kind of . . . migrate. It was the best-worst birthday Bendinger could have had.

"Somebody comes in, like, 'Hey, you know what, fuck this bowling bullshit. Dan Waters is having a big party, let's go to his house,'" she said. "And so we all leave my dumb bowling party and go to Dan Waters's, and that's where I meet Mark and Dan. As uninvited guests of Richard Kind at Danny's birthday party. Sure. And that's my life."

Daniel Waters agreed that their friendship was written in the stars. "[Jessica] came to my birthday, and we have the same birthday and, like, I don't know about her—I don't believe in astrology, but I believe in Scorpio. I think Scorpios are evolved beings, and I know she does too. And we're obsessed with November 10. For some reason, it's the greatest birthday. I've become friends with Zoey Deutch and Walton Goggins, and I was friends with Brittany Murphy, and they're all November 10 too. What is it about this great day? . . . We're not astrology freaks at all. Although she probably is but won't admit it. But anything November 10, we go crazy over. So we were instantly bonded, because we were in the November 10 club, even before we met each other, and then we have, like, obviously, a very similar sense of humor."

From there, a friendship—and ad hoc screenplay critique loop—was born. "[It was a] very weird birthday and the luckiest birthday I ever had," Bendinger told me.

Didn't anyone think it was weird for Bendinger to show up at Waters's blowout birthday bash, complete with what Dan referred to as "a very explicit and honest game show" of trivia about his life ("I think she did better than most people at the game show too, even though she hadn't met me"). "I never thought, 'Well, why wasn't she at her own birthday party?' but I guess it was a slow year," Dan mused when I asked about that fateful first hang.

"We had an immediate connection," Mark agreed.

Los Angeles is nothing if not an industry town, so of course it came up quickly that the Waters brothers were in film (Mark had graduated the AFI Conservatory for directing alongside Darren Aronofsky and would soon release *The House of Yes*), and that Bendinger aspired to be. That's when things got real for her, all Cameron Crowe revelations aside.

"I showed Mark, and Mark is like, 'What do you mean you're writing, show me, show me, show me!'" Bendinger said. "And I was like oh god, oh god, you know, this is real. He's at AFI, his brother wrote *Heathers*, you know, then it—all of a sudden it was very real.

Because then I knew: Oh, they know. They'll be able to tell if I can do it or not."

Bendinger had written a script called *Hit Girl*, about a depressed young woman who gets involved with a mob family, then gets made and made over. "It's very convoluted, it's very much a first script," she told me. "It's got way too much plot and way too much attitude for its own good."

Mark read it.

"You learn very early on that asking somebody to read your stuff is a big imposition, and it was then, too, really hard to get people to read your stuff, and even harder to get somebody who's meaningful to read your stuff," Bendinger said. "You just don't do it unless you have a high level of confidence. And I showed Mark Waters my little, whatever, scraggly pages of *Hit Girl*. And he met me at Starbucks on Crescent Heights and Sunset. And he was very stern, and I was like, 'Oh, they suck, I suck,' I was like, this isn't gonna be good, and I sat down and he was like, 'You're an asshole.' Why? 'Because you can fucking write.' And I was like, oh shit. He was like, 'And you haven't finished this? Like, dude, you can fucking write. You have to finish this.' And he's like, 'Look, here's a problem and here's some rules, but like, you can fucking do this.' And really, I could cry. Bow down to Mark Waters."

"I meet a lot of screenwriters, a lot of would-be filmmakers," Mark told me. "She shared the script called *Hit Girl* with us. And it was interesting because you know a lot of the dreck that you go through—*Hit Girl* was like, this person has a voice, this person has style and knows how to write dialogue, and there was a feel to it that was exciting and I remember telling her, 'Yeah, I don't know if it's easy to get this movie made, but this script certainly shows that you can write, and so it's going to do things for you whether or not it actually gets made.'"

Spoiler: it did not get made. This book is not about *Hit Girl*. ("I was like, if this doesn't sell, I'm done, and it didn't sell and I wasn't done, so, you know, whatever," Bendinger said. "People in their twenties don't know shit about shit, I think was the lesson that I learned from that.") But armed with new confidence and connections, Bendinger took the script out and found an agent and some traction. She started batting around new ideas.

Beth Lapides, the founder of the UnCabaret comedy show in Los Angeles and the "godmother of alternative comedy," according to the *L.A. Times*, had taken Bendinger under her wing. They met for lunch at an Italian place on Los Feliz, where over "some sort of Caesar salad event, I'm sure," in Lapides's memory, Bendinger bounced ideas for screenplays off her.

"She pitched me a couple of things. I don't remember what the other things were," Lapides said. "But I do remember very clearly being like, 'Oh, the cheerleader one, write the cheerleader one.' Her demeanor was very bright when she was pitching it—it seemed super unique. I mean, the thing is, as a writer you can think of a million things, but what's the thing that you need to write, that the world needs to hear from you? And that people want to buy from you, that people want to go to, because *you* did it, and it was just so obviously this movie."

Bendinger had first noticed competitive high school cheerleading on ESPN in her high school years and, given her gymnastics experience, its combination of athleticism and absurdity made an impression. "It's just so funny. It was quirky and weird. Who are they cheering for? It was just so all-American, like of course Americans have everything on steroids. I loved it. I just watched them with this weird rabid interest." The cheerleaders in her suburban town growing up were very much of the iconic, popular, beautiful archetypical mold, Bendinger recalled. "Cheerleaders always held this kind of very strong sway over me, and I just always pay attention to that."

But Bendinger needed just one more sign to fully accept what the Waters brothers, Lapides, and even her own gut knew: confirmation from the universe itself that this cheerleader movie was what she should throw her weight behind.

"It blew my mind," Dan Waters said. "She went to a psychic and asked about her upcoming projects."

Bendinger, today, seemed startled and amused to be reminded of the psychic. "Good job, Dan! I'm very curious and I love the unknown and the mystical and I've always had a fascination with that stuff. When I feel anxious, especially when I was younger, it would certainly kick in. And so I think I would try to regulate my anxiety with some certainty, even if it was paid for." She visited someone she described as a semi-deaf psychic in the Valley whom she'd been to before, one who used a trailer out back for his office and sat in front of an oil painting of himself as a child clairvoyant, holding a crystal ball. She asked which project she should be putting her chips on.

Waters recalls, "He didn't know the title, so he wrote down on a piece of paper, *Cheer Virus*, and Jessica goes, 'Oh my god, I'm doing something called *Cheer Fever!*' and he was like, 'Oh, good. That's a better title."

Cheer Fever—which would eventually become *Bring It On*—was a go. At the very least, the universe (and Bendinger) thought so. There was still the small matter of actually writing the script, not to mention selling it to a studio and actually seeing it through production and release. Details.

"I was like, OK, I got no Plan B, let's just hunker down," she said.

It was 1996, and Bendinger had an agent, a sharp script treatment, and a drive to get the thing made, which was good, because it took twenty-seven meetings and pitches before a studio would sign on the dotted line, finally, at meeting number twenty-eight. To add to the drudgery, Bendinger drove to many of those pitches in the 102-degree August L.A. heat in her old Saab, a sort of bronzey gold with a maroon interior and an unpredictable transmission. Which, it's also worth noting, didn't have functioning air-conditioning. "It was ridiculous. I had to bring a change of clothing," she said. "I'd have to change my shirt in the bathroom before going into the meeting." It feels safe to assume that anywhere she walked was uphill both ways, the way this pitch process went.

One of her first pitch meetings was with Michael Besman, then a producer for TriStar at Columbia TriStar Motion Picture Group, which was owned by Sony. He'd worked on *Sleepless in Seattle* and *Jumanji*, among others. More important for our story, he was (and remains) what I'd categorize as a Nice Long Island Boy, hailing from

Mineola, New York. (I know this type well, having married one who grew up less than ten miles away from there.)

"I didn't know what I was doing," Bendinger recalled of that first pitch, where she was sweating and reading off a sheet of paper, terrified. "I did it all wrong." Besman—"wonderful," "really funny"—kindly leveled with her: it needed some work. "I'm pitching it and he is like, 'Girl, this is a mess. You can't pitch this. You don't know what the fuck you are doing.' And he said, 'I'll help you, write this all down in order,' and I had to fax it to him. It wasn't even e-mail. It was crazy."

"It was all my idea, how's that? I'm still waiting for the check," Besman said wryly. (For the record, Bendinger did send him a framed and signed poster when the movie was released—"It was very sweet," Besman said—and the two speak of each other fondly.) He remembers Bendinger as "lovely and fun and hip" and the story as "lacking movie-star roles," a critique that Bendinger would hear again and again, due to the age of the characters and the skill set required for the cheering, a major stumbling block when it came to convincing producers and executives to buy a movie. Then, as now, the first equation in the *Math for Movie Studios* textbook is "Movie stars = box office numbers." Things changed when Bendinger pulled out the secret weapon of her pitch: the tapes of real cheerleading competitions. Besman was hooked, invested.

"I was like, 'Oh my god, this is, like, special effects time. This is so cool.' It's not just, you know, rah-rah-rah-sis-boom-bah. It's like people flying through the air, you know? So I was like, 'Oh my god, this is so fun.'"

He committed to workshopping and refining the pitch and overall story with Bendinger before it went to any higher-ups. "So it had an emotional focus, and you cared about the characters, things have logic to them," he said. "I just kept challenging her about what happened. 'Why does this happen? Why does that happen?' You know, like anyone would in order to understand the story, and create emotional characters and rootable characters and understand the stakes and things like that. We did that, and she was great. I think I drove her a little nuts, but she was totally into it, and was very appreciative and great."

Bendinger has in fact now refined the pitch so far as to make it into a modern-day screenwriting curriculum, publishing *The Bring It On Book* in honor of the film's twentieth anniversary in 2020. Fans and aspiring screenwriters—and, hell, anyone who's just interested, I don't make the rules—can compare the original treatment for the movie, dated August 26, 1996, with the film's final shooting script. This is an extremely vulnerable move by Bendinger, to put her original work and early writing out there. *The Bring It On Book* is equally helpful in understanding how stories change through revision to become coherent movies that are still discussed decades later. All thirty-nine beats of the original outline, from the opening at cheer camp at North Carolina State University to a finale of Torrance writing to the International Olympic Committee to advocate for cheerleading's inclusion in the games (cut from the final film, but prescient for the real world), are documented.

Max Wong, ultimately an executive producer of *Bring It On*, said, "I have used the pitch to *Bring It On* as an example of why the Writers Guild credits the original writer. Because even though there were rewrites and [new jokes], every single character arc that you see on-screen was in the original pitch, down to the farting, bratty little brother."

Barry Jenkins, who won Best Adapted Screenplay and Best Picture for *Moonlight* in 2019, specifically cited Bendinger's outline style as how he gets started with his award-winning scripts, every single time, in an interview with the Writers Guild of America West. "I don't know if I was in film school or just out of it at the time I read it," he said of Bendinger's technique, which she'd written a blog post about prior to publishing the book, "and she had this simple approach to generating a story outline. It was three beats: the beginning, the middle, the end. And then you craft the beginning, middle, and end of the beginning, middle and end. And so on. You build the story from all these mini-stories within the stories. I always do that no matter what project I'm working on. It's a very simple thing you can always do."

Which isn't to say that the outline was perfect, by any means.

"I think the first draft of *Cheer Fever* had six endings," Bendinger wrote in her book. Five more than you're looking for. A problem. But the bones were there: "It was always *Clueless*, it was *Strictly Ballroom* set at the national high school cheerleading championship, that was kind of my log line," she told me. "The hip-hop piece was really the secret sauce, and that was very much in the pitch."

Besman worked with her to get the pitch into fighting shape. "I just remember talking to her on Saturdays, and she came to my office a few times, talking it over," he said. "I specifically remember a Saturday like really laying into her. Like, what's going on here or why's she doing that, what's happening here, what does this mean?"

Finally, the treatment for the movie was ready. Besman liking the pitch wasn't enough to get it made; as a producer, he had to sell his bosses on it to pay for it and put it into production, make it a real movie. He set up a meeting at TriStar with "a young executive who deserves to be known for passing on it, scumbag," Besman joked. "Now we've laughed about it. I mean, I think we laughed? He laughed."

"We pitched it to [him], and [he] was like, 'Oh my god, this is so great, blah blah blah.' He said, you know, 'That's the best pitch I've ever heard, but I'm gonna have to pass.'"

This was to become an unrelenting refrain for Bendinger during that sticky, stressful summer of 1996, as she visited studio after studio, making her pitch. She knew it was good, she knew people liked it, but for whatever reason, she couldn't get that final rubber stamp. "Sometimes I'd go to a studio and they'd love it and they'd take it to *their* boss and they go, 'We love it!' And take it to *their* boss, and then it would get a pass at the third time."

For Besman, *Bring It On* is still the one that got away. "I gotta tell you, I was so pissed. It was such a success. I love the movie, I've seen it like twenty times," he said. At that point, he had just pivoted to a producer role and had an exclusive deal with Sony, so he wasn't free to pursue the pitch further than he did once Sony passed. "What an opportunity, but what are you gonna do?"

"She went deep, she really researched it," he said. "[Bendinger] really earned this."

Her friends rallied her on, talking her up after the dozens of promising meetings that ultimately went nowhere. Dan Waters remembered, "I think, like, since I had been through the process, and *Bring*

It On and *Cheer Fever* was much more commercial than my thing, I never lost faith. I thought, oh well, for sure this is going to be made. That if *Heathers* can be made, then *Bring It On* can definitely be made. I was probably less worried than she was."

The Blacklist didn't exist yet, but if it had, it's almost certain that *Cheer Fever* would have been on it. The famed peer-sourced roundup of the best unproduced screenplays has been published annually since 2005 to the great interest of curious financiers looking for their next box office hit or golden office-mantel decor, taking great stories and unusual voices from "appreciated but never made" to Oscar bait (*Juno, The King's Speech, Argo, The Social Network,* and *Manchester by the Sea,* all of which won Oscars for their screenplays, are also all Blacklist alums, to name just a few of the list's honorees).

"Honestly, it was so good that it would have gotten made eventually," Eric Hughes said. "But again, it had been out there for a [while] and hadn't gotten made. Who would have been that person that stepped in and kind of believed in it enough? But I think that you just needed that perfect storm of people coming together that believed in it to actually get it up off the ground."

Hughes—now a celebrity interior decorator for the likes of Sarah Jessica Parker and in the late '90s an executive at Turner Pictures who heard Bendinger's pitch—was excited by *Cheer Fever's* potential. Spoiler: though he didn't buy the pitch at Turner, this isn't the last we'll see of Hughes in the *Bring It On* story.

Elsewhere in Los Angeles, Bendinger took what would turn out to be a fateful meeting at Beacon Pictures. To hear Caitlin Scanlon and Max Wong tell it, they were instantly captivated by Bendinger's pitch. Wong, the junior executive to Scanlon's senior, had met Bendinger when they both worked at the music video production house Limelight, where Bendinger had directed the video for Queen Latifah's "Fly Girl." Jon Shestack, another Limelight alum who had brought Wong with him to Beacon, was Scanlon and Wong's boss, so he knew Bendinger too.

"When she brought in this pitch I was just sort of like, 'Oh cool, this girl music video director that I knew is pitching movies now, that's kind of rad,'" Wong said. She and Scanlon quickly moved from "kind of rad" to "absolutely obsessed" when they heard Bendinger's pitch, complete with that footage of real elite high school cheerleaders leaving everything on the floor in competition, her secret weapon in those drab production meeting rooms.

"We always describe it as like a car crash, because you can't take your eyes away from this carnage," Wong told me of the video portion of the pitch. "It's super emotional because in the tape, cheerleaders are getting their teeth knocked out and . . . the sportscaster does the Telestrator where they circle the tooth on the tarmac. And the cheerleader is doing a huge smile and she's, like, got blood gushing out of her mouth and she's finishing her cheer, or the girl who totally biffs it, you just see her face and like she's crying and she's smiling because she knows that she's ruined the chances for her entire squad but she has to maintain her presentation as best she can. It was super emotional in a way that most sports sort of aren't. We loved it."

It wasn't only the tape but also Bendinger's passion for the project that caught Wong and Scanlon's attention. Even after all these meetings, she still wanted it, *bad*. Her belief in the project was infectious.

"That's the thing about Jessica: she in her heart is a cheerleader" is how Lapides described her friend's tenacious attitude to me. She's "more than just enthusiastic, but enthusiastic for things that benefit from the enthusiasm. I mean the specific thing about cheerleading, what separates it from other—I mean, you could be enthusiastic about roses or you could be an enthusiastic coin collector. But [in cheerleading] your enthusiasm has an effect on the thing that is happening. And that's different than just enthusiasm."

Bendinger remembers the pitch to Beacon . . . differently.

"I walked in and I was like, 'Hey, you're not gonna buy this. You guys are making *Air Force One*, you're never gonna buy this,' and there you go," she said.

And, frankly, that's not *not* how it went. Though Scanlon and Wong were captivated from the get-go—they both adored musicals, had grown up spoon-fed on *Grease*, and saw the potential for a female-led sports-movie-cum-dance-flick with musical theater sensibilities—but their bosses, whose final OK they would need to buy the pitch and put it into development were . . . not quite as enthused.

"For us, it was a no-brainer," Scanlon said. She and Wong presented "the equivalent of a PowerPoint presentation, these long memos for our bosses," citing the demographics of filmmaking, teen girl attendance at movies, Black moviegoers that the project would appeal to. "We worked in a very male-driven industry and a male-driven company . . . it wasn't a no-brainer to them."

Marc Abraham, a cofounding partner of Beacon and one of the rubber stamps of approval necessary for the production house to buy a pitch, remembers that Scanlon and Wong "kind of implored" him to read the treatment. "And I read it. And I went, well, OK. I mean, I'm not quite sure what to do with this."

Tom Bliss, Beacon's chief operating officer (COO), was similarly hesitant at first, taken aback by what he remembers as an excess of cheerleading jargon. "When the project came in, Marc and I really weren't interested at all," he said. He found the cheerleading terms "unintelligible," he said. "Probably looking back there were like fifty words that I was like, I don't know what that means."

Still, both Abraham and Bliss now claim that they saw at least a glimmer of what Scanlon and Wong did in the pitch, despite their initial reluctance.

"It seemed kind of light," Abraham said. "But it definitely had a voice. . . . That's one of the most important things. I was able to appreciate that Jessica had a point of view. . . . It was a good piece of writing, but it was unfinished. And a lot of things about it needed to be kind of shaped and honed and edited, like any good script or any piece of material."

And that's when the begging started.

"We literally crawled on our hands and knees on the carpet in front of Marc Abraham, and the only time I had begged on my hands and knees on the carpet of his office was for *Scream*, which they had also passed on," Wong recalled.

For his part, Abraham says, "I don't remember anybody begging on their knees. It would have been me probably as a case, but if Caitlin says it, I'll go with it. She might have, I don't know. I mean, I may have played devil's advocate. I may have thought, you know, in the beginning, it wasn't a good idea. I can't remember. I don't remember that. But if Caitlin says it, I'm sure it was true." (Bliss added, "Oh god, I wish you hadn't told me that," when I brought up the *Scream* story. Hindsight!)

"It was all about trying to get our bosses to spend the money, make the movie," Scanlon said. "We just knew it would make the money, even if it sucked. We figured it would make the money, and we were so enthusiastic about it and were willing to work so hard that we also wouldn't *let* it suck."

"Caitlin and I were both like, Do you not want to be rich? Are you afraid of success?" Wong said. "We sort of kind of shamed them into it. They were willing, just because . . . I think to shut us up."

And there you have it: in September 1996, for the Writers Guild's minimum fee, Bendinger's *Cheer Fever* got a green light from Beacon Pictures.

It turns out that the whole "you only need one yes" adage is absolute BS when it comes to getting a movie made. It takes a thousand yeses, everyone from the writer to producers to studios to actors and theaters and even you, the individual theatergoer. (As it turns out, box office results sometimes speak louder than words.)

"The first big hurdle," Wong said, "[was] actually getting it into development in our company, and then it took four years of Caitlin and I . . . marching it around town, trying to get it to different directors and attach different stars to make it exciting to our studio, and it just wasn't happening. People would call us on it all the time, because we would call them up like, 'Oh my god, there's so much happening with [*Cheer Fever*]!' And people were like, 'No, there's not. Stop.'"

All the goodwill Bendinger had gained in the production community with her must-make pitch and the Beacon green light wasn't *quite* enough to get *Cheer Fever* financed, produced, and distributed. The script, having been written, rewritten, tweaked, and polished by Bendinger, was languishing in development. Wong was also developing what would become Alfonso Cuaron's Oscar-nominated *Children of Men*, and Scanlon was producing the comedy *Trippin'*, among other projects for the duo. But they never gave up on *Cheer Fever*, shopping it around to different studios in search of a distribution and production partner.

"When we say that everyone passed, except for Tim O'Hair, who was our internal Universal executive, all the other executives took turns passing on our project in the meanest possible way," Wong said. "They just really didn't like it, they really thought it was stupid."

Ready to roll your eyes? *Cheer Fever* was broadly seen as a "girl movie." And "girl movies" didn't look like big box office to studio execs and decision-makers.

"There was a moment in time in our business when young girls were not seen as a viable demographic to be able to support a film," Abraham said. "Ironically, it changed. And people got their heads wrapped around it and started realizing that young girls were really incredibly influential. But it was sort of like, well, if the guy wants to go to the movie, the girl goes with them. Of course, that turned out to not be true at all. But at that time, it was [considered] true. And if you look back . . . the teen movies were male-oriented. That's one of the reasons that [*Bring It On*] got so much traction, ultimately, was because it was empowering." But that vital element that would eventually make this underdog movie a champ was then what kept it firmly on the bench.

To vault *Cheer Fever* out of development purgatory and into production, it took that perfect storm that Hughes mentioned earlier, and it turns out that its eye had a name: Jonathan Demme.

Demme won the Best Director Oscar in 1992 for his work on *The Silence of the Lambs* (the movie also captured Best Picture, Best Screenplay, Best Actor, and Best Actress, one of only three films to ever sweep all five major categories; the others are 1934's *It Happened One Night* and 1975's *One Flew Over the Cuckoo's Nest*), so just a few years later, the shine was still there and he had more than plenty of cachet. If the man who brought you Hannibal Lecter feels like a jarring match with a lighthearted cheerleading comedy, consider that Demme later directed Meryl Streep in the rocker musical *Ricki and the Flash* and that his final feature-length film directing project before his death in 2017 was the concert documentary *Justin Timberlake + the Tennessee Kids*. The guy had range, is what I'm saying.

Now, how exactly it happened depends on who's telling the story, but the script for *Cheer Fever* made its way into Demme's hands, and that made all the difference in the world.

Los Angeles is roughly 503 square miles, and the area designated as Hollywood is about a 30.7 square mile slice. To run its perimeter would be a little under the distance of a marathon—not easy, but generally doable. So it makes sense that this tiny little portion of the country that accounts for the majority of the film industry is, in reality, a pretty small town, where everyone knows everyone and looks out for their friends. It's the ultimate insider network.

You may not know Kristi Zea's name at first mention, but you've absolutely seen her work. She was a frequent Demme collaborator, the production designer for *The Silence of the Lambs*, the *Manchurian Candidate* remake, and *Philadelphia*. She also production designed *Goodfellas* and *The Departed*, among others, and was an accomplished second unit director. In the late '90s, while *Cheer Fever* was limbering up and waiting for its chance to fly, she was looking for projects to direct. She knew the Beacon crew in the way that everyone knows everyone and everyone has met with everyone in Hollywood.

"[Kristi] came in for this meeting, we gave her the script, she loved it," Wong said. "There was nothing else like it in the market at the time, and that was something that appealed to her, because if you've ever seen a Jonathan Demme movie, like, her visual style is *his* style. And so she was like, 'This is really weird, but this is really weird in a good way.'"

"I don't know if Caitlin got it to her, or it just was in the ether and her agents were looking around and they said, 'Oh, well, maybe this is a good one for you,'" Abraham recalled. "And so they gave it to Kristi. And then she wanted to direct it. And I met with her. And I really liked Kristi, but I was worried and concerned that she didn't have a lot of [directing] experience. And it was a questionable project at best." (Remember: "girl movie." Since everyone knows girls . . . don't like . . . movies?)

A step back, for a moment, to talk logistics. Beacon had given *Cheer Fever* the green light, but as a boutique production shingle, they needed a bigger studio to put up the majority of the film's shooting budget, then market and distribute the movie. Think of it like a loan: In exchange for the production company, Beacon in this case, paying a distribution fee to the studio, and often a portion of the film's back-end profits or home video revenue, the studio fronts the production budget and marketing fees, to be paid back with the box office revenue. Beacon had a multipicture first-look deal with Universal Studios, meaning Universal had right of first refusal on Beacon's greenlit projects, like *Cheer Fever*. The script had crossed the desk at Universal, but it just kept right on going. As the project was developed, if substantive changes had been made, Beacon would bring the script back for another pass. By the time Bendinger had completed the script and Scanlon and Wong had guided the development process, Beacon COO Bliss, who had a tween daughter himself, had come around and become a champion of the project. He just *knew* it was going to be something. It had to get made.

"This only happened to me a couple times, it was this project, *Air Force One*, and *Children of Men* where I read it, and . . . it's hard to explain because it's an emotional thing, right?" he said. "You can't really put feelings into words, but it just struck me, and this one was just so full of joy, so fun, and, I gotta say, so inexpensive." The financial risk to the studio, he explained, was incredibly low. He became an advocate for the movie, eventually talking Abraham around as well. "It just really struck me as—this could be really great," Bliss said.

Meanwhile, Abraham was having trouble stirring up interest at Universal, even with the award-winning Zea's enthusiasm for the project. "They were very respectful, because she's super talented, but it wasn't getting any real traction in terms of her being a director that would motivate them to say, yes, let's make the movie," he said. "Because, historically, you get the right director—*The Commitments* only got made because we got Alan Parker to direct it. Without Alan Parker, that's not a movie that would have ever gotten made. But Alan Parker is brilliant. And he was at that time a major, major A-list director and rightfully so. So without a director who had some cachet, it wasn't helping us."

Looking for some help herself, Zea shared the script with her friend Demme for a second opinion. He flipped.

"[Demme] was like, 'You are so lucky that you have this movie' and what had happened prior to that is that we had submitted it to Universal and they passed," Scanlon said. "Even with all of everyone's pushing they just didn't really get it."

Demme, a "super guy" and "really menschy" in Abraham's words (*The Silence of the Lambs* star Jodie Foster called him an "unstoppable cheerleader for anyone creative" in her public statement after his 2017 death), called Abraham to advocate for Zea as director.

"He called me up and talked about Kristi and he also talked about how much he liked the project," Abraham said. "I was very candid with him. I said, 'Look, Jonathan, I'm really impressed that you would do this and I'm such a big fan, but I have to tell you that I have some reservations. And I think this will be a really hard rock to push up the hill, because I already don't have a lot of support at the studio to make this.'"

Another person Demme counted as a friend: then Universal chairman Stacey Snider, the ultimate decider of *Cheer Fever*'s fate with the studio.

"I said, 'Well, if you talk to your friend Stacey, would you please tell her how much you like the script?'" Abraham said. "And in fact, he did. And when Jonathan weighed in on the material, and told Stacey that he thought it was really a good idea for a film, that it could be very good, it changed her entire perception of what might happen. To her credit, she respected Jonathan enough that she overlooked some of her own concerns about it enough to say, 'Well, if Jonathan Demme thinks this is a thing, maybe it must have something going on, wow.'"

By now, our old friend Eric Hughes, who had heard Bendinger's pitch and passed at Turner, had landed at Universal as an executive. (Told you he'd be back.) He still loved the script and had followed it with interest, hyping it up internally.

"You're trying to kind of surround the project with as much kind of fairy dust or stardust as possible, so that people get as excited as possible," he said, "because, look, at the end of the day it's much easier to say no to something and have it kind of shuffled off to the side. Someone really has to believe in something and really push it through the studio to get it done. Rarely does something come in where everyone's like, yes, this is amazing, because at the end of the day it's a lot of time, a lot of energy, a lot of dollars, a lot of risk, and all of it that goes into getting a movie made, and so someone really ultimately has to kind of take on the responsibility."

Wong called the sudden shift in the movie's fate "completely surreal." She and Scanlon would spend some days around their office passing the time dreamily discussing what they'd do if they weren't producers. A pivot to a career as a hostage negotiator was often tossed around as a good use of their skill sets: tenacity and keeping calm under pressure. (These days, Scanlon, like Eric Hughes, is a celebrity interior decorator, and Wong does basically everything from advocating for domestic beekeeping legislation in California to producing video games. Neither has negotiated a hostage situation, successfully or not.) Lots of frustrating days wondering whether their little cheerleading movie they'd groomed and polished for years would ever see the big screen.

"Jonathan Demme, god rest his soul, is one of my favorite filmmakers of all time, like bar none, and he really got our movie made, because he completely got it," Scanlon said. "He *completely* got the movie and what was great about it, and was able to express that to Stacey. When a national treasure basically says, like, you're so lucky, make it happen, and then you look at the numbers and it's like, the budget is $11 million, you're kind of like, yeah. So the next thing we knew we had a greenlit movie."

Just days after that phone call in which Demme lavished praise upon *Cheer Fever* to Snider, the Beacon crew found themselves in a Universal boardroom across the table from Snider, with Demme, the project's celebrity champion and patron saint, in attendance for good measure.

"It was an absolute miracle and it was totally weird that forty-eight hours later, we're sitting in this meeting and we get a green light," Wong said. "We get a green light on a movie that has no director and no cast." And if that wasn't enough, the studio put a timeline on when production would start: three months from the meeting.

Richard Devinki, a junior executive working on physical production for Beacon at the time, said that he remembered running an errand at Universal, dropping off a script or something. "I'm on the production-level floor and I can't even remember who the head of production was at the time, I just remember him coming out of the office and he sees me and he goes, 'We're cheering!' and I said, 'What do you mean?' And he goes, '*Cheer Fever*, it's been greenlit! We're making it!'" he said.

"So we went through like four years, four years in the dungeon," Wong recalled. "And then all of a sudden, it was just like, OK, you guys have ninety days to get it together."

Ready? (You better be.) OK.

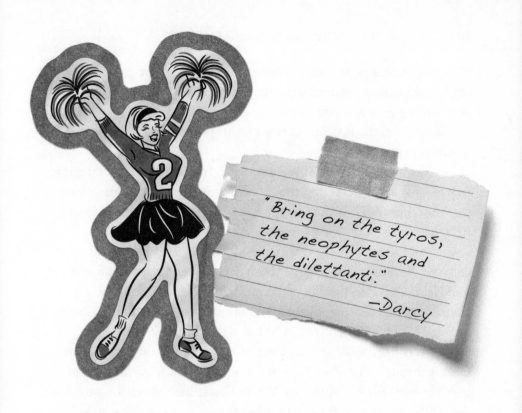

"Bring on the tyros, the neophytes and the dilettanti."

—Darcy

With the green light from both Beacon and Universal and a newly polished and completed script from Bendinger, it was off to the races for *Cheer Fever*. Ninety days, less than a California high schooler's summer break, from the green light to the beginning of production. Three months to find a director, staff up, and cast an ensemble movie, including securing star power that would convince the studio and filmgoers of the movie's box office potential. Hell of a "What I Did over Summer Vacation" essay, right?

"From that point on, we had a lot more support from the studio," Abraham said. The project was assigned two Universal executives, kind of internal hype men who would keep an eye on how things were progressing on the film, collaborate with the team at Beacon, and report back to the studio: Eric Hughes and Tim O'Hair. O'Hair, the junior executive to Hughes's senior, described their role as those of advocates and babysitters of the picture within Universal, a cheerleader for the cheerleader movie that couldn't seem to find its pep.

"You're banging your shoe on the table, saying you're getting good stuff, making sure you maintain attention and getting your picture on and nothing gets derailed," he said.

Meanwhile, the Beacon team was full speed ahead with that tight deadline in sight.

"It was like, OK, well, if we get the right budget, we'll make the movie—we *might* make the movie—but you got to bring us a director," Abraham said of the messages he was getting from Universal. And that director, unfortunately for her, would not be Kristi Zea. "I've always said to everybody who worked for me: deliver the bad news yourself. Because I just believe you have to stand up and take it. So I told Kristi she wasn't gonna get a chance to direct it, and she appreciated that. She was obviously upset, but she appreciated that I called her, and I told Jonathan that. And I also told him that he had helped, and he was like, well, and we kind of bonded over that and became friends through that. Not close friends, but friends. We also bonded over the fact that we both love White Castle hamburgers. So to this day, I have a cup, a coffee cup that he sent me from White Castle."

But if not Zea in the director's chair, then who? The search was on.

"Every time there was a new hot director on the market, we would send them the script," Wong said. "We're trying to get somebody who was in their sort of Cinderella honeymoon, like who just won the Academy Award for Best Short, who is hot at Sundance, who just did this great play in Chicago?" At every turn, she felt she was foiled. "It was literally at that level of bummerdom."

They took meetings with everyone. "We took a handful of directors to the studio," Scanlon said. "And one of them literally said in front of the president of production at the studio . . . 'We don't even need actresses for this movie; we just need hot chicks.' Literally, it was just the most absurd—it was mortifying."

Finally, along came a promising prospect.

"There was this kind of regenerated interest and buzz around it. And I had given it to one of my closest friends, who is a gentleman named Adam Shankman," Hughes said. "Adam has [now] directed the movie *Hairspray* and a number of different movies. He was a choreographer at the time, and choreographing big production numbers in big movies like *The Flintstones*, all kinds of stuff. He had made a couple of short films that were well received, and he was definitely looking around for his directorial debut. So he fell in love with the script."

Shankman met with Abraham and the Beacon crew and won them over. "He made a real heavy pitch for it," Abraham recalled, and "he definitely seemed like a very solid choice. I was down with it, and sold him to the studio."

The studio, it seemed, was also interested. "We'd offered it to Adam," Scanlon said, "and the studio was excited about Adam, and he was a dear friend of Eric's."

And then? As negotiations were underway, a sudden snag.

"At the very last second," Hughes said, "Adam pulled out."

"We lost him, because his sister was producing a movie and he did his sister's movie, so we can't blame him for that," Wong said. Picturing the Thanksgiving conversation if Shankman had passed on his sister's film, for one thing, it's easy to see her point. However, the decision and Shankman's departure left the team shocked. "I was like, 'What do you mean you're not directing my movie!'" Hughes recalled. (The movie that Shankman directed instead, for the record, was 2001's *The Wedding Planner*, starring Jennifer Lopez and Matthew McConaughey.)

Contrary to Wong's point, it turned out that some—like Abraham—*could* blame him for leaving the project. "He crapped out on us," he said. "I never forgave him for that. I mean, I didn't hold a grudge. I just would never hire him again in my life, to be completely honest. It was a betrayal."

The team went into triage mode on *Cheer Fever*, desperate not to lose momentum—or their studio green light. Once bitten, twice shy: the next serious directorial candidate they brought to the head of the studio had to be a winner, or the entire production was at risk.

"You come back with the director and you say, if we have a good meeting, we got a movie; we don't have a good meeting, the movie's off the boards," O'Hair said of the stakes. "And movies get taken off the boards, where it's like, you know what, at the eleventh hour—you read about this, right? You read about the movies where they kind of go in and then all of a sudden, say, 'You know what, this is too much of a hassle,' and it comes down." Losing a strong contender for director, he said, "that's like a wheel falling off your wagon."

Or, as Abraham put it, "A great director who is a friend of mine, Larry Kasdan, once said movies are like patients on an operating table: all they want to do is die. If you let too much go, somebody will walk in the next day with another movie that'll just take that money, and then you're dead."

Abraham's plea to the studio: "'Give us a chance. We'll come back with somebody else.' And that's what my job was then. I couldn't let it fall apart."

The vibe was clear: the next directorial candidate the team from Beacon brought in would *have* to be a home run, or the project would be dead in the water.

The old saying goes that out of good, fast, or cheap, you're going to have to pick just two. Scanlon, Wong, Abraham, O'Hair, and Hughes needed to convince studio head Stacey Snider that their guy—and it would likely be a guy, since even as recently as 2019 only 10.7 percent of the directors of the one hundred top-grossing films of the year were women, according to USC Annenberg's tracking—could be all three, turning a profit and making something of this oddball project that had somehow eked its way through and onto a slate alongside fellow 2000 Universal releases *How the Grinch Stole Christmas* and *The Skulls*, among others. Bendinger herself wanted to direct, drawing on her experience as a music video director, but the first-time screenwriter didn't ever feel she was in serious consideration to make her directorial debut as well. She was given a shot to present her case, but "it felt like I was being indulged a little," given the project's precarious status.

Then along came Peyton Reed. The thirty-four-year-old North Carolina native was not a totally unknown quantity to the lean team at Beacon: he'd been kicking around the scene for a while, cutting his teeth on preshow films at theme parks (directing the intro to the family-friendly 4D Epcot adaptation of *Honey, I Shrunk the Kids* is an early credit) and making-of specials (*The Secrets of the Back to the Future Trilogy*) before moving into directing TV shows like *The Weird Al Show* and Disney TV movies like a remake of *The Love Bug*. He was also a writer, at work on his own bildungsroman high school movie script. He had met with Wong and Scanlon for other projects before, some rewrite stuff, but nothing hugely substantial had come of it. Wong has a self-professed love of the "total treasure-hunting weirdo competition" aspect of production, collecting personalities and skills and filing them away, making and maintaining connections in hopes that someday the alchemy of the perfect match of person and project makes entertainment gold. Reed was one of these treasures.

"He was always the dark horse," Wong said. "Where we were like, OK, well, this is a big-budget romantic comedy, and we need a dialogue punch-up. So let's bring in Peyton to meet with the guys [Abraham and co., in this case], because he's really funny and it was like one of those things where we sort of *knew* that he was not going to get hired to rewrite the big-budget comedy, but part of being an executive is trying to position your favorite unknown people to be discovered by your employers, so eventually you can work with these people that you think are deserving of notice. There's an element of cool hunting, there's an element of talent searching. When you can help somebody over that edge, it is thrilling."

One of the first words that comes to mind when I think of Reed is "affable." He seems to get along with everyone. He's really funny, but he's not going to offend you. He's a drummer and a big music nerd. A "hipster gentleman," as Scanlon put it. He had experience helming projects, but nothing huge that meant he'd be really expensive to hire. He had proven that he could make a movie on budget and on schedule, important for *Cheer Fever*'s modest planned budget. And he had friends on the inside, being old pals with a Beacon marketing exec. He was, miraculously, a viable option to lead the little underdog production.

"It was like the stars aligned in every way," Scanlon said. "Tom [Bliss] could sign off on him because all of the production stuff checked out and he knew how to handle a lower budget with a lot of moving parts, Marc [Abraham] signed off on him because of his creative sense, and he seemed like a good solid person that you'd want to spend time with, because that's a big part of the process. You have to like these people. And then we loved him because we knew he totally got it."

But every job goes both ways: it didn't matter how badly the Beacon team wanted Reed if Reed didn't want them. After tangoing with Disney, he'd moved into directing indie rock music videos and adult-targeted comedy TV shows like *Mr. Show* and *Upright Citizens Brigade* (*UCB*), mulling the space he wanted to move into for his feature directorial debut and reading what felt like an endless amount of scripts. He was also making headway in meetings about getting his "painfully autobiographical" (his words) script for a movie set in high school into production as an indie. If he'd been making a vision board for his career, pom-poms would not have appeared on it in any significant way.

"When I first got the script from my agent at the time, he said, 'I'm sending you a script. It's a high school comedy. I know you've written your own high school comedy, but I know that's been a thing and I would be remiss if I didn't send you this script.' I was like, 'Absolutely,'" Reed remembered. "And he said, 'Don't prejudge this, but the title of the script is *Cheer Fever*.' And I think I said something like, '*Cheer Fever*, what is it, a cheerleading comedy?' I was like, 'Ugh, OK.'"

That changed when he sat down and read Bendinger's revamped *Cheer Fever* script.

"When I cracked that script open, I was like, OK, this is just, I'm gonna read the thirty pages, I'm gonna give it the obligatory read—you know, that's how I like to read scripts. I got sucked in by it, I really did. I remember distinctly putting it down and thinking like, Ah, I can't believe I liked it. I really was taken by it and really, really surprised."

"I felt like I could really do something with it," he told me.

It was epic—"If she had made that original script, it would've been like a three-hour *Godfather*-style movie, it took on so much stuff"—it was voicey and sharp, with that unforgettable roll call opening cheer in place from the very first draft, and it was surprising. Reed—a high school band geek, and, let's just say it's not exactly a *surprise* that he's now making comic book movies—found himself unexpectedly sympathizing with the movie's heroes in teensy pleated skirts.

"I think when I first read it my way into it was the character Cliff, and also the idea of cheerleading as subculture, which was the way

Jessica had really presented it in the script, in a really vivid way," he said. "I had been dealing with sort of like punk rock kids and other aspects of high school subcultures, but this did this very counterintuitive thing and it made a case for this sort of mainstream high school culture as a subculture." Pardon the cheerleading pun, but the script flipped our idea of the social hierarchy on its head.

Beyond that, with Universal already on board, the hardest part— or at least *one of* the hardest parts—was already taken care of, the studio and the money lined up. "I remember sort of doing those mental exercises of 'cheerleader comedy that is there and it is set up and is a movie [that's] going to be made,' and then 'my semi-autobiographical thing that has no traction whatsoever,'" he said.

Suddenly, Reed found himself actually *wanting* to make this cheerleading movie. He knew how it should look. Like Scanlon and Wong, he also loved movie musicals and dreamed of directing one someday, and he saw the potential for a sly and creative nod to the big show numbers that he so loved, just swap jazz hands for spirit fingers. He took the meeting, and he clicked with Scanlon and Wong, saw their passion for the project. They were all on the same page. Just like it was kind of a weird match for Reed to be even considering directing this cheerleading comedy, it was a surprising project for Beacon too. "Beacon at that time was doing big, muscular kind of testosterone movies like *End of Days*, and they've done *Air Force One*. *Bring It On*, even in the context of Beacon, was an outlier," Reed said. He could tell this wasn't a throwaway movie; Scanlon and Wong must have had a legitimate passion for it or it never would have made it that far in the process, with years of development, rewrites, and mental energy poured into it. Just when he thought he was out, they pulled him back in.

For their part, Scanlon and Wong loved Reed's take on the movie: so many movies about young women seemed to treat them and their passions as the butt of the joke, even if they were the ostensible heroes of the story. Reed wanted to take Torrance and the squad seriously.

"It is a feminist movie and it is really empowering, and so we had always seen this as a sports movie, and Peyton saw that," Wong recalled. "And in sports movies, with men, you aren't really seeing the jokes being on the guys unless they're doing something specifically stupid. Nobody ever says to a basketball player, 'Your goal in life to get out of your bad town and go to college on a basketball scholarship is stupid.' You never hear that. But that's what these women in cheerleading also do."

Abraham, burned badly once before on the project, took Reed's measure when Scanlon and Wong brought him in front of him. "He just sort of exuded an air of enthusiasm and confidence about this project, particularly *this* project, that was enticing," he said. And, most important, "I liked him. I really liked him. And I just felt, I felt like this guy, we can make this fly."

Wong considered the ability to examine without criticizing or mocking to be Reed's superpower. "If you look at all the stuff he's worked on, he's very joyful and his humor is not mean," she said. "This is why something like *Bring It On* is successful, is that you can talk about social injustice, you can talk about systemic racism, you can talk about homophobia, you can talk about the hardest, most complicated topics in the construct of a comedy, and you can give those people a voice. And it's a really sly way of sort of giving an audience a look at how other people live. You can't do that if you're mean. You know, he is like Southern Boy Nice. He's super nice, and that shows in all of his work."

The pinky swear was made between Reed, Scanlon, and Wong: together, they'd make this movie happen. Between episodes of the *Upright Citizens Brigade* show he was directing for Comedy Central, Reed went to L.A. to make his pitch to Universal, something that he remembers as "such a bullshitty exercise in so many ways," trying to get across his vision for the tone and vibe of the movie. "You feel like a vacuum cleaner salesman," he said.

Still: vacuum cleaner salesman or not, he apparently didn't suck. (Sorry.) His warm demeanor, his demonstrated experience bringing a project in on time and on budget, and his take on the movie—directing is more than gazing into the middle distance and holding up your hands in a way that implies that you are An Artist, I've come to understand; spreadsheets, data, and even actual math are involved in filmmaking—won the room over.

"Peyton was the right guy," O'Hair said. "I sent a memo to [Universal studio head] Stacey [Snider] saying, 'He's our guy,' and she wrote on it, 'Go for it.'"

Contrary to the years *Cheer Fever* spent in limbo, existing only on paper and in the fervent dreams of a select few, the clock was ticking on getting the actual cameras rolling, making this thing a reality. Ninety days. Tick. Tock.

"It was really quick," Reed recalled of getting the call that he'd been OK'd to direct the project. "They had to make a decision fast, and I think Beacon was pushing because they saw this window open that they might actually get this cheerleader comedy made, and they didn't want it to shut, so it was all about momentum. So my memory is that it all happened really, really quickly. I would say within a matter of weeks. There was no time to overthink anything." The plane ticket, one way to LAX, was purchased quickly.

"When I heard back, it was this immediate 'Got the job, but you got to come back and hit the ground running.' It was a whirlwind."

When Reed says he was expected to hit the ground running, he's not kidding: he recalls going directly from the plane—do not stop at the hotel, do not pass go—to a dinner with line producer Paddy Cullen and actress Marley Shelton, who had cut her teeth as a kid in 1993's *The Sandlot* and was coming off a hot streak with roles in *Never Been Kissed* and *Pleasantville*. These women were meant to be two of Reed's greatest allies in production: The line producer makes sure everything is, well, in line. The actors are making their call times, the director is completing the shot list, everything is costing what it should and happening when it should. Cullen, an industry veteran, was already on board. Shelton—the studio, Beacon and Reed hoped—would be the movie's star, its sunny blonde T-T-T-Torrance, your captain Torrance!

One critique that Bendinger, and then Scanlon and Wong, heard over and over in the pitch process was that there weren't movie-star roles in *Cheer Fever*. Movie stars meant box office money, according to studio math, and established movie stars typically a.) didn't pass for seventeen years old and b.) weren't willing or able to put on a short skirt and be thrown into the air. Details! If they couldn't get a bona fide star, they needed to find the next best thing: the next big thing. Shelton, riding the arc of successful, smart teen movies, was their big bet.

Until she wasn't.

"We really wanted Marley," Scanlon said. "We really, really, really wanted Marley. I remember [casting director] Joseph [Middleton] took her out to dinner with her boyfriend . . . and just really tried to get her to do the movie and she ultimately passed. I could be wrong. I know we were seriously talking to her about it."

Shelton *would* ultimately don that iconic pleated miniskirt, but not in *Bring It On*. "[Shelton] seemed great and seemed like she could do the movie," Reed said, "and then a day or two later we found out that Marley Shelton is no longer interested, she's taken the rival cheerleading movie that's going on. It was a cheerleader heist movie. At the time it was called *Sugar, Spice and Semi-Automatics*."

(A few notes about that movie, eventually released in January 2001, five months after *Bring It On*, under the title *Sugar & Spice* to a roughly $5.9 million opening weekend for its estimated $11 million budget: Shelton costarred alongside Mena Suvari, who had risen to prominence in another cheerleader role in the Best Picture–winning *American Beauty* and the non-Oscar-nominated yet still extremely popular *American Pie* series. *Sugar & Spice* is a scant eighty-one minutes and follows a group of cheerleaders who turn to robbing banks to help their captain, played by Shelton, when she becomes pregnant. The screenplay for *Sugar & Spice* is credited to Mandy Nelson, who doesn't exist. It's a pen name for Lona Williams, who took her name off the movie before its release when she clashed with the producers and director. Another of Williams's most recognizable screenplays? The 1999 cult-classic black comedy *Drop Dead Gorgeous*, starring none other than eventual *Bring It On* Toros captain Kirsten Dunst. Full circle.)

Back to *Cheer Fever*: the talents of casting director Joseph Middleton, who had shown his chops with teen ensembles casting movies like *Go* and *American Pie* (and would follow up *Bring It On* with *Josie and the Pussycats, Legally Blonde,* and even *Not Another Teen Movie,* in a bizarrely meta move), were harnessed, and it was time to dig deep into the rolodexes of young Hollywood—fast.

"The producers [from Beacon] came to us on it," Middleton said. "I was like, oh my god, a cheerleading movie? I love it! . . . We sort of had a niche of young people there. We took it because I thought, oh, it's an ensemble and I think it would be fun and I could travel the world and look for actual cheerleaders. I remember telling an agent, and I remember she made fun of it. But I said, listen, I think this movie is different. Because I am looking at this as if it was a Pepcid commercial. That's what the essence of these people should have. There's a pop and a zest and there's something about them that has to have an energy, and it's not about just the best-looking people. They always have to have this spirit."

They needed to build a squad of believably young-looking actors who could carry a joke and, ideally, perform death- and gravity-defying feats of strength—on beat and with a smile. In the immortal words of Elle Woods: What, like it's hard?

"What was great about our casting director, Joseph," Scanlon recalled, "was that he always, when it came down to two choices and there was a funny girl—somebody who could sell the comedy but wasn't that great of an actress—and a great actress, he always went with the great actress. Because he knew that a great actress will be able to sell the comedy."

The hardest part to cast, according to Reed, was . . . well, all of them. "They were all difficult, because they had to have this combination of—they had to look like cheerleaders, both the guys and the girls, and they had to have some kind of, if not dance training, they had to have some kind of physical coordination, and they also had to be able to act," he said.

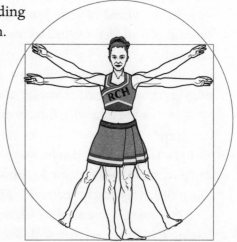

Despite needing to hit light speed by typical industry standards, Reed felt like the three months of prep time he had before shooting was somewhat luxurious. On his prior Disney gigs and on lower-budget TV shows like *UCB*, he'd have very little prep and shoot time, often just twenty working days of preproduction, another twenty of shooting, and another twenty in postproduction for a full-length movie. So the timeline for *Bring It On*, while tight, was a perfect fit for him. Still, casting those specialized actors. In a word: "Terrifying."

"I knew how to do preproduction, and I knew the things that we needed to do," Reed said. But he was anxious about getting the casting right, "because there were the lead roles and then there were a lot of ensemble roles, also very specific needs about actresses who could dance and perform the incredible gymnastics that had to be performed with the cheer routines. So it's all that technical stuff, you know, who was going to do the music, all of this stuff, and it was a whirlwind, it was just *everything*, so fast."

And there was the *Sugar & Spice* problem to up the difficulty score even a tiny bit more: a huge percentage of the actors who ended up in *Bring It On* told me that they'd also read for the rival cheerleading movie, so there were two games in town trying to pull from an already relatively small pool of actors. The coincidence was unwelcome, to say the least.

"I kind of vaguely remember that there was this kind of competing cheerleader movie, which seemed, like, so odd, because you know, how in the world of cheerleading movies did we not have any and then all of a sudden we had two at the exact same moment?" Hughes recalled.

Eliza Dushku, eventually cast as a *Bring It On* lead in the role of edgy gymnast turned reluctant cheerleader Missy, said, "It was like, wait, is this the one with the cheerleaders and the AK-47s, or is it the *other* one?"

In fact, Middleton said he was also offered the casting gig on *Sugar & Spice*, and that he turned it down in favor of *Cheer Fever*. "I didn't like it nearly as much," he said. "That wasn't it."

"Obviously, I knew of its existence," Reed said of *Sugar & Spice*, having had the near-miss with Shelton, "but I also knew what it was about, and it was mining a very different territory than our movie. And I liked our territory more, so I really didn't think of it much after that. I just knew that they were cheerleading bank robbers and we were a high school cheerleader movie."

Michelle Morris, a casting assistant who worked with Middleton on the movie and several other projects over a span of more than five years, said that Middleton's reputation from hits like *American Pie* and critically acclaimed movies like *Go* had made him a go-to for studios looking to cast young ensembles, and for agents to send their up-and-comers who they hoped would break big. He lent credibility to a project that confused some with its heightened language and immersion into the world of cheerleading. "Some of the terminology, actors didn't get, so they passed," Morris said. "I think during this time it was kismet."

The search for the squad was on, before Reed had even officially signed on as director. Middleton and his crew traveled with Bendinger to San Diego, Daytona, Disneyland, San Antonio—in search of pep. Back at home, the cavalry of fresh-faced young actors arrived to read their sides. Here are the stories of how they made the cut, introduced by the original character descriptions for their roles in Bendinger's script.

✳ BIG RED, a sexy 18-year-old with red ringlets and a black heart, commands the floor. RCH in chenille s-t-r-e-t-c-h-e-s across her sweater.

Every story needs its villain. Lindsay Sloane just . . . didn't really realize it would be her. Sloane had gotten her start years earlier in recurring roles on *The Wonder Years* and later played sweet bestie Valerie Birkhead in *Sabrina the Teenage Witch*. She was in that same crew going out on auditions for both the cheerleading projects at the same time.

"There was that other cheerleading movie, *Sugar & Spice*, that was supposed to be like the good one and we were all kind of bummed we didn't get cast in that one, and then all of a sudden it was like, well, look at us now," she said. "All the same people, and it was happening at the same time, so we'd go back and forth and be like, 'Well, what do you hear on this one, what do you hear on that one?' They were just like picking people out. At that time there were fifty of us [seeing each other at auditions]. Between the fifty of us, that's how all movies were cast, the same pool of people."

In her recollection, Sloane never actually read for the role of Big Red, reading sides for Missy and Torrance at her auditions. She was a regular on the casting circuit and felt like she was forever coming *this-close* to getting roles in the teen movies she would come to love when they were released. "*Can't Hardly Wait*, I'm trying to think of like all the movies I got so close on, and it was so devastating," she said. "*She's All That*, all the heartbreak of like, oh, I didn't get that. But I got one that I get to still talk about and that is so fun. And I got the best part. I look back on that and it's the part that I want to be known for." Having fibbed about her dance and cheer abilities—she had no experience with either—this felt like it might be another "so close" moment.

But the real surprise was not just getting cast, but being cast as the one pure and unredeemed Bad Guy in the movie. "I remember getting the offer, and I was like, *Big Red?* I had read the script once earlier before these auditions and I was like, 'Wait, I think she's the horrible one. Isn't she the captain?' And I was like, 'Me?!' Because up until that point, every part I got I was the insecure best friend," Sloane said. "I was never the girl who had, like, a boyfriend. I was just the unattractive one that was so grateful to just be invited to the party. And so I was like, 'Are you sure they got this right?' And then I was so afraid I was gonna get fired, and then every day when it was real and I got to do it, my mind was blown. It was so fun, so, so fun."

✴ WHITNEY DOW, I6, is tan, tan, tan.

"I remember the audition process very clearly," said Nikki Bilderback, who played Whitney, one half of the mean-girl duo who serve as Torrance's foils within the squad. An up-and-coming actress in what teen magazines would absolutely call Young Hollywood, "I'd already done *Clueless*. I'd been doing a lot of TV, a lot of recurring roles and guest spots." With a background as a cheerleader and dancer, she was comfortable with the premise of the movie and knew she could perform.

"I remember when I got a callback," she said. "That was when we had a little more preparation and we had, of course, to do our same scenes that we did for the first call. But then we also had to choreograph either a cheer or a dance so they could get an idea of how we can move and what we could do. And for that one, I had actually choreographed a cheer dance to 'Mickey.' So I went in and I did a whole cheer dance." She remembered Reed and Middleton, plus all the Beacon and Universal producers and execs in the room. "There was a lot of people in the room." No pressure.

Another winning mark in her favor? Her "impermeable bitch face," according to cast mate Rini Bell, an essential tool in the Whitney arsenal. Picture Bilderback's sneer when Eliza Dushku's Missy walks into the gym for the first time, then try to picture *Bring It On* without it. You can't.

"I remember Nikki trying to teach me to be a bitch," Bell said. "She would give me this bitch face. And I could not keep a straight face. I'd just kind of like try to bitchface back at her, and I could not do it. I was laughing. She had such a good bitch face and it was like, impermeable. You could not crack that bitch face. It was solid!"

* **Icy Breck-Girl Blonde, COURTNEY EGGBERT, 16, flips between bitchy passivity and bitchy impertinence. Nightmare.**

And as for the other half of Courtney-and-Whitney: Clare Kramer's journey to donning her Toros uniform as resident ice queen—and redemption-arc star, from hard negging Missy to the hearty "second place, hell yeah!" heard round the world—Courtney was not a short one. While *Cheer Fever* was holding casting calls, Kramer was in town screen-testing for a pilot. When she didn't get cast, she extended her stay in L.A. for a handful of days, just in case. She shot another pilot, a medical drama that was "for sure gonna get picked up," she said, and then stuck around town for a few more weeks, again, just in case. She auditioned for Middleton on another project, which she wasn't right for, but he told her, hey, stick around, I've got this cheerleading project coming up. When she got the script, she "truthfully did not understand the script too much, because it was written in the way the movie is, a lot of jargon and slang and, you know, cheer talk," she said. Still, she auditioned, reading sides for Torrance.

Then she auditioned again. And again.

"I auditioned four times for the role of Torrance," she said. She believed the part was hers to lose. Again, she stuck around and waited.

"Lo and behold, my agent got the call and he was like, well, I've got bad news. Kirsten Dunst is gonna do the movie and I was like, oh my god. You're kidding me," she said. She was invested. If not Torrance, surely she could play . . . someone? "I have to be in this movie," she remembered thinking. "They liked me, there's a ton of other roles, like what about Courtney, you know, she seems like I could play her, you know, or Big Red? I could dye my hair!"

"They keep wanting to bring them back," Middleton said, remembering Kramer's energy as being indistinguishable from that of the real-life cheerleaders he'd seen at competitions. "And she'd fall off the list a little bit. You're like, no, no, no, no, no, don't forget, Clare's really good. They're like, 'Which one? Would she come in again?' I'm like, oh my god, it gets embarrassing for the casting director for the actors. And the further down the line you read them, the more frustrated they must be to be like, we read a thousand times, but at the same time, what my answer to the Clare thing is, she read so many times, is that's how much love we had for her, that we were not gonna let her just fall off and not get in this movie."

Sure, the team said, they'd consider her for Courtney. But she'd have to audition again. She came back for yet another reading, then a final callback, but there was just one hitch: she had another final call the same day, dancing en pointe for the movie that would eventually become *Center Stage*. The auditions were twenty-some miles apart, which in L.A. traffic might as well be the distance between neighboring planets, and were scheduled nail-bitingly close in time. Her agent got real with her: Kramer was trained as a dancer; maybe it was time to let this cheerleading thing go. Respect the laws of time and space, and give up one of the auditions.

"I'm not doing that, I'm not. No way. I worked too hard to get here, and eight auditions, I'm going to that frickin' audition," Kramer recalled thinking. "I'll be there at 7:15 in the morning, or 9:15 in the morning so that I'm the first one there on the sign-in sheet. I said tell everybody, as soon as they start the session, I'm going in first." And she did. She changed in the car, sped from the Universal lot to Santa Monica, and made the next callback, too. The rest, as they say, is history.

"As we know, the dance movie was not that successful and *Bring It On* was. Here we are talking about it twenty-one years later, twenty-two years later," she said. "The point is, always make your own decisions as an artist. So I went to that audition. They let me know not too much longer later that I had been cast as Courtney, and aside from doing the pilots that I had done, and tons of theater in New York . . . this was the first big thing for me. So it was very exciting, and next thing I knew, we were packing up for, I think it was like five and a half months that we were living in San Diego in a hotel, and it was amazing."

✳ Jet-black Lulu bob and movie-star attitude, DARCY ESTRADA is a rich 17-year-old know-it-all. Stacked.

In the infancy of *Cheer Fever*, there was an attempt made to cast the movie with real cheerleaders instead of actors who learned to cheer.

"Joseph and I had gone to a cheerleading competition to see if we could cast real cheerleaders," Wong told me in 2015. "Because that was the really hard thing: How are we going to find people to train fast enough, to be able to do the stunt work that is going to make these sequences spectacular? That's the hard thing with sports movies and musicals: you can't keep doing the same sequence over and over because people get physically tired and that's when they drop each other and injure themselves. So we were trying really hard to find cheerleaders who could also act, and it led to one person: Tsianina."

Tsianina Joelson (now known as Tsianina Lohmann) had grown up in L.A. and was entranced by Drew Barrymore in *E.T.* as a kid. Her acting ambitions had been dashed when she was twelve and her family moved north to Oregon, where she started twirling batons and dancing, as well as competing in high school team sports. She was always fit, a performer who could adapt her physicality to whatever she tried. She got married at nineteen and became a dancer for the Portland Trailblazers basketball team. One day, when she and her then husband were living on-site in a small hotel that they had opened together, she caught a Fitness America competition on TV.

"I was like, I could do that," she said. "I'm very goal-oriented, so I was like, OK, I'm gonna do that, like what else am I gonna do? I'm just cleaning hotel rooms."

She got jacked and started competing, and then she got lucky: through a technicality, she qualified for the top-tier Fitness America competition when a previous competition she was registered for was canceled. Wearing a homemade *Rocky*-themed costume, she danced and posed her way to victory, shocking everyone by winning the contest in her first appearance. She decided it was time to go for it and moved to L.A. to pursue her showbiz dreams, landing a gig hosting a fitness show on MTV.

Things weren't going great in her quest for acting roles—she didn't want to be "the fitness girl," as she said—when the *Cheer Fever* audition rolled around and she read for the part of Missy.

"I was like, oh my god, I was made to be in this movie," she said. "Like, if I don't get this, I'm going home. I seriously should not even be in L.A. if I can't get this job. I auditioned a few times, and me and my girlfriends went to Vegas for a weekend, and on the way back I kind of melted down like, oh my gosh, if I don't hear about *Bring It On* I think I'm gonna have to go home. If I can't make this movie, I maybe wasn't cut out to be an actress, because I've done this stuff my whole life. It comes natural to me."

Again, fate intervened: "On the way back I got the call that I got the part in the movie," playing Darcy, the SAT-obsessed rich girl.

Reed was thrilled with the casting. "She could do all the dancing and physical routines, it was great, but she didn't really have much of a résumé at that point. She really hadn't done that much stuff, but she was just such a striking-looking woman and had the physicality and stuff, so we knew we could work and get her there, and she turned out to be really great."

✳ **Hello, horsey girl. CARVER RIZCHECK is a 16-year-old rep for Thighs-R-Us.**

Um . . . more on this in the next chapter. It was kind of a Whole Thing.

✳ **15-year-old KASEY is a scrawny mess, whose braces are about to blind you.**

Rini Bell had an unusual childhood, starting with being born in Italy, educated in Switzerland and France, then eventually splitting time between New Orleans and New York. She was also unusual in that when she was about nine or ten, by her own recollection, she decided it was time to decide what to do with her life. "One day, I was like, time to make a decision, kid. And I had also simultaneously been in *The King and I* in my school play. And I was like, oh my god, it was fantastic. And then I saw *The Silence of the Lambs*. I was like, OK, I think I have to be an actor." Worried about missing her "child-star window," the ambitious preteen set out to make it happen.

It just so happened that one of her earliest booked major jobs was as "Got Milk Girl" on *The Weird Al Show*, a short-lived CBS variety show from the eponymous musical parodist. The director of that episode? Peyton Reed.

"My big memory from that was the final take," she said. "They were like, we're gonna pour all this milk all over you, like actually pour milk all over yourself. I was like, *okaaaaaaay* . . . And somebody was like, now you should shower so you don't curdle. He was a very silly person, Peyton. I mean, I'm sure he's still silly, but probably sillier then, I think."

Reed remembered Bell as "such an oddball girl" from the show and thought of her for the part.

"I was like, 'Oh, bring Rini in, she's great! She's just got this thing.' And she was easy to cast, because it's like, 'OK, *that* is that character Kasey, I want to get Rini.' She was great," he said.

"I just remember being really nervous, like at every audition," Bell said. "I said I was really bendy. So I took my back foot and I put it over my head and I put it over my nose. Everyone was like, wow. And I was like, 'That's *right*. I have a *very* flexible back. Good for cheerleading.' I couldn't cheer, but I was flexible."

At the callback, when actors were asked to perform a cheer and dance, Bell said, "I did a real cheer. I don't know that it was *amazing*. I tried." She threw out the classic B-E AGGRESSIVE cheer, which she remembered from volleyball. "There wasn't a huge cheer scene" at her high school of four hundred girls.

Wong remembered getting not only a cast member but also a new laugh line for the movie from that audition.

"[Rini] just does her comedy routine, because she is totally not an athlete," she said. "In reality, she's the one who shows up and wears like a Gucci wardrobe and is completely glamorous in real life . . . she came in and she did the 'be aggressive, B-E aggressive' routine, where she didn't move her body at all! She can't dance, and she always knew that. But she was so hilarious that we not only cast her in the part almost on the spot, but we stole that from her and put it in the movie. In the audition sequence, where one of the people comes in to audition for the cheerleading squad, she does exactly an Honorine Bell impression."

When she got the call from her manager that she'd booked the part, Bell called her parents and woke them up. They were excited, but it didn't really seem to click. "It was kind of a bummer, actually. But later on, they got super excited. They just didn't get it, didn't get that, like, I had a really good job. They didn't know the difference. *I* knew the difference."

✳ TORRANCE SHIPMAN, a vivacious blonde 17-year-old, smiles broadly and the poms part ways.

No question about it, *Bring It On* would not be what it is today without Kirsten Dunst as head Toros cheerleader Torrance. Before the heartbreak of Shelton turning down the role in favor of *Sugar & Spice*, Dunst was actually the very first call Middleton made, and she had also initially passed on the script.

"My focus was really about getting Kirsten Dunst, and that kept me up at night," Middleton said. "Because I, somehow in my head, dots dotted up to the idea that she was the right one. And she turned us down."

Morris, Middleton's casting assistant, remembered, "We went to a bunch of people between and then had to keep going back to [Kirsten]."

One of those people was, of course, Shelton, and we already know how that ended.

With Shelton out of the picture—"I could see why she made that choice," Reed said charitably, pointing out that the *Sugar & Spice* script was being touted as edgy and cool, a kind of Tarantino with cheerleaders vibe—it was time to go back to the drawing board. The vibe in preproduction, Reed said, was "these decisions, we gotta make them now, now, now—it's like, well, do I have to skip over the part where we look at lists and names and this is the person who's the lead of the movie?" So without a star already slotted in, Reed had a little more room to think about who would be his ideal fit.

"After Marley was no longer in the picture, that's when we actually went to the lists, and Kirsten was at the top of that list," he said. "I really wanted to reapproach her, and we had done more work on the script and I hadn't had a chance to talk to her. She was in the Czech Republic on a movie. And I think the movie she was doing was a really dark drama."

In fact, "a terrible film," Dunst said. "A terrible, terrible film in Prague. It was awful. Somehow I was making this movie, and I don't know how exactly. My brother still recalls that he just was getting like fat on goulash in Prague as a young kid."

"Who knows why people make these decisions," Reed said of Dunst signing onto *Bring It On*. "I like to think it's because we actually were able to talk about the script and talk about what we wanted do to the script and everything, but part of it may just have been that she was in the Czech Republic doing this dark movie and the idea of doing a fun cheerleader movie seemed like a good change of pace."

"It was a little depressing there," Dunst said. "*Bring It On* came around, and I definitely thought, this is gonna be fun."

"I think the reason I probably didn't jump on it at first is because I think when you're young you really want to be taken seriously. And then when you get older you're like, who cares what anyone thinks. And so I think I just was like, you know what, I like doing comedy. I'm gonna go have a good time."

Middleton recalled that there was also a little hardball involved from the then seventeen-year-old Dunst's team. "Suddenly being in San Diego sounded like a good time to her, but if the money is right," he said. "So we paid a lot of money at that time, and it was right. I'm forever grateful that that worked out, because I've never been able to see anyone else in that role like that. She was so good."

She also had the name recognition that the movie needed, her participation combining with other cast members' to exponentially up audience interest in the movie in theoretical studio mathematics. This was a big deal.

"A moment I remember is when Kirsten said yes," Bendinger said. "I remember crying in the car after that, but hearing that, getting that phone call, that made it feel the most real."

✳ Torrance is flanked by LES and JAN, two male cheer- leaders, who she squeezes for support.

It's only fitting that Les and Jan, the best-bro male Toros who are rarely, if ever, seen apart in *Bring It On*, are introduced together in the movie's script. Life imitated art, and Huntley Ritter and Nathan West, who played the duo, became so close that eventually Ritter was in West's wedding. They remain friends to this day.

Their first impressions of one another, however, were at a cattle call for *Cheer Fever*. It wasn't love at first sight, to say the least.

Ritter was an Atlanta native who had worked a handful of odd jobs to make money and get by, with the vague thought that maybe someday he'd go to school and become a lawyer. His plans changed when he nabbed a gig as an extra on the Aaron Spelling show *Savannah* for ten dollars an hour. On the set, he watched the cast and thought, "I could do that." How hard could it be? He enrolled in acting school, "worked my ass off," and was booking some local day work. Not bad. He was eighteen and handsome and got the advice that with his work ethic and looks, moving to L.A. wouldn't be the worst idea. So off he went, calling up the one person he knew in town when he got there, a cousin he wasn't terribly close with but whose wife was a model who introduced him to a manager, "a real mess. She had this like shitty apartment in Hollywood, like a bunch of cats," he said. "It's hot, no air-conditioning." Still: representation is representation. He networked and researched, handed out headshots everywhere, even in line at the grocery store. He was booking small gigs, building up momentum, when he read for *Bring It On*.

"I get this audition and my agent said, 'Would you play a gay guy?'" Ritter remembered. "And I'm like, yeah, I was like, yeah, that sounds like a good way to win an Academy Award." And with the "super dramatic" sides he was given to read, the role of Les seemed meaty and emotional. He had no problem with that. The hard part? Believably playing a cheerleader. When casting director Middleton said he'd like to bring Ritter back to read for Reed, there was just one outstanding question: What kind of cheer experience did he have?

"'Like, can you do like a cartwheel or something,'" Ritter remembered Middleton asking. "I'm like, 'Yeah, of course, yeah, no, I've done—yeah!' I don't know shit. I don't know anything. I've never heard a dance count in my life. I've never heard '5, 6, 7, 8,' *never*. So I go back to my little apartment and my neighbor is a former TCU cheerleader, and we would hang out sometimes on the weekends. So I went to her and I said, 'I need help. I got a callback for this movie,' I have no idea what this thing's really about, right, but it seems like a juicy, juicy role for an actor. And I said they're gonna maybe wanna see like a cartwheel, so she worked with me on Pico there at that park for like four hours, teaching me how to do a cartwheel. I actually had the acting piece down pretty solid."

At the audition, he spotted West for the first time in the waiting area down a long hall from the room where the auditions were happening. They sized one another up. "It's kind of a tense moment, because you're all kind of competing," Ritter said.

He ended up being right: he did have the acting down, and felt confident that he could bust out that cartwheel when asked. "I do the audition and I nailed it. Like sometimes you nail it, sometimes you don't. But all the pieces were there, all the moments, the emotion was real, everything was good, and Peyton was like, 'Man, you're great, like that was really powerful, really well done.' And I said, 'Well, thanks, is that it?' and they're like, 'Yeah!'"

"I spent four fucking hours learning this cartwheel." He wasn't letting it be for nothing. "The assistant had the door open and I'm like, 'Did you want to see like if I can do a cartwheel or something?'" Long pause. The longest. The kind of pause that can only happen if you're nineteen years old and very earnest. "Peyton is like, 'OK.' I don't think he really cared. So Nathan always told me the story as like, 'I'm looking down the hallway and all I see is Ritter fucking cartwheel across the room.' And he's totally full of shit too, he's never done any of this stuff either, he's a hockey player. I come walking out, I get down there and he's like, 'Hey dude, are they making you do like gymnastics stuff?' and I'm like, 'Yeah, man, yeah, it's hard-core.' I was just trying to fuck with him."

West recalls: "I actually didn't really know what I was getting involved in. Everybody—and if anybody said different, this is the truth on this one—*everybody* lied about having any gymnastics or cheer experience, we all did." He had his own version of the meet-aggro with Ritter: "Did Huntley tell you his little story, that he did the cartwheel coming out? That's how we met." At the time, West was running out of money and desperate for a job that would fund trips to see his then girlfriend, actress Chyler Leigh (who is now his wife), in Florida where she was filming. He vividly remembered sitting on that couch at the end of the hall and Ritter's psych-out. "I was so nervous, and he comes out doing cartwheels. And I walk in, I'm like, Oh my god, you know, what are they going to ask me to do? And luckily for me, they were just like, All right, you're supposed to be kind of, you know, the ladies' man. Do you got washboard abs? and I'm like, yes, and I flexed. [Turns out] they didn't ask him to do anything else other than just read!"

In retrospect, West thought Ritter's Cartwheel of Intimidation™ worked in his favor: "He came out and he was like tap dancing his way out of there, you know? He did this cartwheel and looks back and they're laughing and I'm like, Oh my god. And then I realized he was going for Les, I was like, OK, OK, OK. So he kind of set me up for a win, to be honest with you, because they were just, I walked in that room and they were so warm and they were laughing and it was perfect."

Obviously, we know how this story ends: West and Ritter were cast as Jan and Les, respectively.

Ritter received word of his casting after his agent beeped him (yes, this was the late '90s, and pagers were in full force). Great timing: he was nearly out of cash, and on the way out of the audition had done a random act of kindness that left him even lower on funds. "People had cell phones then, I didn't have a cell phone," he said. "Then when I drove home, I got a call, my agent was like, they want you, they're booking you. And I remember thinking, like, I don't know if I got it because the audition was good or because I do good things in the world. I always kind of felt like maybe I got the part for that."

After that final callback, West remembered, "It all happened so fast. I jumped on the 101. I got a call like fifteen minutes after I left and I'm going on the on-ramp up Laurel Canyon. I get a call from my agent,—he, unlike Ritter, had a cell phone—"get on the phone, and they say, you got it, and I freaked out. I think I went about ninety miles an hour, like up the on-ramp onto the freeway. And then of course it was stopped traffic, but it was an awesome, great moment."

✳ A STRAGGLER walks in. Brunette 16-year-old wearing low-slung cholo trousers. Baroque black tattoos ring around one bicep. MISSY PANTONE looks more like a roadie for Social Distortion than a cheerleading candidate.

It's Torrance's face on the poster, but it's Missy, the outsider whose school, as you might recall, had no gymnastics team and for whom this is a last resort, who sets the movie's plot in motion by revealing that the Toros' cheers were all stolen. The filmmakers needed a foil on the squad for Torrance, someone to contrast with her bubbly can-do determination but somehow also fit as an unlikely friend. Also: they needed someone famous enough in the real world to get more butts in seats when the movie was released. Eliza Dushku was already a name. Where Dunst had budding leading lady appeal with serious, adult-targeted films like *Interview with the Vampire* and *The Virgin Suicides* (among many others), Dushku was a fan favorite on TV's beloved teen drama *Buffy the Vampire Slayer* and its spin-off, *Angel*, as Faith, the badass, snarky alterna-Slayer. The choice, as they say, was five-by-five.

"Eliza was big," Morris said. It was a no-brainer.

"I'm sure at some point there was a second choice, but I can't even remember who it was, because I always just wanted Eliza," Reed said.

Just because filmmakers wanted Dushku, however, didn't mean that she was necessarily . . . enthused about auditioning. Middleton and his team remembered calling on relationships with agents with several potential cast members who had been confused or put off by the cheerleading-jargon-heavy and highly stylized language of the script. We may all get what it means to put the "itch" in "bitch" now, but it didn't quite jump off the page for everyone in the beginning.

"It's just a very delicate dance," Morris said. "And in a movie like this that, yeah, we all thought it would make money, but we definitely didn't think people would quote it years later."

Dushku was one of those who had to be, shall we say, *coaxed* to audition. "I don't remember her just being like, 'Oh, I can't wait to do this!'" Middleton said of Dushku.

"This was an audition that I was none too kind of enthusiastic to attend, as I was, much like my character Missy, not the cheerleader type in high school," Dushku said. "I was a self-proclaimed and very, very real tomboy with three older brothers. You know, someone who spent my high school years as more of an emo kid, camouflage jackets and dyeing my hair with Manic Panic colors and being edgy." She didn't have a hate-on for cheerleaders—she told me her best friend in high school was the captain of the Watertown High School cheer squad, who was a year older and "embraced my emo." Their school's colors were even red, black, and white, the same as Rancho Carne High. Even though she could be close with the head cheerleader, "I never mistook that I could ever be that," Dushku said.

"When I got this audition, I believe I overslept the morning of and showed up a little groggy, perhaps even hungover, and walked into the building," she told me. "Before I even got to the room where the audition sign-in was, there were like people flipping up and down the halls, doing cheerleading moves and stunts in the lobby. I remember just thinking like, this is not for me, but I guess I'm here. I went in, signed in, didn't even try to lie on the form and say that I had any kind of cheer experience."

She absolutely embodied the character in the room, with Reed describing her as the Veronica to Dunst's bubbly blonde Betty. Other auditioning cast members immediately noticed her vibe, that her alphabet went straight from E to G.

"I remember seeing Eliza outside smoking," Kramer remembered of one of the auditions.

For her part, Dushku impressed not just Reed, whom she described as "just warm and welcoming," but also herself at that reluctant reading. "[Peyton] asked me straight up, 'So, have you ever done cheering?' and I said, 'No, no.' He said, 'Do you think you could?' I said, 'I don't know.' He said, 'You ever done a split?' and I said, 'I think so, I can try,' and I, like, dropped into a split. I guess he just wanted to generally see if I had flexibility or a will or the capabilities. I think I booked the job on a split. It was as much of a shock to me as I think it was to everyone that knew me, but it was sort of exactly what that character was."

She read the whole script and talked with Reed and Bendinger, heard their pitch and vision for the movie, then followed her gut. "It had the potential to be something either really special or it would be really, really, misguided and inappropriate, but we had faith," she said. "I think Jessica and Peyton gave us a lot of faith and confidence in the mission."

After negotiations, Dushku signed on, bringing the movie its bad girl and moral center.

⁎ **The CAPTAIN raises her arms like a conductor. Her squad falls silent. ISIS.**

Decades down the line, Gabrielle Union and the character of Isis have become inextricable from one another, and it's impossible for fans to imagine anyone else in the part. The filmmakers share that feeling. Though there was some discussion of stunt casting a musician for the captain of the Clovers—a route that would ultimately be taken for the Greek chorus of Isis's teammates—Union quickly entered the picture.

"Gabrielle was always Isis," Bendinger told me in 2015. "She was Isis at the reading and she was Isis in the movie. She was destined to play that part."

"Gabrielle just came in and auditioned, and she just nailed it," Scanlon said in 2015. "We were all in the room and we were like, 'Oh yeah, that's it, that's her.' She has the most incredible presence, incredible. She just crushed it. She just killed it, *killed* it in the audition. It was just through regular channels. She was sort of a known entity in Hollywood, in the casting world, I'd say, but not so much in the world at large."

At that point, Union was still early in her career but making all the right moves: she'd appeared in *10 Things I Hate About You* and *She's All That*, both successful teen movies in *Cheer Fever*'s cohort. It's worth noting that Union was twenty-seven when she filmed *Bring It On*, though she would continue playing high schoolers for years to come. She was also one of the many who also auditioned for *Sugar & Spice* around the same time, where she was turned away. The cast of that movie ended up having no Black actors. Despite raising her eyebrows at many of the scripted lines for her character, Union signed on to *Cheer Fever*. She said it was the assurances that she'd be able to help shape her character into something she'd be proud of that made her sign on to what would become arguably the most iconic role of her career.

In 2015 she told me, "When I realized we were all kind of working towards the same goal and everyone was very open to getting it right, still keeping it the campy, good time that it is, but also not losing the message either by watering it down with stereotypes that could be harmful to even the campy fun. But everyone was like, let's all work together; let's make this right. That's what sort of kept me involved. Because there were a ton of teen movies at the time that I passed on that were not committed to getting it right."

Morris cast Union in the movie without an extensive audition process, having met her while casting other projects with Middleton.

"We always took time to talk to [auditioning actors] in the room and also get to know them for the reason that—Joseph taught me this—you're seeing people for four or five projects down the road," she said. "Gabrielle always came into our office. I just got to know her as a person."

With that, the Clovers had their captain.

✱ Isis appears. She has TWO CLOVER COHORTS, LA FRED AND JENELOPE.

The named members of the Clovers are rounded out by La Fred, Jenelope, and Lava, played by the real-life musical girl group Blaque. The trio, whose self-titled 1999 debut album was certified platinum and who had no prior acting experience, were cast in a bit of marketing wizardry to cross-pollinate audiences. *Cheer Fever* got to benefit from their pull to fans, and they got a guaranteed spot on the soundtrack with their single "Bring It All to Me," featuring *NSYNC's JC Chasez. Synergy!

This is another case of time eroding an origin myth; the story of exactly how Blaque came into the picture depends on who you ask two decades later. "Likely it was Max [Wong]" who suggested Blaque, Bliss said. "She was much more operating near the ground level, just scrounging for material and younger and hipper and more in the scene than I was."

According to Scanlon, Blaque's agent submitted them.

Wong's take? "It was totally sort of by fluke," she told me. "Jon Shestack, who was the head of production at Beacon, was driving down La Cienega Boulevard one day and he was stopped at that intersection of La Cienega and Beverly. He happened to look over, and posted on one of the poles was a mini poster of Blaque, because they're dropping their new album. He literally got out of his car at the red light and peeled the poster off the pole. We'd been trying to cast the Clovers . . . so we were just looking everywhere and he brought in this image of these three beautiful girls. They were wearing costumes that were made out of bubble wrap. Like, who are these people, because we're not cool. So we look them up and we're like, oh, they're touring with TLC and *NYSNC, so I guess they're huge. We totally lucked out that we saw this and they were in our film."

Shestack remembered grabbing the flyer. In a pre-Google world, he had to. "I had seen a poster for them on a construction site or something on La Brea and I feel like I was questioning my ability to remember how to spell it," he said. "So I just grabbed it. Because I felt like, I'm going to come in, I'm going to say 'black' and if I don't remember that it's B-L-A-Q-U-E, I'm not gonna get it."

Reed said that the idea of stunt casting outside of traditional actors—looking at the worlds of music, comedy, and modeling—may have been his idea in the first place, and was thrilled to have Blaque in the movie. "All three of them had charisma like you wouldn't believe," he said. "They can dance, they look great, and they were so enthusiastic that we immediately cast them. . . . It was at a point where everybody was trying to find the next Destiny's Child or whoever, and they came in and I loved them. Again, I think there was a part of me as a director that was like, 'Eh, really? A girl group? Can they act? Whatever.'"

However they got there, the women—Shamari Fears (now Shamari DeVoe), Natina Reed, and Brandi Williams—were a tonal fit and a win for the movie.

"When we actually met with them, they just had the right attitude, they could nail the lines, they could sing, which translated into doing the cheer routine," Scanlon said. "So it was like, oh my god, this is great. It's a great shortcut. We don't have to see a million more girls for these three to four roles, we can just pop these girls in."

More than that, they were known to young audiences. Wong recalled of the later test screenings, "When we tested it to teenagers, we discovered that 70 percent of the teen audience knew who Kirsten was from *Interview with the Vampire*, but 80 percent of the kids knew who Eliza Dushku was from *Buffy*, but 90 percent of the kids tested knew who Blaque was. Blaque was like the secret weapon."

DeVoe remembered being . . . unimpressed. The group was touring and working hard to promote their album, putting in grueling hours on the road and onstage. "I looked at it and was like, oh my god, this is super corny," she said. "The name of the movie was called *Cheer Fever* in the beginning. So it's like, oh my god, what is this about? So I just thought it was super, super corny and I was like, no way that this is gonna be the number one movie in America and be a cheerleading cult favorite for the rest of my life."

According to *her*, Beacon reached out to Blaque's manager, Johnny Wright, whom they shared with *NSYNC, about being in the movie.

"I was like, you know what, hey, why not? Let me give it a shot," she said. "You know, we don't even have to audition to be a part of it. They're reaching out to us. And they're like, do you guys want to be in a major Universal Pictures movie? So we said yeah, and we did it. Why not? And it's cheerleading, it might be pretty fun. Who knows?"

✷ **Her little brother JUSTIN, 14. He acts like he smells: bad.**

Cody McMains was thirteen years old and his career was heating up. He came by his bratty little brother bona fides naturally: He told me he had gotten into acting because "I always wanted to do whatever my brother did," and the parts started rolling in, with the years leading up to 2000 being especially busy. "I was really starting to dip my feet into being a full-time working actor as a kid" when *Cheer Fever* came along, he said. He read the script in full, though "I feel like as a thirteen-year-old, censorship should have been a little bit more important. But, you know, my parents are very artistic and very freedom of expression, you know, California, bare footers through and through." He thought the script was "very funny," and when he got the role, was relieved to learn that he wouldn't have to attend cheerleading camp with the rest of the cast, something that he'd worried he may have to do despite the fact that the closest Justin would come to a pyramid in the movie would be wearing spankies on his head at Nationals.

"*Bring It On*, it was like kind of like the cherry on top," he said.

✷ **CLIFF, a hunky 17-year-old, glides into the room in a well-preserved CLASH t-shirt, and complete with a Walkman headset. From the reactions of the crowd, he's a new commodity. Dressed differently from the rest of the kids.**

Jesse Bradford's signature one-sided smirk is iconic now, but the role of Cliff was anything but quick or easy to cast. For one thing, Bradford, who had been acting since he was an eight-month-old in a Q-tips commercial and had starred in a Steven Soderbergh movie, *King of the Hill*, as a teen, turned the part down at first.

Many of the eventual stars, Morris remembered, took wooing to get interested in the movie. For the actors with a significant body of work behind them already, like Bradford, a low-budget cheerleading movie was not an obvious next move. "They all at the age of twenty were taking themselves very seriously," she said. "And this movie, obviously, wasn't taking them seriously, but ironically it treated a sort of silly subject like cheerleading with a serious manner. So in a way, it almost like gave them that respect. But on the surface, none of them saw that. So yeah, I just remember a lot of coaxing."

Bradford, specifically, remembered being less than excited about teen comedies, having turned down *American Pie* shortly before getting the *Cheer Fever* script. "I didn't care to be involved," he said of *American Pie*. "Possibly a big mistake, but like it was when you read a script, it either kind of speaks to you or it doesn't, or you think there's a shot for it or there isn't or whatever. With *American Pie*, I was like, oh, I don't know about this, like, gross-out sex comedy. I don't know what's going on here."

For a while, Reed and the producers chased Jason Schwartzman, fresh off his debut role in *Rushmore* and a newly minted indie hero—perfect to play a Clash-loving cheerleading skeptic. It didn't happen, obviously. James Franco also read for the role before *Freaks and Geeks* was picked up to series. Ethan Embry, hot off *Can't Hardly Wait*, read the part in at least one table read. The filmmakers went back to Bradford's team again.

He admits now that when he got the script, he didn't get it. Kind of, *ugh*, cheerleading. "I mean, yes, I was, you know, I hate to say that because I sound, it makes me sound—you know, like an idiot," Bradford told me. "But I think I can claim some defense there in terms of like, I was a twenty-year-old, you know, red-blooded American cis male who was like, you know, not exactly into the cheerleading culture or whatever."

Wong remembered going back to Bradford. "We went back to Jesse and we were like, 'Come on! It's going to be a cheerleading movie.

You're going to be in the sun in San Diego with a bunch of girls! What could go wrong!'" she said. "And he was like, 'Can I get a convertible?' And I was like, 'Of course!' Which was a total lie. Nobody got a car."

"Sounds like me. Sounds believable. I don't remember that, but I'm not going to deny it," he laughed. "And you know what I did? Actually, I shipped my mountain bike, my Cannondale mountain bike that I still have, out to San Diego from New York. And I used that to get everywhere. It was great."

It was connecting with Reed—a fellow music fan, another outsider to cheerleading culture, who saw something in this script and believed in it—that convinced Bradford to sign on. "I think sitting down with Peyton, and understanding the degree to which this character was the outsider to all of that is maybe part of what made me take some initiative on the idea and go, Oh, like this guy's the anti-cheerleader, that works for me and my relatively small-minded view of the world or whatever my twenty, twenty-one-year-old guy's take on things is," he said.

Convertible? No. Deal? Yes.

★ **Their eyes widen upon seeing: SPARKY POLASTRI! His outfit consists of all black. He places an audio-cassette in the deck and stands at attention in the middle of the room, eyes closed in meditation.**

Ian Roberts does not do flips. He does not cartwheel, he does not dance. A founding member of the now legendary improv comedy troupe the Upright Citizens Brigade alongside Amy Poehler, Matt Besser, and Matt Walsh, the then thirtysomething comedian met Reed when he directed a few episodes of the second season of the Comedy Central show by the same name.

"We were friendly, I really liked Peyton. He was a great director and did great episodes," Roberts told me. What came later was a shock to the comic, who still felt like he was finding his footing in being a professional entertainer. "That being said, I was still surprised to get a role without auditioning in a movie! I had never been in a movie. *UCB* was really the first, you know, mainstream commercial thing

I'd done. I'd been in a sketch group, and our sketch group got a TV show—so that was pretty, pretty great to get cast in a movie." The chance of it all still kind of seems to blow his mind, over two decades later, that he'd get his most recognizable film role—not to mention his *first* film role—by basically having someone call him and go, "Hey, want to do this thing?" Um, yes?

"It just so happened that the guy who directed the movie directed our show and thought enough of me from the show [to cast me]. Which, it sure wasn't that he saw me dance that he thought, I'll cast him without auditioning, that he could talk them into doing that. I've had stuff, you know, later in my career, written for me where the character's name is Ian, and I've not gotten the role. So, it's not easy to get someone to just like rubber-stamp you and say yeah, yeah, he can do it."

And what an opportunity: even in early drafts of Bendinger's script, Sparky Polastri was an over-the-top character. In the final cut, he's one of the most memorable characters, even though he has only one major scene. The character underwent some changes to become "Bob Fosse–esque and a little bit of a maniac hard-ass," and Roberts was given the chance to write some of his own lines. Spirit fingers are *gold*, and so was Roberts's experience on the movie.

Auditions finished, deals negotiated, and cast in place, it was time for everyone to put in some blood, sweat, and cheers.

"Front handspring, step out, round off, back handspring, step out, round off, back handspring, full twisting layout."

—Whitney

Now that the movie had assembled its ragtag cast of actors, beauty queens, and honest-to-god cheerleaders, it was time to head to San Diego, where *Cheer Fever* was to be filmed. Some 120 miles down I-5 from Los Angeles and the prying eyes of studio executives, the actors moved into a Marriott in the Gaslamp District to begin training for an experience many in the cast would later call the opportunity and experience of a lifetime.

Originally, the hotel placed the actors—mostly in their early twenties, single and ready to hang and shenanigate—in rooms spread across the hotel, on different floors. But then along came Nathan West.

"This guy right here had this brilliant idea," he laughed, pointing at himself with both thumbs. "They put us on all these different floors and I was like, 'Yo.' I'm a people person and obviously an extrovert, right, so I was like, you know, guys, we should really just take over a wing of the hotel. There's so many rooms and we're all going to want to hang out, we're on a cheer team together, so we should be hanging.

And so it was my idea to go back down to the front desk, and we did, we literally moved in and we had one wing of the hotel where it was like dorm rooms. Every room. . . . It was the best thing [the hotel] could have done, because it was super loud and the doors would just be open and you just kind of walk in, talk to so-and-so, then turn around and go into this room, it's just like a dorm room party."

Bilderback said that just as Whitney and Courtney were inseparable on-screen, she and Kramer became fast friends in real life after meeting at their wardrobe fitting, "pretty much attached at the hip from the get-go," and then living in hotel rooms next to each other.

"There weren't any on-set dramas, there was no catfights," she said of the young ensemble. "We all just got along and loved each other and we hung out and partied and it was literally like being in a college dorm at that hotel. That poor hotel, though, having to put up with us. God bless them. We were probably their worst nightmare."

Once the bags were unpacked, it was time to whip the cast into shape and make them look like, well, cheerleaders. A handful of professional cheerleaders had been hired to fill the ranks of both teams—with several, if you look closely enough at the finished film, pulling double duty in uniforms for both the Clovers and the Toros, given the difficulty of finding competent cheerleaders over a certain of age with some acting chops and a willingness and ability to take the paycheck (NCAA guidelines and labor laws, among other factors, complicated things). Nevertheless, it was important that the teams have their own separate styles, and that the actors, who had mostly lied through their teeth about their dance and gymnastic abilities during auditions, could pass as hard-core competitive cheerleaders.

Enter Anne Fletcher, now the director of movies like *The Proposal* (which I personally watched several times a week during fall semester of my senior year of college) and *27 Dresses*, then an erstwhile dancer and frequent assistant choreographer and creative partner of none other than Adam Shankman, *Bring It On*'s almost-director.

"Adam Shankman and I met as dancers on the 1990 Academy Awards, when they used to have dancers," Fletcher told me in a phone call. "And then soon after that he started choreographing music videos and some things here and there, and then he brought me along as a dancer. . . . Adam would say I was his muse as a dancer, because I understood his choreography so well. And then, as we were going on, I then became his assistant choreographer, because I could—he's one of the most amazingly brilliant choreographers of our generation, truly, but because I understood his choreography, physically on my body, I could also translate it to other dancers. And so I became his assistant and then as the years went on, there was so much work, thankfully, in film and television and the stage that we ended up kind of being partners, because he couldn't be in two places at one time, so then I would just take over here and he would go over there, that's sort of how our relationship went for years. And then he went and directed *The Wedding Planner*."

While Shankman ultimately didn't direct *Bring It On*, he did contribute greatly by recommending Fletcher as the movement lead for the film, championing her in conversation with his childhood friend Hughes, one of the studio executives on the picture. The actors almost unanimously praised Fletcher, unprompted, for her encouragement and humor, two things that proved to be absolutely essential during a grueling multi-week cheer camp for the Toros before filming began. Her nickname is "Mama" for a reason.

"I had no desire to choreograph, by the way. I always just wanted—I'm fifty-five, I would still be dancing right now, honestly, if my life didn't go how it did," Fletcher told me. Still, she took the meeting and hit it off with Reed ("He and I just start joking around, almost immediately. Sarcastic, throwing quips, silly, crazy . . . we just vibed." Reed: "We really fed off of each other's energy, I smile just thinking about Anne, she's just one of the funniest people I've ever met. Amazing.") and got the gig.

"The thing that to this day I always remember about Anne is she has such a positive, energetic energy, like even if she weren't choreographing your movie at that time, you'd kind of just want her around as like a spirit animal," Reed said.

Now to figure out how to make it all happen, and look believable. Because producers were hoping to keep costs low, they were banking on using special-ability extras—the professional cheerleaders—and the actors themselves in the movie's big cheer competition set pieces and the opening number to cut down on the number of expensive stunt doubles they'd have to employ. The background cheerleaders at the competitions would be filled in by real squads.

Fletcher herself had been what she called a "pom-pom girl" in high school, and then later had a stint as a Laker Girl, but her choreography had always been more dance-based, rather than the elaborate stunting the elite cheerleaders of the *Bring It On* world participated in. To bring authenticity to the cheer choreography, she hired cheerleading pro Ray Jasper to work with her on the competition routines for both teams. And to make sure the Clovers had their own style that looked notably different from the Toros, she enlisted the help of choreographer Hi-Hat, a repeat Missy Elliott collaborator and music video mainstay.

The newly cast Toros, with the exception of Kirsten Dunst, who had a conflict with shooting another project and would come to set later, assembled in San Diego for four weeks of intense cheer training.

"We didn't have [Kirsten] until really seconds from shooting, and it made me nervous, because I will say this: one out of a million people, I cannot get to dance," Fletcher said. "One in a million. I can get anybody to dance. It doesn't mean you're going to, you can't learn how to be, you know, a trained Cecchetti dancer, that's not gonna happen, but it makes you look great in this twenty seconds or a minute, given the opportunity. I was nervous."

And so the training began in earnest to turn the eager young actors, many of whom were on their first studio project, into cheerleaders. "We trained from like, I don't know, nine to four or five in the day, and then we had to go to the gym after that to work out," Kramer, who played Courtney, said. "So when I started seeing the level of the cheering and the routines and the gymnastics, that's when I realized, OK, this is not just gonna be a little sports movie, this is actually the real deal."

Huntley Ritter remembered the absolute panic at realizing just how "real deal" it all was. "I get down there and I'm told, 'Hey, you're gonna be picked up by this van, you and this other guy, Nathan West . . . we're gonna bring you here, the girls will already be there,'" he said. "OK, cool. And you know, you don't really know what's going on, it's almost like being in the military, it's like need-to-know basis. They just tell you where you're gonna be, and you're going to do something. So Nathan and I get in the van and we're talking, he's like, 'Hey man, do you know how to do anything?' I'm like, 'No, do you?' He's like, 'No.' 'Did you tell them you did?' He's like, 'Yeah, did you?' I was like, 'Yeah,' so we quickly bonded over how thoroughly we had bullshitted this. And we're in the van ride to rehearsals, and we're terrified, because we're full of shit, total shit with what we can do."

The terror really set in when the duo arrived at the studio to see all the female Toros and pro cheerleaders running through what they'd already learned. An absolute record-scratch moment for the ages. "They're all in position, and [Anne's] like, '5, 6, 7, 8.' And they do all this crap! And Nathan and I are sitting there, we just stop, and we're like, oh crap. It is so fast! *Five, six, seven, eight!* And they're all jammin' into this stuff!"

By Ritter's account, Fletcher quickly realized she couldn't just stick the duo in the back and expect them to pick it up. She pulled them aside: "She goes, 'So boys, you don't know how to fucking dance, do you?'" Playing the role of "deer in headlights" tonight: Ritter and West. "She's like, 'Guys, don't bullshit me, my job, I have to get all you fuckers'—like, you know, Anne's a cuss a second—'fuckers dancing in like four weeks. You need to come clean with me.' And we're like, 'Look, we don't. But! We need this job, don't fucking tell the studio this, we *will* figure it out.' And she's really cool. She's like, 'I'm not gonna tell on you, but we got to figure out how to like—you know what, you guys don't know shit, you don't know what the counts are.' We've never done this in our lives, like he's a hockey player, I'm like, I like, you know, hunting, fishing. We're kind of athletic, but not like *this*."

Speak for yourself, West would say. In high school, he had done a routine to "Ice, Ice Baby" when he won prom king, so he felt he had at least *some* moves. "I consider myself a decent dancer but more of a clown," he said, then couldn't resist clowning on his friend. "And I just remember looking over at Huntley and watching him, stiff as a board, trying to do his thing. I'm going, I'm OK, I'm gonna be OK. I'm gonna be fine. I'm just gonna keep standing next to this guy."

Jokes aside, Ritter and West put in the time, even begging off some evening group hangs to rehearse together. "He and I would like meet up in one of our rooms and we would practice this and practice this and practice this and we got it, we're like, OK, we're not going to get fired," Ritter said.

"We started really slow," Fletcher said of her training regimen. "And we built and we built and then we had two actor boys who were our cheerleaders, Nathan and Huntley. We had to integrate them with the cheerleader guys, and so they all taught each other as, as anyone like dancers, cheerleaders, all the same. We'd have kids break off and start teaching actors certain things, we'd see Ray [the cheerleading pro] break off, then we would try the whole group as a whole. You're starting at the bottom, you're building the little pieces of what are going to work with the actors. And by the way, they just went for it."

That fear of getting found out and fired, working hard to beat out that imposter syndrome haunting almost every member of the cast, helped bond the young actors quickly. "Being a fish out of water, never having done a major motion picture, it was like, you kind of just felt you could get fired at any point," said West, who remembered panicking after an early all-cast table read and feeling like he hadn't wowed. "I remember talking about that with Rini and talking, like, each of us had our own moment with that, because we all were relatively new to the game, or it was our first experience doing a major motion picture, so it was kind of like you always had to make sure. Like, it's not me. You want to be the last person standing, kind of thing."

Eliza Dushku, though initially bearish on the whole cheerleader thing, took a "go big or go home" approach to the training. If you're gonna do it, do it. "I think in some in some funny way, conscious or subconscious, there was even like, Whoa, I get to sort of like relive vicariously my own high school experience that I didn't have and call it work," she said.

The practices were brutal, exhausting. "It was hard work," line producer Paddy Cullen remembered. "Like they would call me every day after practice saying, 'We need a massage. We need a chiropractor.' [I'd say,] like, no! Get back to work. And I mean, they were definitely pushed to the limit. They were rehearsing with real cheerleading squads. . . . Like I said, they were calling me all the time. Like, there's too many of you, and you just need to do this. You know, and they were young and they did it."

"Nikki Bilderback, who played, obviously, Whitney, we had our hotel rooms beside each other," Kramer said. "And I remember she would be like, 'I can't even sit down to go to the bathroom,' and I would be like, 'Me neither!' We were so sore."

"I think my whole body was sore except for my earlobe and my pinky," Bilderback said. "Literally, we could not move. I mean, it was hard-core."

"They had to do special Eliza days," Dushku remembered. "[Fletcher] made me feel so good but then also was able to really break it down to me that, like, I looked like I wanted to—I was hurting people. Physically, I had the moves down. I had the count down, but my face was giving, you know, murder vibes and I needed to learn about Cheer Face. So there were entire days devoted to like, 'Smile, Eliza!' and adding that perma-grin to the moves. I just remember those cheer camp days as being an opportunity, a weird opportunity in a way for me to like go back in time and have been a part of this group that I totally had never felt I was a part of or would have been welcome to be a part of and I ate it up, it was awesome. It was just fun and crazy."

The vibe was positive and the group supportive, but there was plenty of anxiety from the actors around body image and looking good on-screen as well. "I remember us going for lunch and this was kind of the first time I learned about, it sounds really weird, but the first time that I realized that nutrition was really involved with being an actress," Kramer said. "Tsianina . . . was teaching me about 'Well, I'm gonna have like a bean burrito in a tortilla because I've already had my carbs' or this or that, and I was like what?! I wish I could be that naive again. I remember they would put us in a van and take us to the mall for lunch, you know, go out, do our thing at the mall, and then they put us back in the van and we'd come back to continue training. That was always kind of a fun thing, going to the mall with everybody in our little gym clothes. And then I remember going to the gym after training all day, you know, going and spending like an hour, an hour and a half on the treadmill or whatever. Just trying to get really lean for the movie. They bought us gym memberships, so I felt like that was them strongly suggesting that you could go. And it wasn't like we went for like ten or twenty minutes, we went for like an hour and a half after we finished training."

Rini Bell remembered comparing herself to the rest of the cast and feeling like they were all "Glamazons." Freshly eighteen years old when the movie filmed, she said, "In my opinion I was like the real teen on the set, because I was the one who was actually a mess and the rest of the cast had it just so together, and I never felt like that. They seemed really put together. I am a mess. I think I'm crazy all the time."

That fear of getting fired that many in the cast voiced may have seemed a little unreasonable . . . until someone was actually let go. That one-in-a-million person that Fletcher couldn't teach to dance? She had been cast as Carver, the cheerleader who eats it during Torrance's overly ambitious attempt at the Wolf's Wall in her first practice as captain and breaks her leg, setting the plot in motion for Missy to join the squad.

"Here's the bad story," Fletcher said. "I didn't want to tell it, it's so heart-wrenching. It's so bad and it makes me want to cry. . . . Peyton hired who he wanted as actors and then I just had to make it work, and we did have one incident. That's the bad thing, which is one person didn't work at all. So it was the one in a million. And it was tragic and devastating and upsetting. . . . [That] was an awful experience on my first movie, it was devastating because I don't want that for anybody. You want everybody to succeed and win and do great. That's why we do what we do, because we love it."

The cast was unsettled. "The girl who had originally got the part, I remember Anne was working with her and working with her and we were all sort of like, off to the side in the gym," Kramer said. "And I remember a couple people being like, she's not picking it up, you know, like she's not getting the choreography, it's not going well. There was like a sort of, if I'm remembering correctly, there was like a balcony area where you could watch, an observation deck in the gym, and we're all up there and I was just like, I better absolutely be able to pick up all this stuff. I don't want that to be me that they're working with down there, like, doubting. And then pretty soon after that day or the next day they were like, yeah, we had to replace her."

"There was another actress that played Carver and she did get fired, and her and I kind of came in late together," Lindsay Sloane said. "At the hotel we checked in at the same time, we were driven into rehearsals together, and then suddenly when she's gone after we've been making jokes every day, like, go to your room and sit by your phone because one of us is being sent home, and then she does. I was genuinely afraid that I wasn't pulling my weight."

"[The original actress] got down to San Diego and like, just like anything, everybody says they can cheer," Morris, the casting assistant, remembered. "Like, yeah, can you dance? Yes, you can dance. So we trusted people, you know, we didn't have them do huge choreography. And that phone call of like, no, she's really not it. Because physically that was all about tumbling. And you know what I mean, like that was, that was huge. So that was a little bit of a snafu."

Bianca Kajlich, whom Middleton had seen in auditions but who ultimately hadn't been cast, was called in as a replacement.

"I always wanted Bianca," he said. "For me, it was probably just a win. I always wanted her for the role."

The timing was fortuitous, producer Wong remembered. "Bianca got the call, she was I think literally moving out of her apartment," she said. "She was packed up with a truck outside and moving back to Seattle because she was totally out of money because she failed at Hollywood. It was one of those stories that it worked out for her. I totally forgot about that, but that did happen."

"I can't believe I forgot about this! She got fired!" Ritter said. "She got fired, and then Bianca got cast and Bianca fit with us really fast, like she just fell in, we all became fast friends with Bianca. We were terrified, I mean, we didn't even need that, we were always scared we were gonna get fired on this thing."

The firing didn't just have an impact in the moment—Kramer said that ever since then, she's waited until she's well into production whenever possible to announce new roles, just in case.

Reed, too, felt the blow. "It's horrible," he said. "It was horrible. But you know, ultimately it's like when you're out there, it's hard enough to do it with people who have great senses of rhythm and have rehearsed and stuff, it's just, it's hard. So you have to at least have a starting point, that just has to be enough."

With a renewed sense of can-do and eagerness to prove themselves, the squad kept working, some more into the stunting than others.

Rini Bell, who played Kasey, was . . . not into it, to say the least. "I was like really not cool with how gymnastic it was," she said. "But I mean, the dance part was really fun. I loved that. They had me paired with the actor boys in the very beginning. They were doing the lifts. Like one boy on each side, lifting me up. And I'm like the most fearful one. And they couldn't do it, one guy lifted the leg and the other one didn't and I was like, I'm out of here. If you can picture that, like, when each one lifts you up with one hand on each foot, and one of them goes up and the other one doesn't." She decided to stay groundbound from then on. "Something in me just clicked and I was like, 'Let's stick to the non-lifts. Nope. No thank you.'" She watched in awe as her cast mates stunted: "A lot of the actresses just went for it. And when they did the full-on flip really, like scary, like they throw these people way up in the skies! That was really intimidating."

Kramer was one of the ones who got hooked fast. "I was one who always was like getting held up in the stunts, and it was so fun and so outside of anything I'd ever done," she said. "The cheerleaders were just part of the team, we became a team. We became like a family, a family of unruly teenagers. I did not see a separation between us and [the cheerleaders]. . . . At the end of the movie I was like, I think I'm really gonna continue cheering and like be a professional cheerleader! And my parents were like, 'What? That's not a good idea.' That's how fun I found it. It was fun, and nothing really scared me. I was up for trying it all and doing it all and having just the best time. I still, you know, to this day wonder if I could do any of those lifts and stunts and stuff. I mean, I probably think I could."

"Honestly, we were all like, I can't believe we're getting paid to do this," Ritter said. "This is so fun."

Even Fletcher, with her team of choreographers, cheer coaches, and cheerleaders to help, was shocked at the actors' progress. "We had all the actors with the cheerleaders going up and doing flips, going up in the air one-handed, two-handed with the cheerleaders on the bottom, the guys, and the actresses on top, just like, we were having so much fun and they're all kids and just pumped for life and excited to be there and to be having the best time, just a bunch of kids—it just was a great experience entirely."

And when Dunst arrived to train with the squad shortly before filming, to Fletcher and the producers' relief, she was a quick study, especially under the tutelage of her cast mates. "It was unbelievable," Cullen recalled. "The girls all would be like teaching it to her on the set. And they'd always be practicing and teaching Kirsten. She picked it up. I thought there's no way this is gonna happen, there's no way she's gonna be able to learn, we're gonna have to push shooting and I was really nervous about it. And she's such a pro, she came in and learned it so quick, it was really amazing to watch."

Dunst, for her part, had been a cheerleader in middle school and knew a few moves, plus a double was used for certain stunts. "I couldn't do, like, a backflip," she said. "I knew what it was like to be a base and cradle people properly and stuff like that. I've always been into dance and had done dance stuff as a kid, so that wasn't intimidating to me."

"She got to us and just did great," Fletcher said. "She just caught up really quickly, and for that I was so grateful." She'd feared having to figure out how to choreograph around her, which would have been especially daunting given that Dunst played the main character. "If she comes in and she can't dance and she's that one person in a million . . . I can figure out how to make that work. That is my job." Luckily, though, Fletcher didn't need to figure out how to rely on close-ups and cutaways for the movie's lead, a relief for all.

"I never felt like, 'Oh, I'm the lead of this movie,' and there's this pressure," Dunst said. "I never felt that. I just felt like, oh, we're just having a really great time. I think the rehearsal process was great because it was just us getting to know each other and learning dances. So fun. It's like it's a dream job, to just get together and just learn dances together."

Of course, plenty of movie magic was employed in choreographing and shooting the film overall. Purists and nitpickers will love to point out the parts of *Bring It On* that would never happen in real life.

"Where are the coaches on-screen?" they might yelp. Cut for narrative flow and bulk, that's where. "You could never get away with doing those moves in competition!" "That's illegal in high school competition!" Um, it's a movie?

Fletcher said the movie's cheer choreography specialist relished the chance to loosen up a little: "Ray, when I told him, let's get rid of the rules, he lit up like a Christmas tree. . . . You can only be so creative when you've got all these rules and you're trying to choreograph, but there was no pushback. The cheerleaders were beyond excited, because they got to do something [different]."

On the Clovers side of things, the watchword of the day was "different." Choreographer Hi-Hat brought her own take on cheer movement, incorporating hip-hop sensibilities for the Clovers. (For numbers like "Brr, It's Cold in Here" that both the Clovers and the Toros performed, "my memory of it is Hi-Hat obviously choreographed the Clover stuff and then Anne watched it and then did the sort of stiffer white girl version," Reed said. "It was so amazing.")

"I never wanted to be a cheerleader," Hi-Hat said. "It wasn't hip enough for me. There was no edge, no swag to it, so I definitely never wanted to be a cheerleader, never dreamt of being a Laker Girl or, I don't know if New York has cheerleaders. But, yeah, I think the most intriguing thing was, oh my god, I get to change cheerleading just with this little movie. I get to put the swag, the funk, the movement, remove some of the stiffness, you know, that already was. That was cool."

The pressure was on, not just to learn the choreography but to do it quickly: Gabrielle Union, the members of Blaque, and the designated professional cheerleaders who would fill in the Clovers had less time to train, about two weeks as opposed to the Toros' four, due to both limited cast availability and their smaller slice of screen time.

Some of the professional cheerleaders struggled with Hi-Hat's freer, funkier twist on cheer. "The challenge was difficult for cheerleaders who weren't used to dance," she said. "You know, picking up choreography and just a different way of moving your body. Now you're using not only just straight lines and your arms and being straight and stiff, now you got to kind of move your torso."

Oh, and there was the small matter of Union, who has been vocal about her struggles with dance. "I was only a cheerleader in eighth grade, when you didn't actually need any talent," she told me.

"The cheerleaders had a hard time with the dance part of it, Blaque had a harder time with the cheerleading part," Hi-Hat remembered. "Gabrielle had a hard time with a lot of things, but she did great, you can see the outcome. . . . I found myself, you know, encouraging a lot. 'Come on, you can do it!' You know?"

Union, for her part, laughingly suspects she "broke" Hi-Hat. "I feel like the poor woman was so frustrated with my lack of ability."

"She had a hard time with most moves. But she didn't give up," Hi-Hat said. "I know we had lots of talk, a lot of, like I said, encouraging. She didn't break me—no, not at all."

Fletcher agreed, laughing at Union's claims. "I love her something fierce, by the way, she's so funny," she told me, also waving away the actress's belief that she dealt a soul-deep blow to Hi-Hat with her (lack of) coordination. "Oh yeah, I don't know that to be true, I just don't believe it. I mean, I'm sure it was difficult, because the choreographies are very difficult. Gabrielle can dance. That girl, we've done two movies together with dancing. She can dance."

"I think Gabrielle is famous now for sort of saying like, 'Oh, I can barely do it, get out the Bengay, I'm so sore,'" Reed said. "She was only twenty-seven. Come on!"

As you can see for yourself in the finished movie, it all worked out. Union—and the rest of the cast, for that matter—look like legitimate cheerleaders, not out of place among the ESPN of it all.

"They were beaming like the sun," Fletcher said of the actors when they nailed their stunts and put the pieces together. "When they finally got up there, like, oh my god, I did it, and then it just kept going and kept going and they get more confident so we could go a little further. That was the whole boot camp, and then within the boot camp of the cheerleading aspect of it was the dance rehearsal for the opening number, because all of it has to be really dialed in. That's why I step back and go, wow, I'm still—one of the things that I can say I'm really proud of is that movie, because it was a first on my own. It was a massive, massive undertaking. And we totally did this, we pulled this off and it's just amazing."

Just as important as looking believable as cheerleaders, the cast came out of cheer camp looking believable as friends, as a team. They'd bonded with each other and with the filmmakers, resulting in an on-set atmosphere many said they'd never experienced again in their careers.

"Anne, sweet Anne, is the best. We had the best choreographer, Peyton is one of the kindest humans I've ever known, and we bonded," Sloane said. "We all fell in love, we were in San Diego and it felt like real camp, and it was kind of one of those dreamy experiences to have on a set. I'm so grateful that it was like my early twenties. I was a kid. I didn't get to finish college because I was working, and it just was an experience [where] I was like, here is this thing that you don't get to experience often, and now you get to do it."

Dushku summed it up: "I think we were all on a cheer high. I mean, we were infused through and through with the cheer fever."

Here's a math problem: What do you get when you take a dozen and a half–ish people, ranging in age from seventeen to twenty-seven years old? Give each of them one (1) hotel room and zero (0) parental supervision. Oh, and make them all actors, so they're facially blessed, shall we say. And keep in mind that this word problem is situated approximately twenty miles from the Mexican border. Solve for x. Show your work.

If you came to the answer of "x equals absolute shenanigans," you are correct. With its young cast of newcomers, all living together in a hotel (with the exception of Dunst, who was underage and had a rented house in La Jolla with her mother), "it was definitely kind of like *Animal House* a bit," West said. "It was a party. And I don't think you'd blame any of us for doing it, and I wouldn't take anything back, because we had such a great time together."

As if at some kind of adult sleepaway camp, the cast of *Bring It On* spent their nights roaming from room to room in their Gaslamp

District Marriott Suites, some of which, in the case of Bilderback's, were personalized with photos and throw pillows, individual touches to remind them of home.

The days followed a routine. "We would be picked up at the butt-crack of dawn and then work all day," Bilderback said. "Wrap, and then work out or we'd go to dinner, but then there was always partying going, we were always hanging out." Lather, rinse, repeat, with mall food-court lunches of bunless burgers, that staple menu item of the late '90s, to keep their energy up.

"We'd all hang out together," Tsianina Lohmann, who played Darcy, said. "We all did everything pretty much together. We'd go to lunch, we'd hang out afterwards. Yeah, we were just always together, so I guess it's like being at camp, really."

And like camp, the bonds seemed to form instantly, like in the case of Ritter and West, who still consider each other close friends today. They recognized one another from Ritter's fateful audition cartwheel mind trick when they arrived in San Diego and decided they were in for some fun that summer.

"We broke the ice real quick," West recalled of their official meeting. "We had some dinner and hung out and then we're working out the next day, he's in the gym. I'm like, all right, I'm gonna go to the gym too. We became best pals. He's an awesome guy."

Or Bell, who recalled hanging out a lot with Lohmann—whose nickname was Chu, short for Tsianina—in particular, remembering the coffee drink made of "all kinds of sweet garbage" that Lohmann would make for her "like five times a day" to keep spirits and energy up, a silly ritual that makes her laugh now, decades later.

"She called it the Chu Surprise, and it was like coffee and all kinds of garbage in it," she said.

But let's be real: the vibe with the cast of *Bring It On* was a slightly less wholesome camp than any kiddie worth their bug spray ever attended. The word "debauchery" was thrown around in these interviews. More than once.

Maybe Bilderback's comparison is more apt than summer camp. "We were all one big sorority with the guys," she said. "It was literally just all of us and we partied, I mean, you know when you're that age, you can drink it up and have fun and not go to bed till two, three in the morning and still wake up at 6:00 AM, shove some oatmeal down your face, and head out the door and work the whole day. You know, now—now, it takes me like three days to recover if I have one glass of wine."

With a per diem and a dream—not to mention the superhuman liver strength and ability to exist on a sleep deficit of someone in their early twenties—the world was the cast's oyster. Sixty dollars a day, every day: a boon for many of the young actors. "I was like, whoa, I'm making so much money off a per diem. I don't know if I need to worry about the check from *Bring It On*," Shamari Fears DeVoe, one of the members of Blaque, who played Lava on the Clovers squad, said. "I'm not even eating sixty dollars' worth of food. I was racking up money!"

"Twenty-year-olds with a per diem? I was in heaven!" Sloane recalled.

Extra cash, instant friends, and a room of one's own, what more could an up-and-coming actor ask for? When I asked her if she had participated in any extracurricular antics that summer, Lohmann laughed. "Which one?"

Every night was a hang somewhere, fun never farther than a hotel room or two away. A slumber party every night, but this time with booze. There were two rules held sacred amongst the cast:

1. Make the call time the next morning. No matter what state you're in, get yourself into the van and show up for work.

2. Under no circumstances can you let Paddy find out.

Line producer Paddy Cullen's job was to make sure that all the trains on the production were running on time, and, to extend the metaphor further, to make sure the cars were receiving proper maintenance, all the conductors' health benefits were paying out as they should, and all the seat cushions were accounted for and in good shape. She is an industry vet; when you scroll on her IMDb page, you just keep scrolling, it's that long. She is also, in a word, kind of scary. She's here to get stuff done. She knows you know better than that. She's not mad, she's just disappointed. Her job is to make sure everyone is doing their jobs so that Reed, the director, can do *his* job.

"Paddy is *business*," West said. "She's straight up. She had to corral a bunch of twentysomethings, but she did a great job."

For Cullen, the decision to take a job is "more logistics than creative, unless it's something really offensive to you," she said. "Mainly I'm not one genre, you know, I will do a romantic comedy and I will do a horror movie, it doesn't matter to me. They're all fun, you know, they all have their own challenges." And this movie, which she describes as ending up as one of her favorite projects she's worked on, certainly had plenty of both.

"I was kind of the den mother to all the actors too, for sure," she said. "There was Kirsten, who was underage, and the rest of them were fairly young, so that was definitely different, because the whole cast was young, pretty much. So you kind of had to watch over them a little bit more, you know, you're more protective of them than you might have been with adults."

Which, yeah, that makes sense not only when you're helming a project with a lower budget and a rambunctious young cast, meaning that staying on budget and therefore on schedule is extremely important, but when that rambunctious young cast is in San Diego, which, as a reminder, is just a quick drive from the Mexican border and all of the potential (mis)adventures that lie beyond it.

You can guess what happened next.

A few times.

That we know of.

"That's what they get for putting a bunch of young, early twenty-year-olds, deciding on San Diego as your location being so close to the border," Bilderback said. "They had to know. I mean, come on!"

Cullen made it clear to the cast that jaunts across the border were, in Courtney's words, *strictly verboten*. And yet: "They did, for sure," she said. "Definitely. 'Please don't get stuck in Mexico. Don't go there. Please don't do it.' Of course they did. . . . They may have missed the day's shoot because they said they were sick, but no one said they were arrested in Mexico."

They may not have admitted it at the time, but what happened in Mexico didn't stay in Mexico.

"It was definitely me, Rini, Eliza, and this dude named Lance," Jesse Bradford said. "Lance had a 1966 or so teal blue Volkswagen Beetle convertible. The four of us got talking, or I think Lance kind of talked to the three of us into driving down to the Baja. And we got pulled over. What I recall is that we pulled a wonky traffic move, like a U-turn where you weren't supposed to pull a U-turn, and that's what got us pulled over by the Mexican police forces."

"The movie we always say felt in some ways like a three-month spring break in San Diego," Dushku said. "We worked very hard, but also really enjoyed ourselves and had fun and really became friends and did crazy things therefore on weekends. And when Tijuana was a half hour away, it felt natural one night to get in a Volkswagen Bug and then see what kind of trouble we could get into."

And yes, that Bug got into trouble.

"He kind of ran a couple of stop signs," Bell said. "And they pulled us over and they took us to jail. And they were yelling at us, like, you know, you kids, your friends are going to jail. And somebody was saying, 'Don't worry, I know how to bribe them.'"

"They pulled us over and took us all out of the car, and they gave us the world's worst breathalyzer test where they basically just hold like a little postcard up underneath your chin and tell you to like blow at the postcard, and then they put their nose up on the other side and sniff and go, *Ooooooh, oooooooh!*" Bradford said. "Seriously, that was the breathalyzer. And then the police conferred for a little while and came back and said, 'We can either arrest all of you or two of you. And if we arrest two of you, it's *you* and *you*'—and he pointed at me and Eliza, and we took a hit for the team."

Dushku, though "it all blurs together when it's such an exciting night," remembered a potential prohibited item leading to the eventual arrest once they'd been pulled over.

"The officer searched us and was like, pulled out Jesse's jackknife and was like, '*Oh, es muy prohibido.* Get in the back of the truck.' We were like, what's happening? That was an adventure."

Bell panicked: "I was in way over my head, I can't be this cool. I tried, though, because I grew up in New Orleans. I was, like, raised to be cool. But it was too much for me."

Bradford continued, "I remember being handcuffed and put in the back of a pickup truck, a police pickup truck, true story, and then brought to the station, where [Eliza] and I had to wait in line to be seen by the judge, which was a very rapid-fire process. There's a dozen people ahead of us, and they're either getting sent home or put in jail, and the door to the prison area's right there."

He remembered trying desperately to speak Spanish with an "incredibly drunk older local" in line in front of him, trying to telegraph to those around him that he knew what they were saying. (He didn't.)

"I remember he was before us, and he went up in front of the judge, and I couldn't hear anything they were saying but they threw him in jail. And he looked back at me like I was his savior. As they were pulling him through the door he was like, *ahhhhhh!* as he went through the door and I was like, *Oh god, that's gonna be me.*

"And then it was Eliza's turn to go in front of the judge, and I couldn't hear anything they were saying, but he let her go. And that was when I really, like, tried to make peace with the idea that I was going to jail, because she had been let go. So I kind of figured I was going to be the scapegoat. And I got up in front of the judge and he said, 'Well, you guys, you got to pay a fine.' And the fine was the equivalent of like twenty US dollars, and I paid the fine and he like wrote down my driver's license information, wrote it down with a pen and put it in a little Rolodex thing, like a recipe box, put it in like a recipe box. You know, like picture your grandma with like a little recipe box. And basically said, 'We're letting you go this time, but if you come down here again, we've got your information and if you fuck up down here again, you're gonna be in a lot of trouble.' And I was like, yes *sir.* And I've never been back to Rosarito in my entire life."

When the two were reunited with the pack, Bell recalled, "I don't know what happened or how, somehow everyone just got out of jail. And we all went to the club and drank a bunch of really yummy frozen margaritas and partied all night. Only at that age would you go to jail and then go to a club afterwards. And you're in Mexico. I was really scared though, because it was a little crazy, a little wild. And Eliza and Jesse were not worried. They were just so, like, fearless."

Dushku, freshly eighteen years old the summer *Bring It On* filmed, also remembered rallying: "If I recall, we just bounced right back into it!"

Bradford's memories are a little different. "It ruined the whole night, obviously," he said. "We just crashed out. We woke up the next morning and had like sort of a sad and somber, like, 'OK, we got to just get back to America as soon as possible' kind of day. And we got back to America as soon as possible, and no one was the wiser until we told you."

Dushku, twenty-two-plus years after the fact, also laughed it off: "Well, you know, things come out."

Ah, life before Instagram. "There was just a sense of community, because the times were different and life was different and there wasn't social media and you could mess up and go to Mexico and the whole world didn't know about it," Sloane said of the late nights and deep bonds that summer. "I miss the innocence of what that was, for sure. We were all so connected, because no one was looking down, we were all looking at each other."

"It's a fun memory looking back, like it was bonding in that way when you get into trouble with people," Bell said. "But it was also so stupid. It was like silly trouble, you know? Now it's a good memory."

Bradford agrees—and doesn't hold a grudge about word getting out, by the way. "You know, come on. It's fun," he said. "It makes me feel like Keith Richards to have a story like that from my past, you know? And, you know, no harm, no foul, everybody made it through."

And the best part of it all is, they didn't even break either of the cast's cardinal rules: Paddy didn't find out (not until much later, at least), and they made their call time the next morning. "We didn't miss anything," Bradford said. "No, nobody missed anything."

Dushku, in 2015, said, "We were legitimately scared that Paddy would—you know, she was a tough broad. Love her to death. We knew she would not be amused if we didn't make it back for filming."

"I didn't hear about [an arrest], but I wouldn't doubt it, because everybody gets arrested in Mexico," Cullen said. "At the border they do arrest people for no reason, a lot of times."

Beyond a healthy fear of returning to Rosarito and facing up to that handwritten strike one, Bradford still has another souvenir from that night, to this day. "I paid [the fine] in American dollars and I got my change in pesos," he said. "And I kept the change. I could still tell you exactly where that change is. I kept it as a good-luck charm for the rest of my life."

I should note here that when news of the Mexico antics broke—again, my fault—and it entered *Bring It On* lore in 2015, there was one point of contention, depending on who was talking. At the time, producer Wong said that she found out about a bunch of the cast getting arrested in Tijuana and had to step in. "At some point, Eliza and a couple of the actors felt like they were in so much danger they decided to make themselves less attractive by using lipstick to draw all over their faces," she said. "I don't know how that worked, but that was their strategy. Needless to say, I got a middle-of-the-night phone call to bail them out, and I did."

Dushku, in 2015, called BS. "I want to go on the record and say no producers came and bailed us out. There may have been an incident in TJ one weekend, but we got ourselves out of it. I got us out of it and there was no producer bailing-out happening, so that was an embellishment. I am quite a negotiator. I would admit there was an incident, but we got out in that turquoise convertible VW Beetle and were back for work on time."

"We had to pay our own bail," Bradford said. "I've still got the pesos to prove it."

In her own defense, Wong brought up the discrepancy on her own to set the record straight when we caught up years later for this book.

"In the *Bring It On* article you wrote, I was just sort of like, oh yeah, like the cheerleaders totally got arrested, and that happened more than once. I have to say that Eliza Dushku was right: *she* was not in the group that called me from Mexico to bail them out, so if you talk to her about this next, you can say I was totally wrong. I admit it, and next time she sees me she can punch me, OK? Maybe not in the face, but anywhere else.

"We're all unreliable narrators," she said. "Eliza's trip, it was actually Rosarito, not Tijuana. She was arrested in Rosarito."

For what it's worth: "It's not punch-worthy, in the face or elsewhere," Bradford said. "That was the perfect crime at the time. We got back, no one knew, and we went about our business."

"I didn't know any of this, by the way," Dunst told me, decades down the line. "Not until we started talking and having these reunions and stuff, like, 'Oh, you guys like went to Mexico?' I think it was just that they were older than me and I just missed out on it all. I was just at home watching fucking *Dawson's Creek*, I guess."

But wait, if not Dushku and Bradford . . . who did Wong bail out in Tijuana?

The cast remained tight-lipped on whoever else may have gotten caught, but plenty admitted to some extracurricular international travel, like the night that Bilderback said "could have been really, really really disastrous, a disaster," or DeVoe admitting that in her downtime, "I would, like, catch the trolley from San Diego to Tijuana, Mexico just because, like, let me just get out of here." Or Union, who in 2015 laughed when she told me, "It was a pretty good time, there might have been some trips down to Tijuana, perhaps. Unconfirmed! Unconfirmed bribing of federale. The stuff of legend."

"I think there was this unbridled enthusiasm to just experience things," Sloane said. "And look, San Diego is very close to Mexico, you cannot fault that. It's right there, it's basically calling for that."

And then there's West, who said that he and "six or seven of us" ended up dancing in a massive house south of the border, he's not sure whose, when "there were certain points where I was like, maybe this is a really bad idea." The talking-to that he got after, "that was a moment with Paddy that I won't forget. . . . Paddy was pissed. You don't want to piss off Paddy."

And undoubtedly many more stories, lost to time, memory, or just good old-fashioned discretion.

If it seems like all this would raise alarm bells with the higher-ups on the film or the brass at the studio, think again. They didn't know, didn't care, or some combination of the above.

"I spent my life getting up to shenanigans. The last thing I was gonna do was to be den mother," Beacon exec Abraham said. As long as it didn't slow down the production, get anyone hurt, or balloon the budget, it was all harmless fun. "A bunch of young, good-looking kids getting together and figuring out who to be with, that's their problem. I'm sure they did, you may get a lot of good stories about who was doing who, but no, I didn't know and I didn't care."

Universal exec O'Hair, too, was happy to be kept in the dark on the specifics. His job was to watch dailies and act as a go-between for the production and the financing entity, reporting back to Universal on how their investment was coming along and keeping them psyched about the project. On the flip side, he also had a responsibility to *Bring It On* to make sure they knew that the studio was still excited. A Hollywood ouroboros in action with an interest in turning a blind eye to anything that would raise eyebrows.

"Those are things that, unless they became serious, it's not in my best interest to talk about that at a staff meeting," he said. "Your next questions to the filmmaker are 'Is everybody alive? Is it handled? OK.' Just don't go into detail."

Reed, for his part, wasn't totally oblivious, but he was busy. "I was the responsible adult on that movie," he said. "You're on a real need-to-know basis. You're sometimes shielded from that stuff." Picture the on-set producers paddling furiously underwater to keep all the moving parts working together smoothly and the surface of the water glassy and smooth for first-time director Reed.

Scanlon explained that as a producer, "you're overseeing everything. So making sure that you're working hand in hand with your line producer and your director, but it's like you're trying to have to keep as much from your director as possible, meaning as much of the little chaotic things; they need their mind clear to truly be creative and work with their actors."

"I got little glimpses of their shenanigans," Reed said. "All this sort of going down south of the border thing I was blissfully unaware of until after the fact. . . . I knew something was up. . . . I still probably don't know half the shenanigans that went on."

The cast, too, knew where the line was and that they were there to do a job, Bilderback said. "They had patience and understood we were young, but again, we also weren't being irresponsible and we all woke up, we all showed up," she said. "We weren't hungover, we performed, we delivered, so there wasn't any of those issues where they needed to stop and pull us aside and be like, you guys, get yourselves under control. There wasn't any of that, not with us."

It wasn't all close brushes with Mexican authority, either. Most of the time, it was the typical young adult stuff, those nights when you're having such a good time that it's three in the morning before you know it. When you can barely keep your eyes open, but you can't imagine letting the night end. Kids, really. When you say things like "friends forever" without a trace of doubt. With many of the cast over eighteen but still under twenty-one, the party mostly stayed in the hotel, and no last call meant the night could easily bleed into the morning.

"There's a few nights where I didn't even go to bed, you know, then work the next day," West said. "But then of course my role is like, sometimes it was like, maybe one line or look and I'm like, 'Oh, I'm just gonna look tomorrow, so I can totally party,' you know? Like, how hard is that to do? We had a great time, we really did."

Lohmann remembered the early call times and stealing every moment to charge up for the day ahead. "Big bags under your eyes," she remembered. "People did fall asleep in the [makeup] chair from time to time in the morning. That's for sure."

Kramer recalled, "I'll just say this: There were days that the makeup did not get washed off from the day before, and we would show up and they would tilt our chairs all the way back, and we'd go to sleep while they would remove yesterday's makeup and put on the next day's makeup. We were unruly, crazy, definitely. We were on the border there so, yeah, I remember at times thinking, 'Well, if I'm in bed by three and my call time's six, that's two hours and forty-five minutes to sleep.' Ridiculous!"

They'd also spend time with Dunst, at her house with her mom in La Jolla. There were barbecues and afternoon hangs hosted there occasionally.

"We'd go out there and have like soda—very, you know, kid-appropriate time with her and her mom," Union said, "and then we, you know, go back and we drink and etc., you know, head over the border, we'd be down in the Gaslamp District."

Dunst said that though she'd been working in major movies for a decade by then, she wasn't one of those hard-partying Hollywood kids. "I was very innocent," she said of her seventeen-year-old self. And with the exception of "a sneaky drink here and there" that she's sure she shared with the other cast, "they felt older than me. So it would make sense that like we wouldn't necessarily hang out all the time."

Some cast members felt they'd adopted Dunst. "Kirsten was very sweet," Ritter said. "I just felt like she was my little sister. I definitely wanted to protect her."

Bell remembered, "We were like, Why are you partying with your mom? Like, it was confusing why she wanted that. But we managed to get her to hang out with us and party with us a couple of times. We felt like we were doing a special service. Saving you from your mom. She seemed pretty content hanging out with her mom."

"My mom's from Jersey and she's fun," Dunst said, though she remembered the cast party at her place as "not a rager."

"I think they knew they just couldn't bring me into it, because I had my mom there and I wasn't of age," she said. "It would be the same situation now if I was working with someone who was like seventeen and I was in my twenties, I'm not going to totally debaucherize the seventeen-year-old who's with her mom. Is 'debaucherize' even a word?"

As the oldest main cast member at twenty-seven, Union would bounce between groups, sometimes hanging out with the girls from

Blaque or their parents, or bonding with Dunst's mom in La Jolla, as well as the main cast. "We had a fucking blast," she said. "My first few movies, I thought, oh my god, this is how it's gonna be for the rest of my career, this is, oh my god, this is so much fun. Yeah, not so much. So now I look back and it's, it's just—it's just fun. It's pure fun, no pressure, you know, socially, I should say. Sometimes the hardest part of filmmaking is connecting off screen, and finding how do you fill the void with folks that you wouldn't necessarily maybe choose for yourself. That can be the harder part."

It was a safe space for many of the cast members to do a lot of growing up.

"It was definitely lots of hotel parties, lots of, of course, you know, drinking," Kramer said. "No social media, which was a great thing for all of us. I'm so glad, so glad I didn't come of age in the social media age. But yeah, every night, I feel like pretty much every night we had a gathering somewhere. I don't know how we did it. I really don't. But we were always on time!"

In her memoir essay collection *We're Going to Need More Wine*, Union wrote, "Everyone was horny, and there were a lot of marriages that didn't make it to the end of production."

Still protective of one another, the cast stayed vague on breakups and hook-ups. Asked about Union's quote, West said, "I know there was some stuff that went down. . . . I think said person, you know, there might have been more than one, but I know one in particular, for her, I think she was just, she wanted something else in life, and I don't think you can blame someone for that. She handled it the way she knew to handle it."

And, of course, like anything you've had decades to look back on, there are some regrets. Sloane, an actor since she was a kid, called herself "too responsible to be irresponsible," saying that Cullen and Wong "really liked me" in somewhat mournful tones. "They never had to worry about me.

"It's a bummer, it's a lost opportunity," she said. "I allowed myself to have fun up into a certain degree, and I would always excuse myself like an hour before the party got really good. . . . Oh, man, I wish I got to Mexico, just to have that story. . . . I didn't drink enough or experience enough, I just didn't say yes enough."

Still, Sloane and the other cast members gushed about that summer in San Diego as a gilded one, halcyon days. An absolute unicorn of an experience that many say has been unmatched since then.

"For a lot of us it was our first good job in Hollywood and some people it wasn't, but we were all just like—everybody says Hollywood is full of snakes and such, and this was just really a positive experience," Bell said. "Now, I think Hollywood is full of snakes, like I'm that person who's like, 'Oh, kid, watch out for Hollywood.' But really not from that movie. I mean, everyone was so sweet to each other. There was a little bit of pettiness, but it was like youthful pettiness. And we all just really wanted to do a good job and we all really believed in each other."

ANATOMY OF THE SORORITY SQUAT

> "The squad hits an ornate formation in seconds
> flat. Torrance grabs the Stick, handing it over."
> —*Bring It On* shooting script stage directions

It's a classic of the genre: the sorority squat. It is written that in any photograph where five or more women are gathered, there's an 89 percent chance that this pose will be deployed. Just before Torrance sentences herself to an eternity in [cue voice effect] Hades, as New Pope Cheerleader #2 explains, she's taking a picture of another squad with the spirit stick. Kamla-Kay McKenzie, professional model, modeling and posing coach, and author of *How to Become a Model*, shared tips for how to get that picture-perfect sorority squat in your next group pic with the spirit stick.

ANGLES: "If you are someone who wants to just tilt your head slightly, that's perfectly fine. You know, sometimes you just think, oh, the right side of my face is a little bit more my favorite. It's perfectly fine. You just don't want to do too much. You don't want to be too extra."

ARMS: "Both of your hands should be either on your knees or on your thighs, whatever is most comfortable."

KNEES: "Make sure your knees are together; otherwise, it's not going to look like the sorority squat at all."

FEET: "Your feet should actually not be touching; they should be slightly separated but parallel to each other."

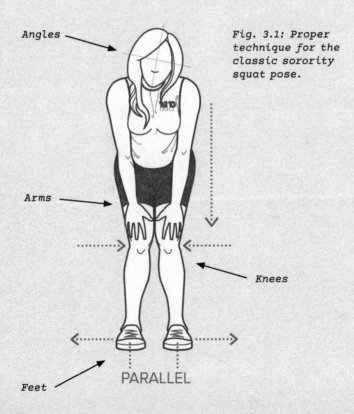

Fig. 3.1: Proper technique for the classic sorority squat pose.

SMILE: "So say cheese, but don't really say cheese. It's a happy moment. Don't be the Cruella de Vil face." If you're tired of smiling, try looking away and resetting your face, sucking in your cheeks to relax your facial muscles, or even laughing out loud. Fake it till you make it!

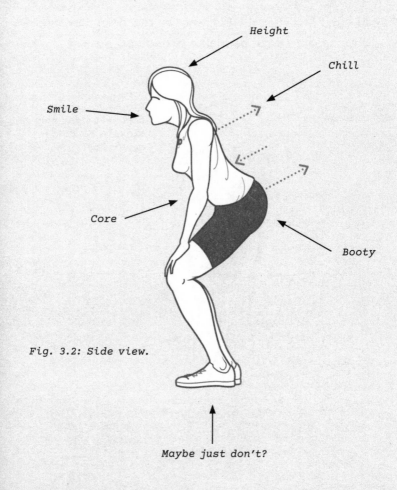

Fig. 3.2: Side view.

HEIGHT: "You're going to bend down to probably about half your height position." This is your height in whatever shoes you're wearing, so take your heels into account.

CORE: "When you're doing this, especially if you're someone that's concerned about your tummy, it's almost like when you're working out or doing yoga, they always tell you when you're breathing that you want to make sure that your belly button is going inward, like you're breathing in and tightening your core. So it certainly helps just in terms of how your body will look. Not required, but I do suggest, just tighten up your core a little bit."

CHILL: "The tendency for most people . . . [is] to tense up and put our shoulders more towards our ears. In this squat, you want to make sure that your shoulders are back and down, and not upwards and towards your ears. So it's almost like you want to relax your shoulders and push them down as you're sticking your butt out. You look chill, but your butt looks great."

BOOTY: If you want to put the "ass" in "association," feel free to arch your back a little. "For someone that really wants to accentuate that part of their body, you're going to do a slight curve in your back, so as you do more of a curve your butt is going to go out and upward a little bit."

MAYBE JUST DON'T: "I would get thrown out of my modeling agency if I sent in my portfolio with a photo of that pose. Let's make that clear. This is not for your modeling portfolio."

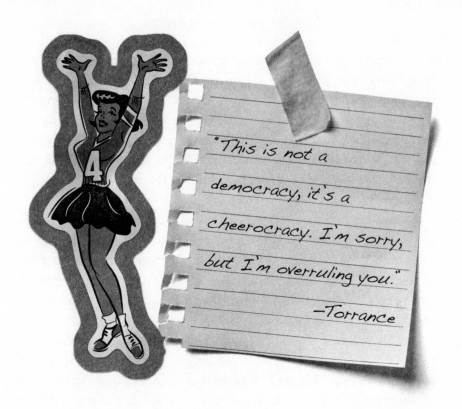

"This is not a democracy, it's a cheerocracy. I'm sorry, but I'm overruling you."

—Torrance

Before the cameras could roll on *Cheer Fever*, there was yet more work to be done. While finalizing the cast, Reed also launched into planning, storyboarding, and finalizing the script to take the story from page to screen in a tidy, ninety-ish-minute PG-13 package, on time and on budget.

"The two biggest things to me that were terrifying were the casting, getting that right, and also sort of corralling the script into shape, because it was too long," he said. He described it as an epic, complete with a subplot about a bitter dance team captain named Pam Anne who had it out for the cheer squad at Rancho Carne.

Reed and Bendinger got to work finessing the final script, a process that often got tense.

"It was tricky in the beginning, because Jessica—and I think rightfully so—was reluctant to change anything in the script," Reed said. "Jessica, I think, would have loved to have seen it shot as-is, don't change a word, but that's most writers, right? Because writers spend a lot of time getting things exactly the way they want them. These words don't just magically appear on the page." And in Bendinger and *Cheer Fever*'s case, she'd spent years developing and tweaking the script already. She had wanted to direct the movie, so it's no surprise that it was an added sting to have Reed arrive on the scene and start quickly overhauling the script—don't forget that tight production timeline, the ever-tick-tick-ticking clock to the first day of principal photography.

"It was my first movie, it was Peyton's first movie," Bendinger told me in 2015. "All the dumb first movie mistakes, we now laugh about it because we're still friends. He's trying to make a movie, and I'm trying to get my movie to be as close to my first script as possible, so there's this horribly combative stuff and I was super inexperienced and a pain in the ass for sure."

Reed's priorities with the script included both narrowing and expanding: tighten the story to cut length, and broaden the appeal of the movie by removing a bit of deep-cut cheerleading material and grounding the script while maintaining the movie's overall attitude and heightened language. No sweat, right?

"There were definitely times early on when we would sit in Jessica's apartment in West Hollywood . . . and work on it and I would have come with possible edit notes because we had to get the page count down," Reed said. "We actually *had* to get it down for budgetary reasons and stuff, so, you know, I started off with Jessica in the sort of quote unquote Kill Your Darlings phase of the writing, right, because we were in active prep. As soon as I came on we were prepping and we were staring at this shoot start date, which was a handful of weeks away. We had to make decisions. So I'm sure that process started really quickly and probably abruptly as far as Jessica is concerned, which is tricky."

Dan Waters, the *Heathers* screenwriter and friend of Bendinger's, remembered that period. "Jessica doesn't need anybody to tell her, 'Hey, fight for what you believe in, don't let them change your life.' We have unsuccessfully tried to be an influence in her life of like, hey, pick your battles, don't fight everything," he said. "Like if I give them one thing, they won't notice I didn't do this other thing. Jessica will fight on every point. Because she knows her way is better. She didn't take our play-nice advice."

"They hadn't worked on it as long or as hard as I had," Bendinger said. She had recommendations and connections for everything in the cheer world, from uniform suppliers to cheer coaches and choreographers, garnering a coproducer credit on the finished movie alongside her screenwriting credit.

Bendinger and Reed pulled teeth and cut lines: farewell to Pam Anne the dance team captain, as well as every adult character in the script, with the exception of Torrance's parents and choreographer Sparky Polastri (yes, yes, we know high school squads have coaches; it's a movie and can only be so long), hello to an agreement to throw the official rules of high school cheerleading out the window and just make it look cool.

Though the script would see continuous tweaks throughout production, like any movie, it was finally time to start filming. *Action*.

At long last, after years of writing, pitching, development, and training, shooting began on *Cheer Fever* at the Stu Segall Productions studio in San Diego on July 12, 1999, the same day the Clovers actors arrived to begin their cheer camp. Up until that first "action!" a movie is a maybe, Universal exec Hughes said. It can be a probably-maybe, but once you start shooting, it's nearly impossible to put the toothpaste back in the tube.

"You really, really do hold your breath until that first day of shooting," he said. "Then you exhale a little bit on that day, completely. Because things can still go wrong once the movie starts to shoot, but really once you get to that first day, for the most part, you think like, OK, we're at least—we're making a movie. We're really doing this. So at that point you feel like it's real."

It was to be forty-four intense shooting days, which Reed had meticulously planned and storyboarded with cinematographer Shawn Maurer, a longtime friend and collaborator whom Reed had fought hard to get hired on the movie, which was Maurer's first big studio feature as director of photography. While the cast continued to bond and have wild nights at their hotel in the Gaslamp, Reed, Maurer, Cullen and other key crew were ensconced in the tony golf community of La Jolla, where they got wild with spreadsheets and shot lists every night to keep production on time and on budget.

"Everybody to me at that point were strangers, like Marc and Max and Caitlin and Universal, the studio, all of it. So I needed somebody there, and Shawn was that person for me . . . someone that I knew and trusted intimately shooting that movie with me," Reed said.

Reed and Maurer had met at a production company called Amblin Entertainment, Steven Spielberg's shingle. They were on the sets of huge productions like *Back to the Future* and *Forrest Gump*, but they were the below-the-lines of the below-the-line, making the behind-the-scenes documentary featurettes about the productions. It was like an extremely meta on-the-job training program, making their own movie together while seeing some of the biggest names in the business make the films that would top the box office on their release. This was in the '90s, before DVD special features were a thing. Remember Laser-Disc? That's where you'd find this stuff. Reed and Maurer would work together on movie sets, then go hang out and nerd out over *other* movies together after work. They learned what to do (and what not to do) partially by watching the setups on the movies they were documenting—the light tricks that the feature cinematographer might use, for example, or how the on-set vibe changed with a word from the director.

"We were all the same age pretty much, and we're out of film school and we're just very eager and just want to do great stuff," Maurer said of working with Reed pre–*Bring It On*. They were close friends, and when Reed reached out to see if he'd be interested in being the director of photography on *Cheer Fever*, Maurer didn't hesitate. There was a hurdle, though: getting studio approval to hire him. Maurer is a visuals guy, pretty laconic in conversation. And he'd never actually *had* a job interview before, he told me, having gotten all of his other work through referrals and friends. By his own admission, he absolutely biffed his first interview with Abraham, describing it as "stumbling for half an hour." Fortunately for him (and the movie), he got a second chance to make that first impression and prepped like mad. "Luckily, I passed the second time," he said. "In hindsight, I think it's so remarkable that I ever got that job."

By having someone like Maurer with whom he had a shared history and who understood his filmmaking style, Reed had a creative compass and rudder. Director and cinematographer would bounce ideas off one another.

For example: "I presented Peyton with a visual, the inspiration I had for *Bring It On*. It's gonna sound nutty, because it was Orson Welles in *Citizen Kane*." Welles's Kane was filmed throughout the touchstone 1941 movie from extreme low angles, so low that the crew had to make holes in the set floor to physically lower the refrigerator-sized cameras into. "It was 1941, black and white, but it was storytelling in a graphic visual sense, and I wanted to relay that to Peyton as like, this is what we should be doing," Maurer said. But of course, "I wasn't going to be digging holes in the sets." DVD may not have really been a thing in 2000, but technology *had* advanced since the '40s. The shot where Union's Isis is introduced—throwing her arms in the air to signal for silence in that gym with its soaring vaulted ceilings, larger than life in her Clovers uniform—is a direct visual reference to *Citizen Kane*.

Those long nights after the long days of shooting, Reed remembers "going through and shot-listing stuff and just everything being on the fly, because the script was in flux and the production schedule is changing fast. . . . We had a shorthand, so if the two of us knew what was happening, everything was going to be OK."

Maurer remembers there being "I don't want to say *no* oversight, but . . .

"We were these geeky film student kids, and we want to do what we like watching, that's how we want to make this movie," he said. "There were no adults in the room. We were on our own. It's strange, because the last six, eight years, I've been doing television. There can be *so many* directors. For this, we didn't have that. Our playbook was just the movies we love."

He remembered evenings fine-tuning the script with Reed. "I would go over to his place in San Diego and he would just spitball ideas at me and I would laugh or not, and he's adjusting the script." It was stressful, he said, but like Reed, he said it was "good stress."

Reed recalled, "I know there were a couple of cookouts or things like that, but that literally is a blur to me, because I was so myopic about, just, I had my chance to direct the movie. I just wanted that to be all it was about."

Producer Bliss would make the drive and stop in to check on the shoot occasionally, but he largely kept to Beacon's Los Angeles offices. He knew the pressure Reed was under. "It was a really quick production," he said. "It was simple, it kind of had a modest budget sort of sensibility to it. I'm not gonna say it was down and dirty, because $12 million is a lot of money. But it certainly wasn't a blockbuster, spend whatever you had to spend kind of mentality and I have a theory, having worked at all budget ranges, that when you have parameters, it actually forces you to think it through. . . . When you're just looking at the paper, the script, and edit in advance, I think you come up with a better product, I really do. And so I think that the mentality of limits really helped all of us, and especially Peyton and the cast, make what I think is a really good picture, a really good picture. Excellent picture."

With a young cast, young production team, young director (see a theme here?), and relatively small budget, there was a thirst for success and excellence, a scrappy sensibility, and a fuck-you attitude while the project flew under the radar. Scanlon and Wong had begged on their knees for Beacon to buy the pitch, worked with Bendinger on development for years, then talked up the project around town to find a studio home to finance the movie, and they were personally invested in its success. It was their chance to be in the driver's seat, whereas on other Beacon movies like *Air Force One*, it felt like there hadn't been room for them in the car at all. That had been an $85 million movie, starring heavyweights Harrison Ford, Gary Oldman, and Glenn Close. The vibe in *Cheer Fever* meetings was different, to say the least. The Beacon brass were fine to have Scanlon and Wong leading the charge.

"Max and I both had experiences of bringing movies into a big company and being sort of taken off them pretty quickly," Scanlon recalled. "Being taken off them because there's just not a lot of room for you. When every meeting has literally like ten people in it because each movie star has to have, you know, as many representatives as humanly possible to protect them and every change has to go through a committee and it just gets watered down and invariably becomes shitty, and sort of because we didn't have a lot of oversight, because when we did ultimately get the green light to make the movie, we were making it for so little money that our bosses didn't really care. It's not that they didn't care, they cared very much about the bottom line, but they didn't pretend to know about teenage girls."

Wong agreed. The stakes were relatively low for Beacon and Universal—everybody wants their movies to succeed, of course, but the budget was so low that the financial risk was minimal—but high personally for her and Scanlon, who had fought tooth and nail for the project. Now that it was actually happening, they were going to make the most of it.

"As hard as it was to be the unbeloved project, I totally agree with Caitlin in that how we got to make this movie was just that nobody cared," she said. "I was on set forty out of forty-four days, and I had to drive myself down there. I lost money on this movie. Caitlin and I were not paid, we're the only people who got no residuals, we got nothing from this movie because we did it in the context of being executives, and my bosses, you know, they were so not interested in the movie to the point where they're like, we don't need you wasting your time on set, you need to be back in your office like making phone calls doing business on other more important projects. . . . I was just like, No, this is important, I'm gonna see this through. I deserve this. It's been four years, and I know what should happen. So every week I would just like get in my car and I would drive like two hundred miles round trip to San Diego, and I'd be down there and I'd drive back up for whatever meeting I was supposed to come up for that week, and the rest of the time I was just sort of hanging out. We were out of sight, out of mind."

Hughes, the Universal exec who was on the movie with O'Hair, said, "Once production is on, then it's like, OK, you guys have everything you need to kind of go off and make the movie now."

ROLL CALL!

Every musical worth its kick-ball-change has one thing in common: The "I want" song. The lovable protagonist, wide-eyed, perhaps naive, lays out what they're looking for. A way out of this small town, love, success, you name it. Wildly successful composer Stephen Schwartz once said that if the "I want" number doesn't happen within the first fifteen minutes of a show, there's a major problem.

It's fitting, then, that *Bring It On* opens—literally first second, first shot *opens*—with what could most accurately be categorized as a "You want me" song. What else would you call an epic cheer that not only gives most of the Toros a by-name introductory spotlight, complete with a signature move that the actors came up with on the day of shooting, but also contains the lines "Who am I? Just guess! Guys wanna touch my chest!" It's a wink and a nudge to the audience, a meta mention from the characters and the filmmakers: we know what you think of cheerleaders, and we're in on the joke.

That opening cheer, which Bendinger wrote all at once and which was kept largely intact from first draft to shooting, was one thing Reed loved about the script when he first read it, and it remains one of his favorite sequences in the film. "Every character gets this exclamation-point entrance into the movie," he said. "Like, almost more so than in a superhero movie. They all come in, and they have very unique—I mean, Kirsten's character literally has a Busby Berkeley musical number as her intro, Missy has this, you know, big, big intro, Cliff

has a big intro, you know, obviously Isis does, but they
all have these big overblown intros into the movie, which I
thought was really fun."

For her part, Bendinger told me in 2015 that the seed of
the sequence had been planted long before she even thought
about writing *Cheer Fever*, with an image created when she
was about seven years old. "That opening number, there was
this famous cover of the *National Lampoon* magazine when I
was a kid, super racy, that I remember seeing when I was little
of a cheerleader jumping in the air and her skirt was up and she
didn't have any panties on," she said. "And that image of being
behind a cheerleader jumping in the air, you see her butt and
the audience's faces, it just always stayed with me. It was so
funny and powerful."

The cheer itself came together quickly, Bendinger said:
"That came to me in five minutes, you know, with me and a
rhyming dictionary."

At one point in rewrites before Universal picked up the
movie, she remembered, the idea of cutting the opening cheer
was floated. "I threw a shitfit of the highest order," she told
me in 2015. "I was like, you cannot have this movie without
the opening! You have to let everybody know that you're in
on the joke that people hate cheerleaders. You've gotta know
that your tongue is in your cheek. You can't lose the opening.
They were like, all right, all right. I was totally that girl. I was the
most annoying Tracy Flick of the movie, fighting for all these
things. You annoy people, but then it works."

It's impossible to imagine *Bring It On* without its hyper-
kinetic dream-sequence opening. It sets the tone—sassy,
energetic, athletic, earwormy—for the entire movie, and is

actually so iconic that all of the franchise's straight-to-video sequels have also started with dream sequences, though none as over the top and memorable. The big opening also played to the secret dream of making a musical that Reed, Wong, Scanlon, and many others had harbored, a *Grease* with a sensibility born in the aughts: "You wanted it to feel like a musical that wasn't *quite* a musical," Reed said of the opening.

"I storyboarded that out pretty meticulously," he said. To add to the challenge, they only had one day slated to shoot the sequence. "As with everything on that movie it was just fast, fast, fast."

Fletcher choreographed the opening number with the idea of giving Reed and cinematographer Maurer a canvas to play on: complex enough in the broad shapes and formations to encourage interesting wide and overhead shots, specific enough in movement that close-ups were compelling, and with the note to infuse it with the soul of that old-school Busby Berkeley–Esther Williams vintage musical charm.

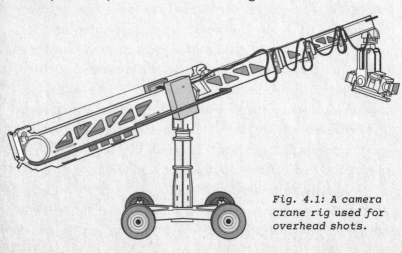

Fig. 4.1: A camera crane rig used for overhead shots.

The squad was given free rein over choosing a quick move for their characters to introduce themselves with, like Bilderback as Whitney slapping her own ass or Sloane as Big Red cupping her chest and winking saucily. Sloane remembered the cast standing around agonizing over what they'd do. "Just being given ownership over anything is so exciting on the set, because it does happen so rarely, but to be so young to be given ownership, and to really try to figure out like what, who would I be, what would my character do, and everyone was trying to have a signature move in some way," she said.

In the end, the translation from Bendinger's vision to the screen was almost beat-for-beat exactly as she'd imagined. "The opening sequence, I was really happy that he really got the Busby stuff," she said. "He really got the lighting, and that flavor felt very bright and correct."

"People kind of left [Peyton] alone," O'Hair remembered. "There wasn't a heavy hand during production from the studio." O'Hair and Hughes would watch dailies and occasionally make appearances on the set, but I can't help but think of a kind of *Don't Tell Mom the Babysitter's Dead* situation: a young, hungry crew making it work and putting together something incredible with spit and glue, absent metaphorical adult supervision.

"The only time that people came for oversight was during the bikini car wash," Wong said sarcastically of set visitors. "You know that scene is a really difficult shoot day, it had many moving parts that just needed more oversight than I could provide."

O'Hair remembered being sent to set that day. "This was in the wake of *American Pie*. I don't know what my language needs to be here," he said. "Essentially, they wanted to make sure that the film had a little bit of sex appeal. And this was the opportunity to put girls in skimpy bikinis to wash cars and throw suds around and have that same thing going on. Yep. And in the staff meeting. I know [then Universal president of production] Kevin [Misher] said to me that he wanted me to go down there and make sure that the film was sexy enough. I was sent down that day for the car wash scene. I don't think people on the show saw me as a suit."

To up the difficulty even more, the movie lost a guardian angel in Scanlon early into filming when she left Beacon along with production head Jon Shestack for a job at a new company, weighing leaving her pet project behind against her long-term career prospects. Shestack had also mentored Wong, and made it clear that there could be room for her to make the jump as well. It was a near-impossible choice.

"I had to tell Jon, my mentor, the person who had always supported me and given me, like, three jobs at this point in my life, I'm not going with you," Wong said. "Because I have to stay with this movie, because this is my shot at being more than a director of development."

It had to work. It just had to.

Wong was a consistent presence on set, working hand in hand with Cullen. After Scanlon's exit, Beacon also called in producer Patti Wolff, with a background in theater working with the likes of David Mamet, presumably to oversee Wong.

"Patti Wolff, to her credit was like, no, Max should totally be down here, absolutely, she knows what's up with this project," Wong said. "So I just had to flout authority and drive myself up and down from San Diego to sort of oversee the project to make sure that, like, what I wanted and what Peyton wanted and what Jessica wanted and what we all wanted was being made and to help facilitate that."

The word you'll hear most about the shoot when talking to the cast is "fun." They loved each other, they loved Peyton, they loved their lives. For Reed, however, the words are "intense"—"but it was a positive intense"—and "stress." The shoot was fun, but the process overall was no walk in the park for the director.

"'Fun' is not the adjective I think of when I think of what I was doing in my off time on that movie," he told me. "It really was, you know, it was stress. Deeply stressful. As it should have been—I can't imagine a version where that's not going to be stressful, because we had a really accelerated prep, we had a limited budget. We had to get a certain amount of shots, because it had to be kinetic and have all this energy. And I didn't really know how to navigate that system. It was my first time out doing that. So stress would be—I was stressing."

And the lack of studio oversight? Did a first-time director even know what the norm was?

"I absolutely knew the difference. And I was thrilled about it. I loved that there was no one from the studio there," he said. "To their great credit, because whether we were such small potatoes they didn't care or they trusted us enough—or they trusted Marc Abraham and Beacon enough, from their point of view—to let us make it, it was absolutely a blessing. Frankly, as it is on every movie. I mean, if there's something going so horribly awry in a movie that you need to call the studio, you'll call the studio. But otherwise it's like, you know, just let the filmmakers do their thing."

"In a weird way," Wong said, "we lucked out. That's something that would never happen now in Hollywood, where there would be this little movie in this big slate and there would be this film that was like, OK, this is a weird project that will just sort of get made, and if it fails, no big whoop, but whatever."

Maurer said, "Thank god. If we had some adults there that were telling us stuff we couldn't do, that would have ruined the movie! That's what probably ruins 90 percent of film and TV, because there's adults on sets telling creative people, 'Oh no, you can't do that.' We were just young and stupid and doing what we like to do. We were trying to make movies that we all liked, and we got lucky."

Away from hovering suits, the pajama party raged on. Reed's stress and the politics of moviemaking didn't seep through to the actors, who were having the time of their lives on set.

"Peyton's the best!" Sloane gushed to me. "Peyton had a bullhorn! Like, happy Peyton with a bullhorn is even better than Peyton without a bullhorn. He's just the best. He sets a tone that was so enjoyable and so fun. I've worked with him since then and he's done it. This is why people want to make movies with him: because he's Peyton."

He was able to coax performances out of actors that really shouldn't have worked, like Torrance channeling pure girlish fun and glee, dancing goofily on her bed with pom-poms to "Just What I Need," the song Cliff writes for her. Just turn on some music and have her rock out, right? Wrong. Not only had the song not been written or recorded yet, but there was no music at all playing during the filming.

"I remember having to do that scene and dancing on the bed," Dunst said. "I was like, oh my god, because I was also at that age where I was like, 'This is so dorky.' I just, in my seventeen-year-old brain, I was just like, this is not cool." But if there was even the hint of an eye roll in the performance, the scene wouldn't work. It needed total buy-in. "I was like, to make this cool, I just have to go for it. How Peyton directed that scene, there was zero song. There was no song. He just talked me through it. He was like, 'Now he said something funny! And now you're gonna get up and now the music is feeling really good. OK, now you're getting really into it.' That's how that was directed. 'And you grab your pom-poms, you go really crazy, because now the song is getting really loud!' So that's how we did that scene, that's a funny thing I just remembered. I was just like, 'I'm just gonna go for it.' Peyton was in it with me in a way. [I was] really feeling it when Peyton's just talking to me." It's a herculean act, getting a teenager to let go of the fear of not looking cool and just go for it.

5, 6, 7, 8

In some ways, music is just as essential to the spirit of *Bring It On* as pom-poms. After all, Reed was a music guy, not a cheerleader. He still drums. He didn't understand the complexities of cheerleading going into the project, but he understood rhythm as a lens through which to comprehend a cheer routine. A huge part of why the Clovers' and Toros' competition routines are so dynamic is the heart-pounding remixes and mash-ups. The echo of *total domination* (*nation, nation, nation*) across the Rancho Carne High gym immediately sets the tone for Sparky Polastri's influence.

And, on the business side, one twenty-five-second music cue was the biggest expense on the movie: Warrant's "Cherry Pie" during the audition scene. "It was probably somewhere in that $40,000 range," music supervisor Billy Gottlieb said. "Which for us was a shitload of money at the time."

Gottlieb cut his teeth as an assistant to legendary music supervisor Karyn Rachtman, working on films like *Pulp Fiction*, *The Basketball Diaries*, and, most important for our purposes, *Clueless*.

"There's a lot of similar DNA between *Clueless* and *Bring It On* in a lot of ways," he said. "So maybe the fact that I was on *Clueless* helped me as well, just because I did have this strange ability to kind of put myself in the mindset of a fourteen-year-old high school girl. That window of it somehow was very comfortable for me. I relate, who knew!"

Gottlieb said that the music process on *Bring It On* was extremely collaborative, with Reed's strong vision for the movie's music. In addition to the subject matter—high school girls—*Bring It On* had something else in common with *Clueless*: lots of music needed, not a lot of money to get it. "We had a shit ton of cues," he said. "It was basically a musical in a lot of ways."

That meant saying goodbye to some dreams, like introducing Cliff with the Clash playing in his headphones, to make room for moments like the Clovers being introduced with a sample of "Let Me Clear My Throat," and of course playing "Cherry Pie" while a would-be Toro auditions with a risqué routine.

"Once it was in the heads of everybody, it kind of was like we can't do anything but that," Gottlieb said. "We knew it would be a fun laugh, so we made that work."

Gottlieb found creative solutions, like working Blaque's "As If" into a few moments like Missy's first appearance in her Toros uniform in her gigantic house's doorway, or the Easter egg of Cliff listening to a song by one of Reed's former bands, Manchild, in his headphones at one point. "We were paid one dollar for that," Reed said, laughing. "Literally one dollar."

One of the most iconic music moments of the movie is Cliff's mixtape song, "Just What I Need," recorded by a band called Rufus King. It's a pop-punk pom-pom moment as Torrance dances on her bed and Cliff wails that he would feed her bon-bons all day.

"I came from the era where all I did in my spare time was make mixtapes," Reed said. "I still have every one of them, by the way. . . . Whenever I was dat-ing a girl or wanted a

Fig. 4.2: The classic cassette mixtape was historically part of the adolescent courtship ritual.

girl, I would make a mixtape, this became the thing. We also were at the time where we would make recorded band demos and send them back and forth between myself and my song-writing partner and stuff like that. We all had four-track Tas-cam cassette recorders. It just felt like a thing this guy would do."

Gottlieb found Rufus King through a friend in A&R and sent the band a few notes on what Cliff's song should include, along with a VHS of Dunst dancing in the scene, which had been temped with a track by the Donnas.

"I think they turned it around in maybe like twenty-four hours," Gottlieb said, "that kind of vibe, and it was like, wow, is it that easy to get such a great song for such a perfect moment?"

Octavio Gallardo, the band's bassist, said that basically, yeah, it can be. "Some of our best songs were just literally written in an hour, you know, they just come together super, super fast."

Gallardo and his bandmates had gone to high school together and were making a go of it in L.A. in the late '90s when they connected with Gottlieb. The group convened in their hometown of Woodlawn, California, and popped the tape into the VCR, getting right to work. The instructions included "Torrance," "cheerleading" and the direction to make it sound "Ramones-ish," Gallardo remembered.

"It came together pretty quick," he said. "I remember collaborating on the lyrics down in my mom's basement."

Reed and Gottlieb loved it, and it made the movie. The band broke up shortly after the movie was released, which Gallardo calls "one of the biggest breakups of my life," but they attended the premiere together, where they were "super surprised" to hear "Just What I Need" mixed into the final Nationals cheer routine music. (That iconic Cliff head-banging moment.)

About that mix: for everything that exists in the world, it's someone's job to make it. It was Mark Bryan's job to make that mix, as well as the other cheer mixes in the movie. The thirty-year-old had gotten his start DJing at a nightclub at a Marriott in Pennsylvania, where a cheer choreographer heard his mixes and introduced him to the world of ultra-high-energy cheer remixes. In Bryan's mixes, the song changes every few seconds, sound effects are introduced at key moments—an old favorite of his is dropping the whip-crack sound effect sample from "Baby Got Back" to put an exclamation point on a big move or formation—and the energy is frantic, charged. It dares you to keep your pulse down.

Ray Jasper, the cheer choreographer for *Bring It On*, suggested Bryan for the mixes. "He was like the Sparky Polastri of song mixing," Gottlieb remembered.

They flew Bryan and his wife and young son to L.A. for three days, which turned into five days, which turned into ten days, with Reed and Gottlieb checking in on progress at the end of each day. Bryan remembered mostly the inside of his hotel room and the studio, while his family explored L.A.

"I got to try In-N-Out," he remembered as a highlight. "It was fine. I don't eat fast food that often, but it was fine."

Bryan said that the only time he's seen the movie all the way through was opening night in theaters, when he went with a group of family members to see his name in the credits. Though he remembers "a little cheesiness," in his opinion working on the movie "was definitely a life-changing experience," a calling card that led to more opportunities.

Gottlieb, who is still working as a music supervisor on major TV productions, said that he saw the movie again recently. "I was like yeah, this holds up pretty well!" he said. "I did a pretty good job on this! I was watching it like, did I do that?"

That on-set attitude of Reed's, the sense of safety and faith that the cast brought up over and over again, is not an accident. "[Positivity is] a big thing for me as a director, and I like to think that I come by it naturally, but I also worked for so many years as a director of making-of documentaries and got to witness many, many directors working," Reed said. "Great directors, you know, good directors, and then a few not-so-good directors, and it was so illuminating for me to watch these directors work and see what made the great ones great and how they all related to crew people and actors. I also came up doing all these random jobs: I worked in props and I worked in transportation and I worked as a location manager and as a PA [production assistant], I worked in all these different positions, so I understand what all the department heads in different positions need to do on a movie, and I remember how much it meant to me when a director would actually, like, acknowledge my work." He tried to create a safe space for his cast, veterans and newcomers alike, where they could "relax and feel like they can try weird stuff and they can fuck up.

"I kind of felt a bit like a camp counselor," he said.

The shoot days were long and physical. *Bring It On* is a high school movie, but there's actually only one scene in the film that takes place in a classroom. The world of the Toros and Clovers is one of gymnasiums and competition floors, cheer routines going full-out, complete with absolutely manic smiles and widened eyes, as if the squads could enthuse their way to a perfect score. Which, actually, they kind of can.

The summer of 1999 in San Diego wasn't unusually hot, with temperatures mostly hovering between 65 and 75 degrees. However, even the most comfortable of climates can quickly become uncomfortable—in more ways than one—when you're a young actor thirsty to prove yourself and look good while doing so. Again. And again. And again.

West remembered the cheer sequences as being the most fun but also the most strenuous to shoot. It wasn't just the athleticism but everything that came with it. "When you go through and do [the cheer scenes], there's a technical side to it, even just [keeping track of] the camera," he said. "You get done doing something like Nationals and you would nail it and then like, OK, no, no, we got to go again.

You have to perform every time and make sure you did your part and you didn't mess up."

For Reed, there was the balance between getting enough coverage to have options for the editors (and remember, this was 1999, so digital wasn't a thing yet—this was all shot on film, and film is finite and costs money), plus getting the best performance out of the cast and making them run through the routines as few times as possible. "When you're shooting something like that, you're just on pins and needles about getting it the best it can be, but also about you know there's a high percentage of a chance that someone's going to fall or tweak an ankle or something," he said. "It was really nerve-racking."

Kramer, who had wholeheartedly embraced her new cheer skills, remembered shooting the Nationals routine as an especially intense day. "It was such a hard routine, and we kept having to do it full-out like the whole time. It wasn't like, 'OK, let's do it once. Now let's do a pick-up shot here.' No, it was like, 'OK, do it again. Everybody recover for ten minutes and then go full-out again.' And it's a very hard routine, especially for the guys, and we're trying to mimic like what it would actually be like at Nationals in this scenario. So we're running on, you know, very amped up, the energy level is super high. And when you have that in real life, in real competition, you really can only do the routine once, because you're so energized. And here we were doing it again and again and again for two days."

Even in the scenes where everybody's feet remained firmly planted on the ground, Reed had to make some compromises to make it through his shot list, like scrapping a planned tracking shot through the Toros locker room early in the film, a "one-shot wonder," as he called it. Take after take, the cues weren't quite lining up.

"He did get somewhat of like the flowing roving shot, but it wasn't quite as Scorsese as he wanted it," Kramer said. "Finally, it was kind of funny on the day, he was like, 'All right, fuck it, I'm not doing it. Let's just try to break it up.'"

West, for his part, had a big plan for his character's real-world intro after appearing in the dream sequence opener. He decided it was time to show off the back handspring he'd learned to do at Fletcher's cheer camp. "I'm like, yo, this is the moment," he said.

"I was gonna back handspring into it, and the first take that Peyton goes through and I literally got into the back handspring and land on my head," he laughed. "Everyone was rolling [laughing]. I didn't hurt myself. I got up. . . . You know, I don't take myself too seriously. So after that, I was like, hey, you know, maybe, um, maybe I'll just stretch it out. Peyton's like, yeah, we wanna make our day, so that's a great choice for you."

The cast wasn't just concerned about hitting their marks; they also wanted to look good while doing so.

"It was a lot of like, you know, tanning salon, and there was the routine of rehearsal and tanning salon, tanning salon/gym combo," Sloane said. "It's also just young women wanting to look a certain way on camera." She remembers "working out like crazy.

"There was a lot of, I don't know, an awareness of wanting to look strong and thin, and also in a way that probably no one would care about at this point. I was completely worried," she said.

Bell, too, remembered seeing the inside of a gym more than she ever had. "I was just not skinny enough," she said. "Like, you can't get skinny enough. And I was so scared of the bikini scene coming up, you know?"

Just like they did everything else together—eating, drinking, practicing cheers, working out, all of it—the cast also chatted about their insecurities and strategized together. Kramer recalled an idea that she came up with in the makeup chair to avoid the appearance of stomach rolls in a locker-room scene, picking up clothes off the floor with her foot instead of bending over: "I was like, 'Oh, good idea, I'll do this totally weird thing where I like throw my shorts up into my hands.' I would rather have not bent over and looked weird and not have stomach rolls. I stand by it."

The guys, too, wanted to look jacked. West remembered of the car wash scene, which he called "such a fun day," "I remember after getting done with every take, Huntley and I are literally dropping to the ground and doing push-ups, like, trying to be pumped up," he said. "I must have done like five hundred or six hundred push-ups that day. That's actually a good trick. It does work."

Wong eventually caught wind of the cast's nerves. "They were doing push-ups between takes, all of them were starving," she said. "I found out about this, and I felt so bad. They were all like, on these horrible diets because they were so nervous about the bikini car wash, even the guys. I was just like, What is going on? I made everybody come with me to In-N-Out after the bikini car wash. So I was just like, have milkshakes, everyone, milkshakes on me."

That wasn't the only speed bump that came with working with a young cast. In the case of the women of Blaque—Shamari Fears DeVoe, Natina Reed, and Brandi Williams—especially, there was a learning curve to contend with.

The featured Clovers were no strangers to the camera, but their experience had been on music videos, or performing onstage with cameras capturing them for the Jumbotron. The camera was the audience, and the fourth wall was not a thing. Not to mention, none of them had seriously acted before. In the music video for "As If," the single that landed on *Bring It On*'s soundtrack and the group's biggest hit, the trio played . . . aliens? Who lived in a box and danced with holograms, potentially? It was high concept, but it didn't have much complex character work.

"I do remember one of the first days we were shooting with them, because they had only ever done music videos," Reed told me in 2015. "We were doing a scene, I think it was one outside the Clovers' high school with Gabrielle when they confront Kirsten and Eliza. We were shooting the girls' coverage, and when we started shooting they were all just looking right into the lens, delivering lines right into the lens."

In casting, there had been some concern over their lack of experience, but it was decided that they'd lean on Union's influence and the group's charisma. "The secret was to just let them be, you know?" Morris said. "And they were good."

It ended up being a reciprocal relationship, with the group members helping Union with the choreography and cheer, and Union providing not only acting tips but also a more grounded performance in contrast with Blaque's more unrestrained line readings. DeVoe remembered "definitely taking guidance from [Union], because I really, really was really nervous. I'm super hard on myself sometimes. I didn't have acting before, so I kind of felt out of place, because I didn't know if I was doing it right. Should I just be myself, or what should I do?"

Blaque were also new to film sets and in the middle of touring even while shooting—"in the crucible of stress," as Wong put it, working on both the movie and promoting their album. They hung out with Union some, but since they came into camp with their own friend group, so to speak, and often had to take time away for shows (they were protégées of TLC's Lisa "Left Eye" Lopez and toured with *NSYNC), they didn't really fully mesh with the rest of the cast. "Their career seemed a little more important," Ritter recalled. When they were around, though, Lohmann called them "super funny and a kick in the pants to be around."

Even within their group, there was tension, with stories of a fire alarm being pulled at the hotel in a moment of high band drama, or a puppy being brought somewhere it shouldn't be and pooping somewhere it shouldn't, among others.

"No, we were not getting along during the filming," DeVoe told me. "No, no, no, no, not at all. Me and Natina were great with each other at that point. Girl groups are hard, OK. Me and Natina, we were cool. But me and Natina weren't cool with Brandi during filming. And then once the premiere came, me and Brandi weren't cool with Natina."

Union recalled of Blaque, "They were over it and over each other. It was some typical teen girl stuff, you know, and I think also working to that degree and nonstop and traveling the world and not having a break, and on what should have been a break, you're doing a movie. I think was a lot on them."

"I love everybody to just get along," DeVoe said. "I don't like drama. So it's kind of hard to know that you're at odds with your group member, your sister, and then film a movie and try to stay focused. But yeah, you would have never known that if you're just watching the movie."

UST: UNRESOLVED
SEXUAL TOOTHBRUSHING

> "Cliff joins Torrance at the sink, totally sidling up to her. Torrance is coyly trying to cover. . . . A playful interlude, bursting with romantic tension."
>
> —*Bring It On* shooting script

It's roughly fifty-one seconds that launched thousands of sexual awakenings: *Bring It On*'s infamous dialogue-free toothbrush scene. After an eventful football game at Rancho Carne—highs include Torrance having scandalous "cheer sex" with Cliff in the stands via extended eye contact, the low would have to be the Clovers showing up and making the Toros look like absolute assholes by making it clear exactly who came up with those sideline shouts—Torrance spends the night at Missy's parent-free mansion. After she watches Cliff roll around in his boxers on the floor riffing on his electric guitar with cartoon hearts in her eyes, Torrance and Cliff brush their teeth side by side in what is somehow the cutest and most chaste yet most sexual-tension-laden scene in all of teen cinema. Who knew fluoride could be so erotic?

"In one scene, when Torrance and Cliff surprise each other while brushing their teeth, it ascends to the frothy, sublimated seductiveness of classic screwball," A. O. Scott wrote in his *New York Times* review of the movie. "Ms. Dunst's expression as she emerges from the bathroom, having done nothing more risqué than spit in the sink, is perfectly enigmatic and completely convincing, a mixture of mischievous amazement and unconscious arousal. It's a wonderfully subtle moment—exactly what you'd expect from a cheerleader movie."

"Let's talk about the toothbrushing scene," Dan Waters said. "It is one of the greatest scenes in cinema, right? I mean, first of all, tooth brushing is gross . . . the fact that it's a) toothbrushing, which I don't want to see, and b) that it works as a romantic moment on so many levels. And without being hot and heavy but it was, it *is* hot and heavy. To me that's an amazing scene."

In fact, the scene wasn't originally in Bendinger's script but was a result of a writing session between her and Reed to strengthen the romantic relationship between Cliff and Torrance.

Reed remembered the inspiration as the film history of decades past. "It's something that you would see right out of a romantic comedy from the '50s or '60s," he said. "We always talked about those. Frank Capra, *It Happened One Night*, there's a scene with Claudette Colbert and Clark Gable. They're on a road trip, and they have to stay in this little lodge, a motel, and they share a room, and of course it's twin beds, but

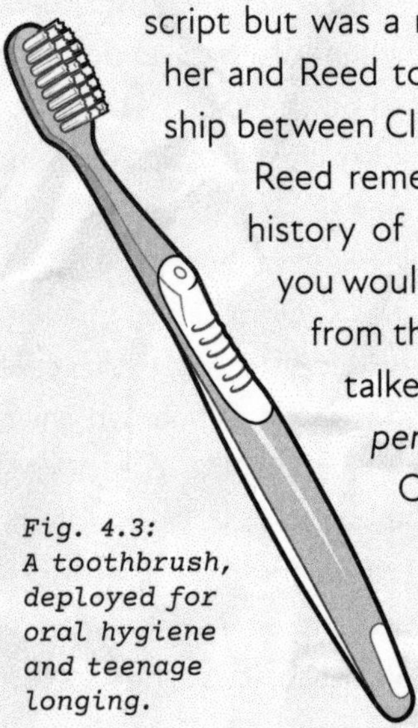

Fig. 4.3:
A toothbrush,
deployed for
oral hygiene
and teenage
longing.

because it's the '30s they string up a clothesline with a blanket over to separate them and it's just this very innocent thing that's also fraught with sexual tension. That was the vibe that I was after for that thing. And it also just kind of hit—Kirsten plays it so well, and to me when I watched that movie, for some reason that scene encapsulates who Kirsten was at that time, even though she's obviously playing a role in the movie, but kind of who she was at the time. She had just turned seventeen. She was so young, and it really like encapsulated who she was at that time."

"I knew those feelings very well," Dunst said.

"In the script the whole scene was like a quarter of a page," recalled Jesse Bradford, who played Cliff. "Jessica wrote it and then Peyton, I think like, knew that he wanted to make a meal out of it instead of just a snack, you know, because you can always downgrade, right? I mean, they could always cut the scene out, but I think he had a certain giddiness about what he wanted to accomplish with that scene that I remember feeling off of him."

That's not to say Reed knew that it would work when he shot it. One word for how he felt after he came out of that tiny bathroom space with simple, head-on shots: relieved.

"Very early on when we did the master of that thing [we were] saying, 'Oh, this is—they're really good together, they really have chemistry, they really have a thing going on on-screen and it's nice,'" he said. "Sort of like thinking like OK, this is something. When I was thinking about the movie and teen movies in general, this is the kind of moment that I love in those movies, and maybe we're going to be able to actually have a legitimate one of those moments in this movie that's entirely separate of all the cheerleading and all the other plot-driven stuff in the movie. It just felt like one of those teen Movie Moments."

And a Movie Moment it was: "I feel like probably a solid chunk of my sexuality was awakened by that scene," cultural commentator, podcast host, and *A Girl's Guide to Joining the Resistance* author Emma Gray told me.

She's not alone. Comedian Lane Moore tweeted about the clip, saying, "Truly this scene in *Bring It On* had everything: a brief scene with minimal dialogue, doing something mundane, fully clothed, and yet you watch this scene and you are unbelievably horny and fully believe this is what true love, or at least the promise of it, will feel like. ICONIC." Not to mention, she goes on in a threaded tweet, "the overwhelming horniness of this scene is not talked about nearly enough tbh." As the poets say, where's the lie?

Asked in 2015 about his memories of shooting one of the landmark teen-movie scenes in history, cinematographer Maurer simply said, "I just remember them getting very tired of brushing their teeth. I'm sure their teeth were very clean after that day of shooting."

Beyond the motivations behind the scene, the old-school movie sensibilities, and the enduring legacy of the sequence, Bradford admits, "When I think about that scene, or think about that moment, the first thing I think of is actually how many times I brushed my teeth. I was just like, Ooh boy, I'm minty for days now."

And then there's the matter of the strike.

On a shoot so intense that Reed described it as "really just about trying to fly and do everything, every day," time is not on your side. Remember those rules that the young cast swore by? One of them was to show up. Didn't go to sleep? Doesn't matter, show up. Sore from performing superhuman feats of cheerleading-related strength? Show up.

So the day that the *crew* didn't show up, that's a huge problem.

Let's take a step back: what we as an audience see on the big screen represents barely even a fraction of the story. There's the pitching and development, years of it, in Bendinger's case. More pitching. Preproduction and planning. Casting. Lots of stressful conversations and spreadsheets to hash out over overpriced salads. Those early mornings, late nights, every swipe of mascara to make the cast look picture-perfect and fiddle of the focus to actually make the picture perfect—all those untold people and hours and effort.

To keep costs down on the modest-budget sports movie—a rarity—*Bring It On* was planned as a partially nonunion production. Note the "partially" there: Reed is in the Directors Guild, Bendinger in the Writers Guild, and the actors in the Screen Actors Guild. It was the crew—lighting, props, hair and makeup, all that—that were nonunion positions and therefore more of a budget choice, not subject to the same minimums and requirements as union positions. This was not unheard-of, though it's uncommon for productions to go this route now. Stu Segall Productions in San Diego, where *Cheer Fever* was set up, is a massive property with soundstages to build sets on, and a roster of crew to pull from as well. The company also hosts a branch called Strategic Operations, or STOPS, that uses movie magic to create hyperrealistic scenarios for military and security training. This company sniffs out needs, finds opportunities, and comes up with services to fill those gaps.

The production found a home at Stu Segall in the way that you might rent a furnished apartment: you bring your favorite elements—

director, director of photography, writer, cast, script—and the rest is already set up. You didn't necessarily choose it, but it does the job.

That is, until someone forms a picket line.

Because *Bring It On* was the biggest production shooting at Stu Segall, when one faction of the studio's crew decided to try to unionize, they needed leverage to force the Stu Segall brass to the table. It's impossible to ignore a disruption to the shoot day for the biggest scene in the biggest movie on the lot. So the day that shooting on the Nationals sequences was set to begin, the union picketed the production.

When the cast showed up to the set, they found the hair and makeup trailers empty. "I think it was Eliza Dushku who called because she was like, 'I showed up for hair and makeup, and they're on strike,'" Wong recalled. Producers ran around moving props or taking shouted directions from crew members on the other side of the picket line.

"I was very naive and didn't know much about union stuff at that point, other than that I was union," Reed said. "I was Directors Guild, obviously, the actors were SAG, and the cameras were all the IATSE guilds. But we got picketed. And they decided to picket us to hurt us where they could, on the biggest crowd days. I remember, again, not finding out about it until the morning of, like, 'Hey, you should know there's some picketers out there, they're going to try and make noise and disrupt filming.' It's like, well, there's no amount of noise they can make that's going to disrupt filming, because we're doing a cheerleading competition."

Bilderback remembered studying continuity photos and the cast helping one another with their hair and makeup. The planned shots for the day were wide angles, but that doesn't mean an actor feels great about having their own makeup efforts immortalized on-screen.

"I think I had like little diamond studs in my hair and I remember what happened, trying to place them exactly where the hair department put my little studs," Bilderback said.

"I mean, no actor wants to go on set without their hair and makeup," Cullen said. "It doesn't matter what the angles are, I mean, I just can't believe we did it, to be quite honest."

That they pulled it off, or that the day wasn't canceled? I asked. "Both, actually."

There was a sense of being stuck in the middle of things: the filmmakers and cast are pro-union, they said, but they were also pro–*Cheer Fever.* The crew, they said, were also caught between two interests. The show, they said, must go on.

"The whole movie was like a team," Ritter said. "The crew and the cast, we were a team. It was like, fuck 'em, let's make a movie. I remember there were people holding signs in the back [of the competition scene]. They just put extras around them. They put like 'Go Toros' next to them, in front of them. It actually worked out, because it gave us more bodies."

It was a difficult day, and the first real hitch in the production's giddy-up. A business reality dropped like a lead balloon into the love-fest of making the movie.

"That was like the biggest issue and that was something that we had to work through, and we lucked out because the on-set culture was really, really good up until that point in time," Wong said.

Reed, as a first-time feature director, said that he didn't fully grasp the financial arrangements that were allowing the movie to be made. "I just got this attitude of 'I am shooting every single shot that I have on my shot list today and I don't give a shit. I'm shooting every shot and everyone else can go straight to hell, I'm making my movie.'"

The cinematographer, Maurer, also couldn't hold back. "There was way in hell I was going to stay away from filming it," he said. "This was my movie. It was mine." He called it "the most stress-inducing part of the job."

And, Reed said, "that's what we did, we just powered through the thing and did it. And again, it's like being completely ignorant of that situation or whatever deal was made until that moment," he said. "It taught me a lesson too as I went forward, to producerially know all of those aspects of what was going on. Yeah, but it was a tough situation."

And, yes, he and Maurer got the shots. The show went on, and a deal was reached to keep cameras rolling. Things were back to normal the next shooting day.

Though the resolution was quick, the ripples lasted. "It was probably, I would say, one of the worst days of my career," Cullen said. "Not an easy day."

Through it all—the friendships, the cheer training, the rewrites, the experiences, and stories that could fill a cheercyclopedia—the underdog *Cheer Fever* team made a movie.

There was still the editing and marketing process and, *gulp*, release to get through, but the summer camp that was the *Cheer Fever* shoot had to end sometime.

"[Peyton] hated to be the authority figure, because it was so fun, and he'd have to pull it out every once in a while, but for months and months after we wrapped this movie we would go over to Peyton's house and have barbecues and hang out," Sloane said. "We just never wanted the experience to end. I mean, it was like a genuine lovefest."

"Peyton was so gung ho too, he was our head cheerleader," Dunst said.

Wong, who had been on the sets of more than two hundred features, music videos, and other productions by that point in her career, also called out how unusual the experience was.

"It was super fun," she said. "I remember telling Peyton, being like the total Debbie Downer, I'm like, 'You know this feeling you have? Enjoy it, because this is unusual. This may be the best experience you ever have on a set.' I just wanted him to completely enjoy the experience because there are some great movies that come out of sets that are just so dysfunctional and horrible. There's terrible movies that come out of sets where everyone stays friends their entire life. Movies have come out of terrible work situations, and some horrible stuff has come out of great work situations, but I feel like we got a great movie that came out of a great work situation.

"I feel like our movie is what it is because everybody jumped on our shared delusion. The Jessica, Max, and Caitlin virus was spread to everybody else. I remember, like, this specific scene: I came to work one day and the dolly grips were standing around with the camera operator and they're looking at the sides for that day and they're laughing. I walk up and they immediately stop laughing, which is, like, not necessarily good. I'm like, OK, what is going on? And they're like, 'We're just reading the script!' And I'm like, 'No, what is going on?' And finally the camera operator's like, 'You know, this is a *really good* movie. This is a really good movie.' And, you know, it was like in context, this is the same crew that works on *Silk Stalkings*, they work on a lot of genre television and so this was like, you know, a bigger project, but it wasn't like they had a choice. They took this movie because not everything shoots in San Diego, so they're like, oh, I can like drive home at night, I can work locally, I'm gonna take this job, that's how a lot of them got on the project. But then at a certain early point in filming, there was a switch that got flipped, and you could just feel it, because everyone was just like, 'Oh my god, this could be really good.'"

"Here's the deal, Missy. We're the shit, the best. We have fun, we work hard, and we win national championships. I'm offering you a chance to be a part of that."
—Torrance

"There's the movie you write, the one you shoot, and the one you cut," Bendinger told me. "Three totally different movies."

Bendinger wrote her movie, Reed shot his, and all the while, up in L.A., Larry Bock was cutting his.

Bock is a guy who loved jazz and wanted to make documentaries when he went to USC, then realized he had an eye for editing. He cut *Critters*, *Rock 'n' Roll High School*, *Don't Tell Mom the Babysitter's Dead*. He's pretty sure he got the gig for *Bring It On* because Wong thought he had cool glasses and took an interest, then his work took it from there. And of course, he met Wong in the first place because they were both getting their kitchens redone by the same woman, Laurie Crogan, who "makes these great designs on linoleum," Bock said. Wong needs an editor, Crogan knows an editor. Wong met Bock, thought his glasses looked cool, the ball gets rolling, and it's time to have a meeting.

"Sometimes you just go in cold, you don't know anybody," Bock said. "That's how I remember it." He clicked with Reed, and the gig was his.

A film editor's job begins about the same time as principal photography. While the cast shimmied and flipped their way through the days in San Diego, Bock papered an edit bay in L.A. with inspiration and posters, a room-sized mood board: images from *Pulp Fiction* and *Sweet Charity*, a felt Clovers pennant, a poster for the pulpy 1973 movie *The Cheerleaders*, in which a squad sabotages their rival football team by, ahem, keeping them up all night before the big game. He does this for every edit he's on, to set the vibe.

And the vibe is important, especially on late-'90s and early-aughts productions like *Bring It On* that were shot on film, when an editor might have spent twelve-hour days assembling scenes. We're talking weeks in this small enclosed room, handling physical film, eventually huddled with the director putting together *their* cut of the film. Luckily, Bock called Reed "the funniest director I've ever worked with. The coolest."

"It was amazing," Reed said of his rapport with Bock. "Now on movies, I have a lot of daily contact with my editor, who's very good about letting me know, like, Oh, we didn't get this or whatever, whatever. That movie was so low budget and so fast, and we were shooting in San Diego and Larry was in L.A. And it was also not digital, it was film at that time. So Larry and I didn't have tons of talk, like it was maybe like once every week or two weeks during production."

So Reed would shoot in San Diego, then the footage would make its way to L.A. via the Pony Express or marathon messenger or what have you, to Bock in his edit bay. Bock had the script and had met with Reed about the tone and the goals. He was putting together a rough assemblage of the movie with an eye for comedy and overall story as the movie shot, ready to refine and share with Reed soon after the shoot ended. His assistant editor, Erik Andersen, focused on putting together the high-octane cheer routines. The shoot ended, and Reed came to Los Angeles for the moment of truth: the first cut.

"Directors hate looking at first cut," Bock said. "It's like all the things that they thought were going to work in a certain way, the editor does it the way he likes it. I guess it's quite a shock for directors."

And for a first-time feature director, that first cut feels exponentially more momentous.

"I had seen a couple early cuts," Reed said. "There was a couple of early cuts that Larry sent down that I was like, ugh, I don't know if this is good. And I've since come to learn that that's my reaction to every assembly, and any director will tell you this when you see the assembly, no matter what's good about it. You want to just like hang yourself because it's not—it's like, oh, they didn't use this right take or the timing's wrong, not what I had in mind, just because you haven't had a chance to work through it with the editor."

But overall? "We saw his assembly," Reed said, "and it was thrilling, because of course it was too long and there were different takes, but you saw like, oh, the movie's *there*. The movie is gonna work."

But to work, of course, the cut needed work. Never mind Reed's tweaks for story and style, there was an expectation that the movie that would eventually come to be known as *Bring It On*—we'll get to that title in a bit—would be roughly ninety minutes, and that it would come in with a PG-13 rating. It needed the rating so that the teens and tweens in the movie's target audience would be able to go see it without their parents, a box office necessity if this movie was going to sell any tickets, which . . . the studio didn't seem terribly confident that it would.

Length could be cut from the movie, sure. But there was one big problem. "When we put this up for ratings, we got a hard R for language," Wong told me. "Like, they were not having *any* of it."

Reed recalled, "We were coming out in the shadow of Universal's own success with *American Pie*, which was R, R, R, hard R. This movie was never ever *ever* going to be R, but it was gonna be PG-13. And I remember everyone talking about like, we want to try and push the

PG-13 as far as we can," he said. And then there's the territory that comes with a cheerleading movie almost as surely as a pom-pom: that duality of cheerleader as all-American sweetheart and sexpot, all in one pleated skirt. "Jessica and I talked a lot about that sort of dichotomy about perception and cheerleading's place in American culture, pre–competitive cheerleading, whereas they were always supporting a male-dominated sport. There was always this wholesomeness about it and yet this sort of flaunting sexuality about it. That was something we always found fascinating about it. So how was this movie going to deal with that and balance all that sort of stuff?"

While Reed and Bock figured out how to tone down the film, they'd watch pulpy '70s cheerleading movies on lunch breaks, just for fun and inspiration. Surely they could keep *Cheer Fever*'s edge while still permitting the fourteen-year-olds of the world to hand over their allowances at the ticket counter?

The first thing they could address was the language. PG-13 movies can have "a single use of one of the harsher sexually derived words, though only as an expletive," according to the July 2020 edition of the MPAA's guide to ratings. So you can say "fuck," but only once, and not when talking about . . . fucking. That would be an immediate R, unless it passed a special override vote. Got it. Another key word in the ratings description is "inconspicuous." A movie might be a little filthy, but as long as it may go over younger viewers' heads, it may still squeak in at a PG-13. This was a line *Cheer Fever* hoped to walk, very carefully.

For example: "One of my jobs on this movie on set was to come up with alternative swear words that they could say," Wong remembered. "The original line in the script when they're at the football game and the Toros football team is losing really, really badly, and the rivals say to them, 'How does it feel watching all the cheer boys steal all your pussy?' That was the original line, 'steal all your pussy.' Well, you can't use 'pussy,' so we just changed the word to 'squirrel.' And that's what they used in the film, and which to me sounds even more disgusting. So that's what we did through the whole film, just changed words out."

The same for the distinctive zingers the movie is known for, with lines like "She puts the 'itch' in 'bitch.'" They're in the script, and the editors leaned on them to put the "F-U" in "perfunctory effort to keep things ratings-friendly."

"We were trying all the time to splice new things and come up with new put-downs and have them describe things," Wong said. "Like 'putting the cum in comfortable.' Like yeah, you're totally saying a bad word, but it sort of slides by, because you have deniability."

Even so, Bock remembered having to tone down some of the filmed language to make ratings. "Oh yeah, we had to cut out a few words," he said. "They were funny. That just really pisses you off. I don't remember what they were, I just remember being so mad."

Next came the sexuality edit. Overall, the finished movie is largely chaste, relying on winking references to spanky pants and playful booty slaps that manage to vaguely gesture at sex without coming near the bedroom, the quick table-dance scene at the cheerleading auditions playing raunchier than the bikini car wash, for example.

"There's a lot of implied sexuality, but it's very clean," producer Bliss said of the movie. "It can kind of ride that bubble, where it could be a family movie and your seven-year-old's not going to get it, but your kids that are older can get it and you can live with it. You know, it just all depends on how prudish the parents are. Today this movie would be very tame."

With, of course, one exception: The scene where West's character, Jan, "lets a digit slip" while lifting Kramer's Courtney at the football game. There's more to unpack on that scene and how it's aged, but here let's talk about how the ratings board felt about it: not great!

"We totally got in trouble," Wong recalled. "The ratings board had a conniption."

As shot, a mischievously smirking Jan lowers Courtney to the ground, where she swats at him as he lifts his hand to his nose and openly sniffs his finger.

"That was something we had to trim," Bock recalled dryly. It came down to the individual frames of footage, pushing the moment to the very limit of what the ratings board might find acceptable.

"Larry Bock, the editor, sort of figured out how many frames Nathan West can lift his hand," Wong said. "So he still does it, you still know what he's doing and he holds his finger up, it just doesn't run all the way to his nose."

Once the ratings issue was out of the way, PG-13 intact, there were still more approvals to get, this time from panels of strangers: the marketing team and its focus groups.

Marketing considerations had been baked into the process from the very beginning, lest you think otherwise. Remember the search for nontraditional actors to fill in the Clovers' ranks, leading to the casting of Blaque? That's a marketing play, a long game to reach audiences who may not be a shoo-in to see the movie. "Anything to kind of get some name recognition or something to get people to show up to this cheerleader movie, right?" Reed said. You want the best people for the roles, yes, but you also want people whose fanbases vary, ideally, and can draw the broadest swath of moviegoers.

Then, after a movie has been cast, shot, and edited together but before it comes out, the studio's marketing team gives various test audiences a chance to see a rough cut of the film. They fill comment cards with their thoughts and reactions, the marketing teams interprets said comment cards, and then the filmmakers make changes and test again. Often this means polishing and reediting the existing footage, but when test screening and marketing response is particularly emphatic, it can mean shelling out for additional filming.

The filmmakers had their own wish list for additional photography, places where Reed wanted more coverage of scenes or they wanted to address story notes or adjust the vibe. (Bock remembered looking for more comedy toward the end of the movie.) They asked for a few days. They got one.

"On movies the budget of *Bring It On*, you have to go begging and scraping to get that day," Reed said. "And fortunately, they believed in the movie enough to say yes to the one day. I'm sure there were other things that we ideally wanted to shoot but couldn't do it in one day."

They shot some gags at Nationals—McMains's bratty little brother character Justin walking around with spanky pants on his head, a girl from another squad barfing hugely and impressively—and some character moments, like a new take of the Toros learning they'd come in second place ("Hell yeah!") with additional angles, and Ritter's Les having a flirtatious moment of connection with a guy from a rival squad, a sweet romantic pause in the midst of all the hubbub and drama of Nationals.

They got that additional photography they'd asked for, and on another day, they also shot scenes of Union and the women of Blaque—specifically for the trailers, at marketing's request.

"I think doing *Bring It On* was the first time I realized how much power the marketing department of any studio has," Reed said. The focus groups had shown that audiences were excited about the Clovers and wanted to see more of those storylines. One big problem, Reed said: "[Those storylines] didn't exist."

The poster you remember for *Bring It On* is split down the middle, Dunst as Torrance on one side, Union as Isis on the other. Though that image is fifty-fifty, the story of *Bring It On* is indisputably Torrance's. She's the main character, and Isis serves as her foil. The movie had already been shot, and would not be reworked and reshot entirely to expand the Clovers' story to make them fleshed-out characters in their own right.

But that didn't stop the marketing team from wanting to make it look like they were.

In the trailer for the movie, we see the Clovers in street clothes, hanging out in a gym, Union cutely kissing a guy against a locker. "That all comes from that trailer shoot," Reed said, recalling the extra marketing cash infused with the directive of capturing the trailer-specific, nonmovie footage of the Clovers. "None of that stuff was originally in the movie, or was cut out of the movie from what we shot. In fact, we constantly felt like we wish we had more and used as much of the stuff as we possibly could that we shot right when we were cutting the movie itself."

In the reshoots, they shot the Clovers tooling around the gym, hanging out. A lot of shots of the Blaque women breaking the fourth wall with direct-to-camera dialogue including the line "bring it on."

Union, in a 2020 episode of the podcast *Keep It*, recalled, "In the original script and in what we actually shot we're in it like a third of the film. But what actually happened was when they started showing

Bring It On to test audiences, the reaction was we need more of the Clovers. But by that time it was too late, because we'd already finished the movie. So we shot additional footage for the trailer that was not in the movie to fool people into thinking that we were in it like fifty-fifty."

Wong remembered the marketing conversations and the realization from the studio that, wow, people may actually go see this. "When we were trying to figure out the trailer for this film, I kept getting these trailers, and the trailers were just not good," she said. "And I was like, OK, let's take a page from Jerry Bruckheimer. Jerry Bruckheimer does a trailer for ladies, a trailer for gentlemen, and a trailer for an urban audience, which is not monolithic. One of the trailers has to be a trailer that explains to men why they have to see this movie. And I'm like, the reason they're going to see this movie is because we're going to use every tit and ass shot we have in this picture in the trailer. And we're going to use the scientific voice-over from our test screening that says, '73 percent of men polled said they would not be willing to see a movie about cheerleading. Here's why you should see a movie about cheerleading.' And then cut to the bikini car wash. I think our trailer campaign was really successful in terms of showing the different parts of the audience this movie would appeal to. . . . We sort of surprised them, because it wasn't just young girls seeing this movie. It was teenage couples and college students, and the Black audience turned out in droves."

Bendinger, who by then was working on a movie with Jonathan Demme and was out of the daily loop of the production, said, "They basically did a commercial shoot with Blaque. They were super valuable. I always felt bad about that, because if a kid was waiting for that scene in the movie, that wasn't even in the movie, but that was way out of my pay grade."

"We ran a full scam," Union said on the same podcast of the additional trailer footage. But the sentiment, she said, was overall good, even if it didn't result in a film centering the Clovers. "It's rewarding for me, for people to have left that, the experience of the movie, with us on their minds, because that really wasn't the original intention. But it's, you know, it's nice. It's nice that people were like, No, I still see you, you and the Clovers and your plight is, it was still central to my viewing enjoyment."

And remember the worry about *Sugar & Spice*, the competing cheerleader movie? With the giant footprint of the Universal marketing department's efforts, *poof*, worry be gone.

Hughes, one of the Universal execs on *Bring It On*, said that the studio made sure that *Bring It On* totally eclipsed any other cheerleading movie (*Sugar & Spice* was released in January 2001, about five months later). "This is where being with a big studio and having a picture like this in a big studio really helps, is that that marketing machine has a way of really taking over and making sure that if there is something else that that's out there competing, it gets lost in a little bit of a shuffle, because everyone's really talking about *your* movie."

Needing to check so many boxes, from budgets and schedules to marketing to audience members who are just there for the short skirts, it's hard to believe a movie—any movie—comes out of the editing process with any kind of soul.

"The marketing worked on the movie," Reed said. "And that is the way marketing works. I mean, it is what it is."

Finally, the studio needed to decide when to release the movie, and what it would be called. *Cheer Fever*, the name Bendinger had given the story years before, as in "You must be sick, you've got cheer fever," had to go. The studio had made it clear early on that it was only a working title. Suggestions abounded.

"The process I remember being painful," Reed said of the name change. "I remember lists and lists, and I have some of these lists somewhere in storage with tons and tons of every possible title of the movie. I remember Marc Abraham was very big on *Made You Look*. I remember there were millions of different titles, and I really hated all of them."

Even during filming, the cast and crew were invited to throw alternate titles into a hat, a proto-crowdsourcing campaign. "I remember Kirsten was like, we should call it *Spread Eagle*," Bell said.

A contender that stood out to Bock? *The Skirt Also Rises*.

Ritter remembered thinking *Cheer Fever* was a "horribly embarrassing" name. "*Cheer Fever*, that's the best we've got? That's horrible."

West disagreed with his friend: "I still think it was a great name! . . . I would have gone with *Cheer Fever*, personally."

"We went through a ton of names," Abraham said. "Ultimately, it got down to marketing, and they did a damn good job of marketing. We always wanted to change the name of the film, I myself wanted to change it, the studio wanted to change it."

Reed had the same objection I do: Isn't it weird that the movie is called *Bring It On*, but Isis merely challenges Torrance to "bring it"? It's so close that the omission stands out, right?

"No one says 'bring it on' in the movie, they say 'bring it,'" Reed recalled thinking at the time. "Let's just call the movie *Bring It!*" He was told "bring it on" was "in the lexicon."

"I remember leaving that meeting thinking, like, I have to stop it. I remember thinking in the car like, Ugh, this movie is going to be called *Bring It On* over my dead body," he told me. It was kind of one of those things where someone asked what he thought the movie should be called, but they're not really *asking*. The poster mock-ups with the title were already made, and didn't they look nice?

Bendinger, too, heard the changed title as a done deal when Reed called her with an update. "He's like, 'I know, I know,'" she said.

Reed: "And then here we are today."

Eventually, there's nothing more to do. The movie is finished. Bock said that at a certain point, you're fiddling with tiny things just to fiddle with them.

"I used to call it frame-fucking," he said. "At the time I thought it was really funny.

"You get everything the way you want it," he said. And then you get notes from the studio and recut. The cut is tested, notes from the test screenings, recut, notes from marketing, recut, notes, recut . . . no more notes. "And then they take it away from you."

Finally, editing done, test audiences satisfied, marketing teams mollified, the final piece: the release date. *Bring It On* would be released in theaters on August 25, 2000, the weekend before Labor Day.

For the filmmakers, it was anything but a long weekend to look forward to. "I don't remember alternate dates being presented, but I do remember in the year 2000 that late August was a dumping ground," Reed said. "That was where movies went to die. That was my perception of it, anyway."

He wasn't wrong. Late August? That's not a tentpole weekend by any means.

"It was filler," O'Hair remembered. "It was released almost on Labor Day in the dregs of the summer. That's almost a punishment!"

Reed, faced with the inevitability of his feature directorial debut coming out in the absolute dog days of summer, when kids have been hanging out for so long they're almost itching to go back to school, just for something different, a change of pace from the sweaty doldrums of summer, grasped at anything he could: Maybe it was a back-to-school movie, maybe kids would go see it in a burst of last-gasp enthusiasm before they packed up their backpacks with their uncreased notebooks and freshly sharpened pencils.

"When you're in that position and they're telling you when you're going to be released and you just—you're clinging to anything," he said. The studio seemed excited about the movie, the test screenings were going well, but there weren't any comps that could predict how audiences would react to a female-led sports movie, and what comparisons they could draw weren't exactly box office blockbusters.

And on top of all that, *Bring It On* would open against *The Art of War*, the presumed number one draw of the weekend, starring Wesley Snipes. They were dead in the water before they'd even grabbed a suit, it seemed.

All that was left to do was to let the movie open and hope for the best. "We were always an underdog of a movie. . . . It's a strange feeling, [and] you've just got to like, make peace," Reed said. "You've got to know how you feel about your own movie before it goes out there and everybody judges it publicly. I felt like I liked the tone of the movie, and was proud of the movie, and I was braced for it to just get ripped apart, but I think that's true of every movie I've ever made. . . . It was also my first time through that process of finishing something that you've been a control freak about, and then it's out there, and you have no control over it. And that feeling can break your brain, it's crazy. You have to just kind of go with your gut, like I know what I like about this movie and if I like it I know somebody else, at least two other people, will like it."

The day finally arrived: August 25, 2000, just a few days after the movie's red carpet premiere, *Bring It On* opened in theaters.

About that premiere: you've never seen so many spaghetti straps, and Blaque's Natina Reed attended the event in a full red-and-black leather take on an angel ensemble, complete with wings. Hired cheerleading squads stunted in front of the big screen in Westwood, L.A., in an event presented by '90s standby brands Candie's Shoes and *Teen People* magazine. Rufus King, the band that recorded Cliff's song, "Just What I Need," was in attendance, with the band Sugarcult as their guests. Actors Ben Savage and Taye Diggs were there, with the former wearing a souvenir ringer T-shirt from the Crazy Horse Saloon in Miami. Multiple cast members wore handkerchief-style formal crop tops. The carpet: red. The heels: kitten. The choker necklaces: plentiful. It was the first red carpet for many of the cast, and the first time many of them had seen the movie at all, and they didn't know what to expect from the end result of that wild summer, now a year past.

"I didn't really know what to wear," Kramer said of the premiere. "So if I had to do that over, I would definitely change what I wore. But I remember being like, this is a really good movie, this is fun."

"When we went to the premiere, did we know it was gonna be big? I don't think anybody knew what it was gonna be," Ritter said.

While Reed had been working with the team on getting the final touches done for the edit, marketing, and release, the cast and crew had moved on to other projects. Camp was over, but the video year-book was finally ready for them—and the world—to see.

"I kind of like left it and it was kind of out of sight, out of mind," Kramer said. "And then I remember a couple months later my manager called me and he was like, 'OK, I just saw a screening of *Bring It On* and it's a really good movie!' And I was like, really? He's like, 'Yeah, it's, like, *really* good.'"

Choreographer Hi-Hat remembered, "It came out, and I was very shocked that it wasn't *Cheer Fever* anymore. Like, 'Oh, *Bring It On*, oh, OK, that's the cheerleading movie!' And you're excited to see the outcome."

Bendinger had seen a near-final cut of the movie on a VHS tape in a hotel room in upstate New York, where she was working on another movie. With a click track standing in for the movie's music, the elaborate cheer routines performed in surreal near-silence. The story that had lived in her brain for over a half decade by that point was there on the screen in front of her. It kind of freaked her out, to say the least. It didn't feel bad to see it, but it didn't feel great, either. "It's very disorienting," she said. Later, going into her first big-screen showing of the final cut, a friends and family affair arranged by Universal just ahead of the premiere, she felt "pretty panicked, insecure, and anxious."

She was flanked at that screening by friends and fellow filmmakers Dan and Mark Waters. After encouraging her for so long and seeing the genesis of *Cheer Fever*, they had a different relationship to the movie than anyone else in the audience. They wanted it to succeed, and badly. Seeing their petrified friend, they were as nervous for her as they might be before the opening moments of one of their own movies.

"It's so nerve-racking before you go in and then it's just like, instantly, fifty-pound weights get lifted from your shoulders, and you're like, oh my god, they got it," Dan Waters remembered. "It's working, oh my god, they didn't try to change it, they went with the whole Jessica-ness of it, and it's working on every level. From the opening moments, like, oh my god, I'm in heaven. This is great."

Bendinger didn't feel quite that same elation.

"Did they tell you how I was devastated after the [Universal] screening?" she said. "I just was so upset. Danny was like, 'This is gonna be a huge hit, you're totally crazy.'"

It wasn't so much that she thought it wasn't good, it was just . . . a lot. "The best thing I can relate it to for people who have never had the experience is seasickness, and it's not that you don't like boats or don't like the ocean. It's just that you feel a little woozy. You may end up having a perfectly great time; you may end up throwing up over the side. I didn't end up throwing up, I ended up having a perfectly great time, but I felt I didn't have sea legs yet. That's all. And that's fair. And nobody prepares you for this, because everybody is so fucking invested in your dreams coming true in Hollywood. . . . There's no proxy for that, you just have to go through it."

Reed, of course, hadn't had a break from the movie, not really. He'd poured everything into it, obsessed over every last frame and poster, and after turning in the final cut, he just kept going.

"I wanted to be working when the movie came out, which I was," he explained. If it didn't hit, at least he had momentum, at least he was already onto the next project. "I was reading, reading, reading," he said, already casting around for his next movie. He signed on to direct a few episodes of the WB network's new Darren Star show *Grosse Pointe*, reuniting him with Big Red herself, Lindsay Sloane. His run of episodes started shooting the Monday after *Bring It On* was released, one hell of an insurance policy. "That's every young director's fear, that you do your first movie and it bombs and maybe you never get another job or another chance," he said.

We know now that he needn't have worried—he has a superhero franchise in Marvel's *Ant-Man* and its sequels, as well as his roster of other successful comedies since *Bring It On*—but that Friday in August, that presumed death sentence of a release date, he didn't wake up feeling so sure.

A few of the production's key players—among them Wong and Scanlon, returning to the fold to witness the opening of the movie they'd fought so hard for; O'Hair; and Dunst, nervously awaiting the public reaction to her first true lead role—gathered at Reed's place in Laurel Canyon, where a van rented by Universal waited to take the crew around to a few theaters in town, something of a time-honored opening-night tradition. Pop in, stand in the back for a few minutes, hope you hear some nice audience reactions, move on.

The vibe at the gathering was friendly and excited, celebratory but not jubilant. "I remember the night started off like, it's good that we're together," Reed said. "We're gonna get good news or we're gonna get bad news, and it's good that we're together. Let's celebrate the fact that we made and finished this movie, and it's opening in theaters, and we know what we like about the movie, and anything else is gravy."

O'Hair, the sole Universal exec in attendance, said, "I was told in advance, keep the budget down, don't spend any money. We had our dinner at Buca di Beppo up at Universal CityWalk. Not exactly a fancy movie dinner." Buca di Beppo is a cheesy-on-purpose (pun intended) red-sauce chain that serves family-style meals and calls out per-person prices on the shared dishes on the menu. There's one in Times Square. I have a feeling that it wasn't a coincidence that this Universal-footed meal was taking place on Universal-owned property.

The group's first stop on the van tour was a theater in Century City. "My biggest memory is that, OK, there were people in the theater, which is not a given," Reed said. "I had two feelings walking into that first theater. I was thrilled there were people in the theater who seemed to be engaged with the movie and laughing. And I also remember, you know, after you've gone to all this trouble of color correcting the movie and stuff, I remember that on the opening night, the print already seemed a little scratchy and was kind of like weaving a little bit." Ever the director.

O'Hair remembered that the first theater or two, they weren't full. There were people, but there were seats open. "The mood in that van was kind of like tepid, like what's going on," he said.

Reed: "As you're driving around, you're trying to remember this hopefully inspirational thing that you've said, while the other part of your brain is not believing it at all because you really want the movie to succeed and you want people there, so it's scary."

But then they drove farther south, and one of their stops was the Magic Johnson Crenshaw 15, a multiplex in the Baldwin Hills Mall. Baldwin Hills has a predominantly Black population, including many musicians and actors who call the area home. And the Magic Johnson theaters—besides that one, there was one in a Maryland suburb of DC; more in Cleveland, Dallas, and Atlanta; and one that's still open in New York City's Harlem—were an eponymous project to bring multiplexes to predominantly Black communities. And that theater was *packed*. O'Hair recalled being told that the movie had been sold out all day there.

"I remember going in where there was a predominantly Black audience and experiencing that audience and that audience's reaction and being so excited that it was playing to both audiences," Reed said.

The next theater they visited was also packed.

"Every theater we were going to was completely sold out," Wong remembered. And that's when the phone calls started coming in. "My friends in Nashville called me and were like, 'OK, we've gone to three theaters trying to see *Bring It On*, they're all sold out, we're in line now and there's cheerleaders in their costumes who have come from the football game and they're doing routines in the lobby.' These are not paid performers, because this is Nashville. My sister had the same issue: she lives in Los Angeles and she ended up seeing a 1:00 AM showing in Simi Valley, 'cause she kept driving and driving. She called me and was like, 'I'm in Burbank and the line is around the block filled with cheerleaders doing stunts on the sidewalk.' When she actually got into the movie theater, there were cheerleaders doing stunts in front of the screen before the movie trailers started. What are teenagers going to do after seeing a football game with cheerleaders? Go see the cheerleader movie!"

Dunst remembered, "It wasn't a surefire hit or anything. They kind of left us alone in San Diego and we made a movie. It wasn't like we had any pressure to be that kind of a movie either. So we just, like, made a fun movie. I remember my brother saw the movie before I did and he was like, 'Oh, Keeks, it's gonna be a hit.'"

Dushku, too, remembered that sense of uncertainty before the opening weekend. "There was initially, even from executives or agents, this idea that, like, this *Cheer Fever* movie didn't have the sort of gravitas to be a real movie," she said. "I mean, there were even conversations about this maybe being a straight-to-video. No one really knew what to do with it or where to put it."

But all around town and across the country, the same thing was happening: The kids were lining up. The seats were filling.

West called the scene at the theater he went to on opening night in Orange, California, thirty-some miles from L.A., "absolute madness." He grabbed his family and girlfriend and some friends and bought tickets, "not knowing how it's going to do or anything."

"We went and watched an earlier screening, and then we came out, and the lineup was, I mean it was, like, so crowded," he said. "All these cheerleaders in their outfits and stuff, some of them going back to watch the second time. So I was walking out, and I saw these cheerleaders and I just said, you know what, I'm just gonna go over and say hi. Half of them had already seen it, so they freaked out, of course, and then they all wanted pictures and I was trying to leave and then they chased me out to the car and surrounded my car. I took a picture with every single one of them. It was madness."

"Here we were, like, hoping to have a $3, $4, or $5 million weekend and then we had this like crazy hit opening weekend," Dushku said.

Kramer went out with three other cast mates, "I really cannot disclose who," in their pajamas on opening night, high on the buzz of the movie's success. "We went to like a very popular place in L.A. and one girl got thrown in the pool, then we got kicked out," she said. "We had a couple crazy nights there celebrating."

Dushku, however, *did* disclose: "I remember, yes, being with Clare and some of the other ladies and traveling down to the Sky Bar and at the end of the night, screaming, 'We have a hit movie!' and jumping in the pool. It was jubilant. It was exciting. And all of a sudden we were all on this train to having this hit movie that everyone was talking about. Looking back, there are a few times that you as an artist and as an actor get to ride that train."

Bradford, for his part, was on the East Coast and nowhere near a theater on opening night, but the *Bring It On* hype machine came for him anyway. "I didn't know it was going to be big until it was upon the world," he said. "What I distinctly remember is that the weekend it came out, I had plans to go see Dave Matthews Band play in New Jersey. And I did. That's where I heard how good the movie was doing. I literally noticed people kind of looking at me like, 'Is that the guy from that movie that's out right now?' You know. So that first opening weekend is literally when it kind of hit me that we had made some kind of lightning in a bottle."

In her hometown of Chatsworth, California, Sloane recalled "that feeling of watching the movie with a full audience, and it worked. All of a sudden that opening sequence happened, and it was just like, *bam*, and my boyfriend at the time turned to me and he was like, 'Um, this is a big deal. This is really special. This is working.' And then just walking out with the crowd and hearing people quote it and talk about it and seeing them cheer—it was magical."

In 2015 Blaque's Williams, in Atlanta, told me she remembered seeing full cheerleading squads in their uniforms in her sold-out theater. "They actually let the team sit on the floor to watch this movie. And I was like, oh my god, I couldn't believe how huge it was."

Back with Reed and the opening night tour crew, excitement was mounting. Reed had wondered whether preconceived notions about cheerleaders would stop audiences from coming. "I felt confident that if you could get people to see the movie, they would enjoy it, but it's getting people out to the theater to see it," he said. "People were in the theater, which was great. Because I mean, again, you're going out with a cheerleader movie. You know, on an [off] opening weekend, a low-budget cheerleader movie, I mean, there's a huge chance, probably more of a chance than not that no one's going to show up."

"The studio had very moderate expectation, at best," Beacon's Abraham told me. One industry friend had run comps and tracked it to make about $6 million for the weekend, he said, not great for a movie that cost over $11 million. It was a low financial risk as far as movie budgets go, sure, but you always hope for a movie to earn back its budget. "I didn't feel the best about six for the weekend, but

I've had many times of disappointment, so you kind of get toughened to it," he said. "I think we were hoping to get like, nine. . . . I was a little bit, you know, hoping, but I didn't expect anything major to happen."

Plus, remember, *Bring It On* was up against Wesley Snipes and *The Art of War*. It wasn't even supposed to be a fight.

The group made one last stop before their dinner reservations at Buca di Beppo. "I remember going to Universal CityWalk the night it premiered and going and looking in the different theaters and it was all packed," Dunst said. "It just it really felt like, wow, we did something that was unexpected."

Wong remembered the unusual freedom they'd had while filming. "I don't want to make it seem like the studio was 'meh' about us," she said. "They had bigger fish to fry, and we weren't the problem child. So they kind of left us alone and it was fantastic, but they never expected it to work out. And since there was nothing in the market to compare it to, their comps were completely off."

Abraham had a friend in marketing and distribution at another studio who would get the first numbers straight from the West Coast theaters on Friday night, from which he could extrapolate the weekend's numbers.

"He sent these faxes around every Friday night, they'd come around twelve, one o'clock, and they would have gotten the key numbers out of the theaters," Abraham said. "This was all, you know, subrosa. There was no Internet, there was no box office, people didn't know what was happening." So Abraham, at home in L.A., gets this tracking fax, those first numbers. He picks up the phone.

At that family-style dinner where they're literally breaking bread together, an extended metaphor on a budget, O'Hair remembered, "a call comes in. I think the studio calls Marc Abraham and then Marc called Max or Peyton. And they say, 'You made X million dollars.' And you go, 'X million!' Like $6 million, or whatever. That's great, right? Next word comes out: 'tonight.' And people started crying. It was a great deal of pent-up emotion at that moment."

The movie had blown past its expected earnings for the whole week in one night, and would top the box office.

"Kirsten heard from her agent and then she started crying and saying, 'I have the number one movie,'" Reed said. "It was just adorable. It was great. Her mom was with us."

"We were this little movie in San Diego," Dunst said. "I mean, we were a Universal movie, but it was such a low budget and I did not think—this was the first movie that I was the lead of that was number one at a box office, you know what I mean? A huge deal."

Dunst wasn't the only emotional one. Reed had not only carried his feature directorial debut across the finish line, made an entire *movie*, but that movie was now succeeding. People wanted to see it.

"I knew I wanted to be a director since I was twelve and started shooting with a Super 8 camera," Reed said. "I worked as a driver, I worked as an assistant props person, I worked in set dressing and all these different positions, location manager on low-budget movies and things, and all the while I was sort of writing and editing and trying to get my own movie made. So yeah, it was really, really rewarding. It was very, very exciting."

Bring It On had bucked the odds.

"We kind of blew the doors off for that kind of movie," Abraham said. "Late August, not the time you open movies. Basically a 'girl movie,' and about cheerleading—it just came out of nowhere. It defied tracking, it defied the genre, it defied everything. We were euphoric about it. We couldn't believe, I couldn't believe it. I was getting all these phone calls from everybody going, 'What the fuck? How did you? What?' Like I was a genius or something. But I had no clue. If I knew it was gonna make $17 million [in the opening weekend], I would have probably tried to make a better deal."

And suddenly, all those studio higher-ups who hadn't had much time for the movie in years prior were *very* interested, O'Hair said. "Of course, all the calls are coming in and the congratulatory things. The Monday-morning quarterbacking, you know? The 'success has many fathers and failure is an orphan' quote comes to mind."

"Everyone was like, blown away. Thrilled. Thrilled!" said Hughes, who remembered toasting opening night with Bendinger. "Champagne."

Director of photography Maurer was on location in Hawaii shooting behind-the-scenes footage for the John Woo–directed World War II movie *Windtalkers*, starring Nicolas Cage. "I was still working a day job," he said. "I was driving a Dodge minivan. And it was a used minivan, it didn't even have power windows." The weekend after *Bring It On* came out, he overheard a conversation between two crew members: "The second AC tells the first AC, 'Oh man, I went to a really cool movie this weekend. I took my daughters. We saw *Bring It On.*' I'm like, 'I shot that movie!' They're like, 'Bullshit.' That was the number one movie of the weekend. So there I am on set. And I have a video camera on my shoulder. I'm nobody. I have to convince him like, yeah, no, I actually shot that. He's like, 'Oh, damn. What are you doing here? Good job!' That was the turn of my career."

The movie that took twenty-eight pitches to get a green light won the weekend. The little movie that could. An unprecedented success.

"All these years later, I have such a warm feeling," Reed said. "I remember being thrilled but in disbelief. It's a really deeply emotional experience. I'm sure I got a little misty-eyed. I can get emotional about that stuff. I'm pretty even keeled about most things, but you know, you do look back and realize how much hard work and intensity go into something like that and it's like, OK, yeah, I can—I need to allow myself to enjoy this. Because if you can't enjoy that, what can you enjoy? It was a thrill."

"The box office really tells a story," Paul Dergarabedian said. "It really represents how much people were interested in that movie. It's a big deal."

He would know: Dergarabedian is a senior media analyst for Comscore, meaning he's kind of the Guy when it comes to box office numbers and interpreting them, a sort of astrologer for the Hollywood producer set. He told me he's done box office reports every Sunday morning for thirty years, skipping it maybe twice in those three decades. He's not only a movie buff, he's a movie *fan* and one who can marry the inscrutable numbers with what they actually mean.

He remembered going to a trade screening of *Bring It On* back in the day. Movies show in advance for critics, entertainment writers, plus-ones who have palled up with them—industry folks. You tend to see the same people when you go to these screenings, over and over, and it's in the little huddled groups that cluster on the trampled-down, faded lobby carpets of the AMC Empire in Times Square or other theaters like it—usually just normal multiplexes, the same place a typical moviegoer would shell out $7.25 for a ticket to whatever on a Thursday afternoon—that's where the fate of upcoming releases is often decided. Those hunch-shouldered groups in their hoodies and ball caps, even and especially then mostly older white males, talking amongst themselves after the screening, hashing out their instant reactions. *What did you think?* Visions of pull quotes on newsprint dance in their heads.

"I remember seeing the trailers and then getting the invite to the trade screening and thinking, 'Oh god, what is this going to be?'" Dergarabedian said. "I think everybody underestimated this movie. I was at that trade screening when everyone walked out and they're like, 'This is gonna be a hit.'"

If real audiences loved the movie, the critical reception was mixed-to-good. Intrigued. Excited. Baffled, in not a few cases. Roger Ebert gave the movie two stars, but the *New York Times'* A. O. Scott said of the movie, "Underneath this movie's tight acrylic sweater beats an unapologetically feminist heart." He recognized the master sommelier–level pairing that the movie was presenting: respect for Torrance, Isis, and the rest of the squad members, and a middle finger shielded by a pom-pom at all those who sneer at them or cheerleading, with notes of heightened drag queen–inspired dialogue and ahead-of-its time messages about cultural appropriation and the importance of creativity. "If Mr. Reed's camera can't help ogle Torrance and her teammates, Ms. Bendinger's script manages to respect their hard work and their aspirations," Scott wrote. "It may be impossible to dispel the notion that cheerleading is a silly, trivial enterprise—a notion upon which much of the comedy in *Bring It On* depends—but this movie rarely feels cynical, condescending, or cheap."

Reed told the AP that he was "obsessive" about checking reviews when they came out, and Bendinger shared that she "burst into tears that he got it" when Scott's *New York Times* take was published.

The *Chicago Reader* called it "earnest and arch," "so fast paced its formulas are wonderfully obscured." The *Oregonian*: "The newest, and probably first, true cheerleading movie." Wesley Morris, now a two-time Pulitzer honoree with the *New York Times*, then a fledgling film critic at the *San Francisco Examiner*, wrote, "An army of rolled abs and their owners give the state of American race relations a beginner's workout." "Unexpected," said *Salon*—and *USA Today* said, "Could be worse." (Sure.) Film.com knighted it "the most exuberantly funny and smartest teen movie this summer." "Who would have thought," the *Globe & Mail*'s review read, "that a film about competing cheerleading squads would turn out to be the one very pleasant surprise in this very dismal summer season of moviegoing?"

Stephanie Zacharek, writing for *Sight and Sound*, the magazine of the British Film Institute (her criticism has also appeared in *Time* and the *Village Voice*, where she was a Pulitzer finalist in 2015), wrote of the movie, "Conscious perhaps that the world doesn't need a biting satire of cheerleading, *Bring It On*'s director Peyton Reed gives us a pointedly funny and good-natured picture, one that takes the silliness of its subject as a given and moves on with intelligence and verve. *Bring It On* opens with a neat dream sequence featuring the Toros, a prize-winning school cheerleading team, which spells out everything that cheerleaders are thought to be—stuck-up, catty, super popular, aggressively attractive, shallow—and then wallows gloriously in it."

With the hindsight of two-plus decades, Zacharek told me she remembered going to that press screening for her review. While she didn't come out crowing about how we'd still talk about it in twenty years—"I just don't think that way"—or kinging it on her top ten list of the year, it did strike a chord.

"I do remember thinking, wow, I just saw something, I just saw this great modern comedy," she said. "It's about a lot of things, but it's also, you know, really cute cheerleaders and cute guy, cute love interest, in addition to this cultural saga of theft. I guess what I would say is I think that was special, even at the time, for that reason, but it would be a lot more special now. Especially because it doesn't come from this kind of doctrinaire, 'We're gonna make the movie about how the white girls stole from the Black girls.' I mean, it isn't like that at all. Well, that's what the movie's about, but it's very—look, if this is medicine, it goes down really easy."

Audiences evidently agreed.

Some cheerleaders and bored high schoolers were kind of a given, but that's not enough to make a hit. The *well-I'll-be* attitude of critics convinced some unusual audiences to show up, see what this was all about. They told their friends about this strange little confection, an infinitely quotable little movie that was much smarter and better than it really needed to be.

Typically, movies get their biggest hype and box office on opening weekend, then rapidly lose steam. To make money, you've gotta open big. So there's something in box office analysis called the opening weekend multiple. Basically, it's a movie's overall North American gross, divided by its North American opening weekend gross, to make one simple number.

Bring It On's multiple tots out to 3.92, a success by anyone's math. "That's like a Jordan Peele, *Get Out* kind of multiple," Dergarabedian said, noting that non-tentpole movies are lucky to get a multiple of 2, thrilled to see 3.

"To have a movie make its budget back plus $5 million, $6 million in its opening three days? How do you argue with that?" he said. "I'm sure that the accountants and bean counters were happy with that."

In fact, *Bring It On* won not only its opening weekend but the next weekend, over Labor Day, as well. (*The Art of War* dropped from second to number four in its second weekend, and ultimately had a domestic gross of around $30.2 million.) It was unseated in its third weekend by thriller *The Watcher*, another Universal release, which it was later revealed Keanu Reeves reluctantly starred in when a friend forged his signature on a contract. Wild.

Though the box office reign was short-lived—but two weeks on top is two weeks more than anyone thought this movie had a chance of winning—the numbers of *Bring It On* tell of audience word of mouth and staying power: Between the first and second weekend, grosses only dropped 34 percent, which Dergarabedian noted was "actually really low." The next week it dropped 40 percent, but the week after that, only 25 percent. And every week, the movie showed at more locations, adding theaters steadily for six weeks, until it was showing at 2,466 locations domestically—86 more than it had opened in.

"When you have a big multiple of opening weekend, when you have small drops week to week, theaters being added, screens being added week after week, most movies it's the law of diminishing returns," Dergarabedian said. "*Bring It On* was additive. Because of the conversation surrounding the movie, word of mouth. This movie was so much fun, and I think people had fun dragging people to see it who they thought might like it or who they thought might hate it, and then getting caught up in it and loving it."

Bliss said that there's a luck factor always at play in the box office: "The weekend, what it's up against, that there wasn't like an electrical storm shutting down the East Coast," he said. "So many factors go into opening the movie. It's always really, really scary. You can have a great movie, and it just does nothing for reasons that have nothing to do with the movie and you can have shitty movies that do well. In my opinion, this is a good movie that did well. The fact that it still resonated, it's fantastic, I couldn't be prouder."

In O'Hair's opinion, it wasn't luck that won *Bring It On* those numbers. "The movie overperformed," he said, "and overperformed in spite of obstacles placed in its way. And that just shows that the audience at the end of the day is smart enough to find the picture."

Even the actors were stunned. "It wasn't supposed to work," Sloane said. "It wasn't a huge box office hit, but it made money, and they weren't expecting that."

Bell remembered, "Our first residual check was so big. And that's when I realized [how well it had done], that's how you know."

The cast were vindicated even further a few months later. "There was that other cheerleading movie, *Sugar & Spice*, that was supposed to be like 'the good one,' and we were all kind of bummed we didn't get cast in that one," said Sloane, who was one of the many who had auditioned for the rival cheerleading movie. "And then all of a sudden it was like, well, look at us now."

"I wasn't surprised," Fletcher said of the movie's performance. "I wanted the movie to succeed for Peyton more than anything, and the kids. But in all honesty, it's like the golden ticket afterwards. We had the best time making this movie. That is actually the prize. The prize is we had the best time making something that we love. And here's the golden ticket: everyone else loves it. What?! You're beyond excited, because you have no idea what's going to be happening in the world, how people are going to receive it. You have no idea. You're hopeful, you know, but you just don't know. Nobody does. Nobody in our industry knows what's gonna work and what's not gonna work for audiences. But knowing me, I was thrilled back then, and knowing who I am today, same person, was thrilled for everybody involved, but I probably was on to my next job, you know, surviving. You go, 'It worked, great, like awesome. Couldn't be happier. I gotta go.'"

Fletcher may not have been surprised, but *Bring It On* was the surprise of the summer for many, and the long tail of its legacy remains an unexpected wild card.

"I remember thinking, wow, like, what a delightful and beautifully made little movie," Zacharek remembered of her initial reaction in 2000. "When I say 'little,' you know, I don't mean it in a pejorative way. But, like, I wasn't expecting *this*. Fantastic."

PART II

TAKE A BIG WHIFF

Spirit Fingers

The Legacy

"Count the trophies."
—Torrance

When I told people I was writing a book about *Bring It On*, I was largely met with something along the lines of one of the following reactions, or a combination thereof:

"Oh my god, I love that movie!"

"Spirit fingers!"

"I need that book!" (Thank you, if you're reading it now!)

"You know what I love? That toothbrushing scene."

I'm talking my friends, my dermatologist, the various research librarians (read: earthly angels) who helped me go beyond Google, the gal at the gardening store, Instagram mutuals, film critics I know socially, fellow day-care parents killing time in the evening pickup line, everyone.

Considering the warmth and enthusiasm I'd been met with for the topic of the making of *Bring It On*, its cultural impact, and an investigation of why this lowish-budget cheerleading movie is still so popular,

I was shocked by the first question I got from several people involved in the making of this movie.

Due to the constraints of both geography and a global pandemic (potato, po-tah-to), nearly all of the interviews for this book, not only with the cast and crew but also with fans, academics, cultural commentators, critics, and more, were conducted either over the phone or video chat. Typically, we'd begin with introductions and some context on my project. I'd explain my background (journalist, writer, former tween), my past with the movie (former tween who just wanted Torrance's cute hair, eventual author of the oral history project around the fifteenth anniversary that became the viral and until now definitive text on the making of the movie), and then the big question I wanted to answer: Why in the heckity are people still talking about it, two-plus decades after its release?

"Are they? Who is?"

This question was posed almost exclusively by folks who had a career in the movie business and/or for whom *Bring It On* is one in a long list of film credits, an accordion folder in an overstuffed filing cabinet of past projects and reviews and box office numbers and line budgets and congratulatory notes, the bubbles of that celebratory champagne long since gone flat. For me, a person who has spent countless hours watching and thinking about and reading about and talking about this movie, it was less of a query and something more akin to an existential crisis. Was . . . I the only one talking about it?

I'll cut right to the chase and answer that now: No! I'm not. It's not just me. But certainly I and people like me ("like me" means a lot of different things here, in age, interests, and more) are a huge part of what's keeping the legacy of the movie alive and introducing it to new audiences.

I don't need a quiz about music tastes or TV references to guess at what generation I am: I am a millennial, my birth year positioned firmly in the midrange of the era. And millennials were absolutely primed to be into the movie, even those (like me) who had yet to start high school when the movie opened, the same way we all read *Seventeen* magazine as tweens. Teen-focused media invites comparison and planning: Does my life look like this? *Will* my life look like this? It's a fictional control group, an impossible model for us to hold up to the light and examine, turning it this way and that to spot the differences.

Generational impact is important when considering the enduring popularity and legacy of *Bring It On*. Just as cheerleading is often a multigenerational activity—former high school squad members grow up, have babies and dress them up in adorable tiny pleated skirts and spangled hair bows as big as their noggins, and set them up on Tiny Tots teams almost as soon as they can walk without involuntarily tumbling—*Bring It On* spanned generational cohorts. Just think: when the movie was released for home video (very good DVD extras, by the way, robust selection) and I watched it with my friends, I was doing so on the house's big TV in our family room (ever the literalists, we called it the TV Room). We were in the central area of my home, and my parents couldn't help but see it. (Over. And over. And over. I was a very thorough child.) We didn't have a direct connection to cheerleading at all; to my knowledge no one in my immediate or extended family has ever been a cheerleader or shown any interest in being a cheerleader. I grew up in Eugene, Oregon, on the same coast as Torrance's sunny San Diego but much more granola in flavor, and certainly significantly damper and gloomier in climate. I loved movies; I wanted to have hair like Kirsten Dunst's; I would eventually be voted class clown in my senior year and was already a goofball; I was a multisport athlete and an ardent musical theater enthusiast. All of these things contributed to me seeing and liking *Bring It On* and bringing it on into my home (sorry, had to).

Now imagine if I had been on a cheerleading squad and had gone to see it in a group with my team. Imagine if one of my parents had been a cheerleader and we saw it together, or a grandparent or an aunt or uncle. Imagine, even outside of those possible family connections, that a person sees the movie and shares it with someone else, either a friend or at a team gathering or somewhere else. Ripples. The influence spreads. But that's nothing unique to *Bring It On*; that's just how any movie would find its audience, with the added benefit of the subject matter being about not only a group activity but one that multiple generations are likely to have participated in or at the very least have strong opinions about. Many of the people who loved *Bring It On* when they were young now have children they're showing it to, like former cheerleader Amy Cavner, now parent to twelve-year-old Blake Cavner, who spends an estimated twenty hours a week on her cheer commitments. "My mom showed it to me," the younger Cavner told me of her first *Bring It On* exposure. "I like the movie and I figured some of the innuendos would go over her head," her mom said.

This core audience of *Bring It On* fans—of which I (and the senior Cavner) am a part—has aged, since that's a thing we tend to do as time passes. Nostalgia and revisiting the person you were and the things that person loved as a youth is nothing unusual, but throw in a pandemic, like what we've lived through in 2020 and 2021, largely confined to our homes and with streaming entertainment to keep us company. Brains overloaded with anxiety and an underlying current of fight or flight as a default, binge-watching and rewatching old favorites, allowing our mental state to sink into a comforting warm bath of a movie where we know exactly what's going to happen next, the dopamine spike of hearing Courtney bark out, "You're being a cheertator, Torrance, and a pain in my ass!" exactly when we expect it, became a daily ritual. In fact, a 2013 study published in the journal *Psychological Science* found that whether a person is baseline anxious or just in an anxiety-inducing situation, the tendency is to maintain the status quo and repeat old actions, such as watching movies you've seen before, as a source of comfort, control, and an unwillingness, conscious or not, to process new information. We can't know what kind of workout DVDs got in 2020, and *Bring It On* has been on and off streaming services (which don't typically provide hard viewership data anyway) more times than Whitney curls her lip in the movie, but as an exhibit, a Nielsen study in 2020 found that though overall viewership of comedy shows on broadcast TV dipped 9 percent, all eyes were on classic sitcoms. *Friends*, which bowed from TV in 2004, jumped 30 percent in viewership year over year between 2019 and 2020, for example, and viewership of *Roseanne*, which ended its original run in 1997 (an additional finale season was revived in 2018) leaped by an eye-popping 70 percent from the year prior. Stuck at home, people filled their days with the familiar and tried to find something to laugh about. In another study, this one by MRC Data with numbers collected in April 2020, soon after stay-at-home orders, 68 percent of people said they were engaging with movies more than they had two weeks prior, and over half of respondents said that they were seeking comfort through nostalgic entertainment from their pasts. No pandemic needed, honestly—the pressures of adult life are enough to raise anyone's heart rate and send them scurrying back to old favorites any day.

Cultural critic and *Keep It* podcast cohost Ira Madison III was one of those who returned to touchstones like *Bring It On* during the lockdown. "It's a rewatch for me," he said. "I definitely watched it during the pandemic, during lockdown." It's the equivalent of pulling an old blanket over your lap, the sense memory as important as, or maybe even more important than, what's actually happening on the screen.

Culture journalist and *Carefree Black Girls* author Zeba Blay started even earlier, as a balm for political angst. "I went through a phase when it was on heavy rotation, and again in 2016, because [Donald] Trump had just won [the presidency] and I was depressed," she told me. "It's like some comfort food."

Little kids do it too, by the way. If you've ever seen a toddler ask for the same book over and over (and over), they're building confidence via predictability, among other things. When you're very small in a big world, it's soothing to have a sense of control and understanding, knowing exactly how the little mouse is going to trick the Gruffalo next. Unfortunately, much as we'd like it to, no matter how many candles are on that cake, the "very small in a big world" vibe never actually goes away. The best we can hope is that it bubbles to the surface just a little less often.

That same Nielsen study about comfort rewatches, by the way, found that older sitcoms with more diverse casts saw truly wild surges in viewership as audiences sought out shows that not only provided the pop culture equivalent of a long hug with a comforting back pat but also were less homogenous and more in step with the real-life social circles and racial awareness of current years. For example, *Family Matters*, which centers around the travails of the Winslow family, who are Black, saw a 392 percent increase in viewership between 2019 and 2020. It's easy to see, with this data trend in mind, how *Bring It On* could have seen a renewed surge of interest in the period—not that a movie with five sequels ever could have truly faded out in the first place.

Also worth noting: a 2013 series of studies published in the scientific journal *Emotion* concluded that nostalgia is "an antidote to boredom," and a 2018 article in the *Review of General Psychology* discussed how nostalgia "helps people find meaning in their lives" and "acts as a buffer against existential threats."

It's worthwhile too to take a look at what few numerical metrics we *can* point to for interest in the original *Bring It On* over time. A look at Google Trends data, which was cataloged beginning in 2004, four years after the movie's release, is illuminating. When you pull up a line graph demonstrating search interest in the original 2000 film specifically, it's as jagged and uneven as an unpaved road, with dramatic peaks in interest at irregular intervals. Just when you think things are calming down, whoa, hold onto your butts, here comes another one! OK, sure, you may say, people Google it sometimes, seems normal. However, compared to the search interest analysis of other movies that could be considered peers based on subject matter and time period—say, *She's the Man*, the 2006 Amanda Bynes and Channing Tatum–starring, gender-bending, soccer-flavored take on modernizing Shakespeare— the difference is obvious. *She's the Man*, which I can tell you using personal anecdata has not flown under the radar with the *Bring It On*– loving crowd, sees a spike in March 2006, when it was released, then another in August 2006, potentially a reaction to its home video release in late July of that year. Beyond that second jump, the data for the next fifteen years describes a landscape of gently rolling hills, nothing your Apple Watch would ping as flights climbed, really. Like, it's out there, but it's just sort of . . . peacefully existing. The contrast between the interest in it and *Bring It On* is unmistakable. The same gentle texture of the line chart's progression is also true of movies such as *Not Another Teen Movie* and *Save the Last Dance*, two more peers in both era and subject matter, the former sharing archetypes and tropes as a spoof of *Bring It On* and the latter a studio-released dance-based teen movie that overtly deals with differences in race, though through an interracial romantic relationship between Julia Stiles and Sean Patrick Thomas instead of via rival cheerleading squads. Not only is the interest in

Bring It On dramatically higher overall than those other two films in the period from 2014 to 2021, but also the peaks are more frequent and more dramatic.

"Here's the thing of films from that era," Madison said. "There's a lot of teen movies from that era, it was sort of one of the big booms, and there are a lot of them that are bad, that are very forgettable, you know? I mean, I enjoy the film *Get Over It* that Kirsten Dunst is in with Ben Foster, but when I bring that film up to other people, some people are like, Huh? It's not as good as *Bring It On*, so it didn't really hit. Nostalgia can only get you so far. You need to be able to rewatch it or want to rewatch it and have like a good memory of it and enough people to celebrate that they have a good memory with it."

To answer another question posed along with the "Are people really talking about it?" skepticism/astonishment, let's again use the search interest data for *She's the Man*, *Save the Last Dance*, and *Not Another Teen Movie* as a quick comparison. And this is not at all to pick on them—I saw and enjoyed all three movies, and Julia Stiles's New York Mets halter top at the 2001 MTV VMAs was like the *coolest* thing I'd ever seen when I was a thirteen-year-old, before I had an inkling that I'd marry into a hard life of Mets fandom myself years later. But let's take a quick look at milestone anniversary interest. I was asked whether people like, ahem, me, when looking for something to feed the ever-hungry beast that is writing about entertainment and pop culture on the Internet, just trot out movies like *Bring It On* on their fifth, tenth, and subsequent anniversaries, gush about them, and get people riled up and sharing links, essentially creating false demand and perpetuating the illusion of interest. It's the same idea as never feeling so beloved as on your birthday, a circled date on everyone's calendar that reminds the world to tell you how great you are, when you're the same ding-dong you were on Tuesday when no one was baking you a cake. Everyone loves a party, right?

Google says: nope! The data for Augusts 2005, 2010, 2015, and 2020 for *Bring It On*—the fifth, tenth, fifteenth and twentieth anniversaries of the movie, respectively—doesn't show a dramatic spike in search interest, despite much to-do being made of the milestones in the press with tributes, interviews, and articles, my own coverage included.

The comps for the other movies don't show a pronounced jump either, despite the same type of coverage. Even when the marketing machines participate in promoting an anniversary, like the 2021 fifteenth-anniversary Blu-ray release of *Bring It On* packaged with new materials, and included a Blu-ray collection alongside *Clueless* and *Mean Girls*—very nearly a declaration of teen girl movie queendom to be placed in a trio with those titles—didn't lead to a notable peak in interest.

Then, you may ask, what *did* make *Bring It On* spike above its already-high baseline level of interest so many times? First of all, people just wanted to watch it. Several of the peaks over the years correlate with times that the movie was added to or leaving streaming services like Netflix, lists of titles that entertainment websites make a habit of publishing monthly as surefire clickbait wins. See that *Bring It On* is coming to Netflix, think, Oh, I love that movie!, and search it. Another data point gathered. This is also supported by the number two question asked worldwide about *Bring It On* since 2004, according to Google Trends: "Where to watch *Bring It On*." (The number one question, as I know you're wondering, is "How many *Bring It On* movies are there.") If there's a better indicator of ongoing popularity and longevity to be had than people asking for two decades where they can watch a movie, I'm not sure what it could be.

Another data point in favor of it being part of the cultural conversation, having a life beyond its ninety-eight-minute run time, is the proof that it's in the cultural conversation. When Ariana Grande paid homage to the movie in her record-breaking 2018 music video for "Thank U, Next," the movie enjoyed a corresponding boost in interest. Ari's not the only one to have nodded at the movie and cemented its iconic status—but it's an undeniable proof point.

All this to say: not all teen movies are created equal. A teen movie can be good, and a teen movie can be enjoyable, and a teen movie can be profitable—and those are often three very different things— but not all teen movies are iconic. And, it's worth saying, *Bring It On* is *good*. Some initial reviews, in my opinion, fell victim to the internalized and unconscious perception of teen-starring and teen-centric movies as lesser, and movies with teen *girls*? Whoa, pass. Internalized misogyny ahoy; if teen movies weren't examined seriously as art, then societal misogyny made one about teen girls dead in the critical water. Take a look at the re-reviews and reconsiderations of the movie, and you'll see the change. Even Roger Ebert changed his mind, as we'll discuss in the next chapter.

Entertainment journalist Joe Reid, host of the podcast *This Had Oscar Buzz*, pointed to the quality of *Bring It On*, that it's so much better than it needed to be. "I think there are these movies that exist in a genre where you could probably get away with doing something a little lower effort and a little junkier," he told me. "This one did not take that route. This one did the work, and we love to see that."

Using that earlier method of looking at the data, *Bring It On*'s curve is more akin to those of *Clueless* (1995), *Legally Blonde* (2004), and even *Heathers* (1988), which has persistently been of interest at a high enough level through the years to rank here, while other movies' lines appear almost totally flat, so dwarfed their numbers are by the interes in their competition. These titles are teen-movie canon, and hugely influential in culture and the movie biz. They're sleepover classics and nostalgic faves. *Clueless* is hailed as an early reigning matriarch of teen girl–centric comedies that are funnier and smarter than they have any right to be. *Heathers* is every aspiring screenwriter's ambition and an indisputable classic of the genre. *Legally Blonde* is an endlessly quotable evergreen favorite, a box office smash that continues to see new studio-produced sequels and spin-offs involving the original creatives, like a reality show to choose the next lead of the Broadway musical adaptation and a planned third installment starring Reese Witherspoon, an apples-and-oranges comparison of how a film franchise of this type can continue through decades while staying loyal to its original fans and concept, while *Bring It On*'s extended universe consists of spin-offs with new casts and thematically similar plotlines. Not all teen movies live forever, but those lucky enough to reach immortality status don't all do it the same way.

Beyond being sexy and cute, it all adds up to *Bring It On* being popular to boot—not only upon its release in 2000, and not only with my then-tween crowd. More than two decades later, it's time to acknowledge officially what we all know: *Bring It On* is here to stay.

revised
6/24/99

CHRISTINE
JOHN WOO
J546

July 1999 CHEER FEVER

Sunday	Monday	Tuesday	Wednesday	Thursday	Friday	Saturday
				1 *START GAFFER KEY GRIP TECH SCOUT TORRENCE SW (TRAVEL A.M.)	2 TECH SCOUT	3
				FDS TRAINING WEEK 2		
4 I WEEK OUT	5 4TH OF JULY HOLIDAY	6 *START 2nd 2nd A.D. & SCRIPT SUPER - 8:00- 12:00 MAKE-UP/ HAIR TEST	7 9:00-12:00 PROD MEETING CAST READ THRU (PM)	8 CAMERA ELECTRIC GRIP LOAD TRUCKS- LA L FLIES TO FLORIDA	9 CAMERA ELECTRIC GRIP LOAD TRUCKS- LA	10 MARK + KATHRINE GET MARRIED
				15	16	17
			R TRAINING WEEK 1	22	23 steve	24 ALL CLO LEAVE HI HAT 1
		WEEK 2 OVER TRAINING		29 RICHIE VENS		31

June
S M T W T F S

August
S M T W T F S

Director Peyton Reed in the edit bay,
which editor Larry Bock decorated with
vintage cheer cutouts and movie posters for
inspiration during postproduction.

Director Peyton Reed described the shoot—with its accelerated timeline, limited budget, and kinetic energy—as stressful and intense, but "a positive intense."

"When I started seeing the level of the cheering and the routines and the gymnastics, that's when I realized, OK, this is not just gonna be a little sports movie, this is actually the real deal." ——Clare Kramer

"I think we were all on a cheer high. I mean, we were infused through and through with the cheer fever," Eliza Dushku said. Front row, L—R: Bendinger, Ritter, Bell, Dushku, Lohmann, Kramer, Bilderback, Dunst. Back row, L—R: Fletcher, Reed, West.

$2.50

IND 38370

All New Material

NATIONAL LAMPOON®

1964 High School Yearbook Parody

Plus: School Newspaper, Literary Magazine, Basketball Program, Report Card, Diploma, Detention Slips, Fake ID, Cootie Catcher, Cheater Slicks, Beaver Shots, Feel-Ups, Fake-Outs, Gross-Outs, Chug-a-Lugs, Wheat Jeans, Pressed Ham, Hang-a-Louie, Go Bent

The 1974 *National Lampoon* magazine cover that stuck with Jessica Bendinger and inspired the vibe of the opening cheer montage. "You see her butt and the audience's faces, it just always stayed with me," she said. "It was so funny and powerful."

"We all fell in love, we were in San Diego and it felt like real camp, and it was kind of one of those dreamy experiences to have on a set." —Lindsay Sloane

"CHEER FEVER" NEW TITLE LIST C
Possible Titles

SMELLS LIKE TEEN SPIRIT
SMELLS LIKE TEAM SPIRIT
TEEN SPIRIT
TOTALLY FREAK ME OUT
EVERYTHING YOU'RE NOT
SPIRIT FINGERS
WE GOT SPIRIT
GIRLS IN SHORT SKIRTS
I GOT SPIRIT
I WAS A TEENAGED CHEERLEADER
MAKES ME WANNA HOLLER
SWEATER MONKEYS
KICKS
KICK IT
LOOK AT ME
BLOOD, SWEAT AND CHEERS
SIS BOOM BAH
ALL FIRED UP
GET FIRED UP
SHOUT IT OUT
GET PSYCHED
GET READY FOR THIS
BE AGGRESSIVE
HIT IT, STICK IT
FEELS LIKE FIRST
ALL TOGETHER NOW
NEVER LET ME DOWN
TRUST ON THREE
GROOVE ME, BABY
LIFT ME UP
POM-O-RAMA
Jump
Bring It On ← **THE WINNER**
The Spirit Al...

A list of possible titles pitched for the movie during postproduction. "I would have gone with Cheer Fever, personally," Nathan West said. "I still think it was a great name!"

Kirsten Dunst, Eliza Dushku, and Tsianina Lohmann sing karaoke at the wrap party for the film.

Real-life cheerleaders filled out the ranks of both teams, and the whole group bonded and helped each other. "They all taught each other . . . dancers, cheerleaders, all the same," choreographer Anne Fletcher said.

Universal Pictures Presents

BRING IT ON

(Left)   The cast of "Bring It On": (From top) Torrance (KIRSTEN DUNST); (second row, from left) Courtney (CLARE KRAMER), Missy (ELIZA DUSHKU); (third row, from left) Kasey (RINI BELL), Isis (GABRIELLE UNION), Big Red (LINDSAY SLOANE); (bottom, from left) Jan (NATHAN WEST), Cliff (JESSE BRADFORD), Darcy (TSIANINA JOELSON) and Les (HUNTLEY RITTER). (Top, right) The Toros' Torrance (KIRSTEN DUNST); (Bottom, right) Torrance and the Clovers' Isis (GABRIELLE UNION), captains of rival cheerleading teams, face off at the national championships.
5536-1

Photos by Mark Seliger, (left); Ken Jacques (right)

A publicity handout shared with the press ahead of the movie's release.

Director Peyton Reed on set in makeup for his cameo, credited only as "Silencio Por Favor."

Kirsten Dunst initially passed on the role of Torrance. "My focus was really about getting Kirsten Dunst, and that kept me up at night," casting director Joseph Middleton said.

(left) Dunst and Reed on set with Richard Hillman. Cute as hell, just not boyfriend material.

(below) Peyton Reed offers Eliza Dushku a dollar to just get the take right already.

CHEER!

CHEER FACTS

HISTORY

Ancient times – Spectators cheered for runners in footraces held in the Olympics

1860 Great Britain – School age students begin cheering at competitive sporting events

1865 Princeton, NJ – 1st cheer club created 1st recorded cheer at a football game. It was:

"Rah, Rah, Rah!
Tiger, Tiger,
Sis, Sis, Sis!
Boom! Boom! Boom!
Aaaaaaah!
Princeton, Princeton, Princeton!!"

1889 Minneapolis – 1st official cheerleader makes his debut at U of Minnesota. Student Johnny Cambell is elected "Yell Marshall" and leads crowds in cheers. His cheer:

"Rah, Rah, Rah,
Ski-U-Mah-Hoo-Rah
Hoo-Rah!
Varsity! Varsity!
Minn-e-so-tah!"

1900s First widespread use of the megaphone

1920s Men leave for war. Women begin as cheerleaders

1930s Paper pom poms are introduced

1940s Lawrence Herkimer puts together the 1st workshop to train cheerleaders, it later develops into the NCA (National Cheerleaders Association)

1965 Fred Gastoff invents and introduces the vinyl pom poms

CHEER STATS

97% of all cheerleaders are female, however, 50% of all collegiate cheerleaders are male

12% of all cheerleaders are aged 5 -13 and 12% of dancers are as well

81% of the nation's cheerleaders are between the ages of 14 and 18

83% of cheerleaders hold leadership positions in school organizations

83% of cheerleaders have a B average or better

62% of cheerleaders are involved in another sport besides cheerleading

The largest growth of cheerleaders is from juniors

During a typical gridiron game players may get breaks, but cheerleaders go flat out for three and a half hours in all weather.

Tsianina Lohmann, Clare Kramer, Bianca Kajlich, and Nikki Bilderback vamp on set.

Some Clovers in the atmosphere: Union and the members of Blaque——Brandi Williams, Shamari Fears DeVoe, and Natina Reed——between takes while filming the cheer-off scene.

A handout from the movie's press kit.

IS CHEERLEADING A SPORT?

Webster defines "sport" as 1) an athletic activity requiring skill or physical prowess and often of a competitive nature 2) diversion, recreation; a pleasant pastime. According to this definition, cheerleading would be categorized as a sport.

Cheerleading, unlike other sports, does not have a unified set of universal rules, thus causing a debate as to whether or not it is an official sport.

International Cheer contests have more than 210 squads competing and draws over 12,000 spectators.

It costs an average of $1500 to $2500 a year to keep a kid in competitive cheerleading.

Texas is the Cheerleading capital, housing The National Cheerleading Association which was first founded in 1947.

The athletic aspect of lifting another by means of strength and skill in cheerleading is dominated by men.

"Stunting" is any kind of flip or specialized move in cheerleading including lifting another person up.

A liberty heel stretch involves a guy holding a girl by one foot.

"Pinch a Penny" in cheerleading is keeping your body taut by imagining that you have a penny stuck somewhere in your body (hint – the lower region of the body) that you must pinch to keep it in place.

Samuel L. Jackson was a cheerleader.

The Spirit Stick, invented by Lawrence Herkimer, is given to an individual or team for exceptional spirit at cheer camp.

Competitive cheerleaders must be trained in dance and gymnastics.

The National Cheerleading Association was founded by Lawrence Herkimer in 1947.

Aaron Spelling was a cheerleader.

Funny-man Steve Martin got his start as a stunter in college.

The most common competitive cheerleading injuries are busted lips and broken arms.

Colleges give out full cheerleading scholarships to men for stunting.

Dwight D. Eisenhower was a cheerleader.

FAMOUS CHEERLEADERS

Paula Abdul
Marliece Andrada
Gladys Bankston
Toni Basil
Kim Basinger
Angela Bassett
Halle Berry
Sandra Bullock
Belinda Carlisle
Charisma Carpenter
Ana Maria Carrasco
Katie Couric
Courteney Cox Arquette
Sheryl Crow
Cameron Diaz
Calista Flockhart
Vivica A. Fox
Leeza Gibbons
Kathie Lee Gifford
Janet Gunn
Jenilee Harrison
Schae Harrison
Teri Hatcher
Tina Hernandez

Lauren Hill
Lauren Holly
Ashley Judd
Cheryl Ladd
Tina London
Shirley MacLaine
Debra McMichael
Madonna
Debbie Matenopoulos
Lenda Murray
Kelly Packard
Annie Potts
Priscilla Presley
Donna Rice
Diane Sawyer
Alicia Silverstone
Meryl Streep
Kirsten Dunst
Uma Thurman
Cheryl Tiegs
Kiana Tom
Sela Ward
Raquel Welch
Karime Zarate

BRING IT ON

Opens Nationwide August 25th 2000

"CHEER FEVER" ONE LINER AS OF (9-23-99)

/SCENE	DESCRIPTION
01-02	OLD SCHOOL, WHITE BREAD-AMERICANA CHEERLEADERS
03	THE SQUAD PERFORMING "THE MIGHTY TOROS" CHEER
04	OUR GIRLS INTRODUCE THEMSELVES INDIVIDUALLY
05	SEXY SYNCHRONIZED MOVES .TORRANCE LIFTS OFF INTO NUDITY
06-08	FOOTBALL ... BAND REACT
09	GREEN SC ... ANCE SCREAMING
10	AARON PIC
11	TORRAN
12	AARON B
13	AARON
14	AARON
15	MONTA
17	THE GIR
19	BIG RI
20	TORRA
21	THEY
22	THE SO
23	ESTA
24	TORR
25	INTE
28	KAS
29	WE
30	CLI
31	TH
32	ST
33	T.
34	ST
35	
36	
38	
39	
40	
41	
4.	
4.	

Dushku was initially reluctant to audition, seeing herself as the anti-cheerleader. "[I] didn't even try to lie on the form and say that I had any kind of cheer experience," she said.

TORRANCE A ... O M ... HEADS UP THE ON-KA...

Union, the oldest cast member at twenty-seven, has joked about how hard the dancing was for her. "I was only a cheerleader in eighth grade, when you didn't actually need any talent," she said.

Dunst takes a break while filming the infamous dialogue-free toothbrush flirtation scene.

Universal Pictures and Beacon Pictures cordially invite you and a guest to the World Premiere of

BRING IT ON

Tuesday, August 22, 2000

7:30pm

Mann Bruin Theatre
948 Broxton Ave., Westwood

Followed by a celebration at
Barfly
8730 West Sunset Blvd.
West Hollywood

This evening is sponsored by

Teen People   **candie's**

RSVP to 818-777-1405

This invitation is absolutely non-transferable

The invitation to *Bring It On*'s world premiere. The late August release date was seen as "almost a punishment," Universal's Tim O'Hair said.

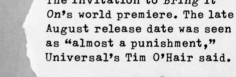

Dunst and Dushku filming the lead-up to the big reveal that Big Red was a big thief.

Bring It On's home video release coincided with DVDs becoming more available, and the movie found another massive audience in sales and rentals.

The Toros huddle while shooting the film's opening dream cheer sequence, which was inspired by Esther Williams and Busby Berkeley.

"She had just turned seventeen," Reed said of Dunst during filming. "She was so young, and it really like encapsulated who she was at that time."

Bring It On in New York City.

Producer Max Wong, Peyton Reed, and Kirsten Dunst getting the call that Bring It On would top the weekend box office. "It was a great deal of pent-up emotion at that moment," Universal's Tim O'Hair said.

On opening night, some of the film's key personnel drove around L.A. and stood in the back of theaters. "My biggest memory is that, OK, there were people in the theater, which is not a given," Reed said.

Ranking This Week	Last Week	Title (Distributor)	Reported Weekend Boxoffice	Pct. Change	Per Engagement Average	# Of Engagements This Week	Last Week	Cumulative Reported Boxoffice	# R
			$17,362,105	—	$7,295	2,380	—	$17,362,105	
1	—	Bring It On (U/Beacon)	10,410,993		3,959	2,630	—	10,410,993	
2	—	The Art of War (WB)	9,676,012	-45%	3,982	2,430	2,411	33,745,083	
3	1	The Cell (New Line)	6,514,903	-31%	2,331	2,795	2,835	63,709,955	
4	3	Space Cowboys (WB)	5,906,038	-47%	6,750	875	847	21,213,02	
5	2	...of Comedy (Par)	4,612,974	-32%	1,796	2,568	2,760	130,919,54	
6	5				1,500	2,717	2,754	30,777,66	
7	4							4,051,9	
8								109,992,7	
9								26,822,	
10									

"It wasn't a surefire hit or anything. They kind of left us alone in San Diego and we made a movie," Dunst said.

Bendinger and Reed in L.A. on opening night, hearing about the surprise box office sweep.

First Alert

Preliminary data for the week ending Feb. 18

VHS sales

Rank	Title	Supplier - distrib.
1	Dinosaur	Disney-BV
2	The Silence of the Lambs	MGM
3	Left Behind	Cloud Ten
4	Digimon: The Movie	Fox
5	Erin Brockovich	Universal
6	Manhunter	Anchor Bay
7	The Road to El Dorado	...mWorks-Uni
8	The Green Mile	...arner
9	Chicken Run	...Uni
10		...a

DVD sales

Rank	Title	Supplier - distrib.
1	Bring It On	Universal
2	Gladiator	DreamWorks-Uni
3	What Lies Beneath	DreamWorks-Uni
4	Dinosaur	Disney-BV
5	Get Carter	Warner
6	Me, Myself & Irene	Fox
7	Bless the Child	Paramount
8	Coyote Ugly	Touchstone-BV
9	Gone in 60 Seconds	Touchstone-BV
10	Manhunter	Anchor Bay

Source: VideoScan, a service of VNU and A...

The movie's success on DVD may have contributed to the decision to continue the franchise with straight-to-video sequels.

THE No.1 U.S. SMASH HIT!

"EXHILARATING!"
NEW YORK POST

"FUNNY!...
LIKE 'AMERICAN PIE' AND 'ROAD TRIP'"
ASSOCIATED PRESS

"CLEVER, EDGY FUN!"
NEW YORK DAILY NEWS

"THE BEST COMING-OF-AGE STORY
SINCE 'CLUELESS'"
LOS ANGELES DAILY NEWS

A COMEDY ABOUT THE CRAZY THINGS GIRLS DO TO BE ON TOP

BRING IT ON

Marketing played up the movie's sex appeal. "The reason they're going to see this movie is because we're going to use every tit and ass shot we have in this picture in the trailer," producer Wong said.

SATURDAY SEPT. 11

CHEER FEVER
CREW CALL: 6:30P
TUESDAY SEPT 7, 1999

TABLAO FLAMENCO
5567 DEL REY STREET
(MAP ON BACK)

CHEER FEVER
WRAP PARTY

STARTS 8 PM

FOOD   FUN

DANCING

CHA CHA CHA!

"Y'all are such an inspiration to us."
—New Pope Cheerleader #1

Bendinger's friendship with Daniel and Mark Waters while developing and writing *Bring It On* wasn't just a nice chance clique and script critique circle, it also happened to be a creative brain trust of teen-movie powerhouses of the era, with Bendinger's *Bring It On*, Daniel Waters's *Heathers* (1988) and Mark Waters's direction of *Head over Heels* (part of Freddie Prinze Jr.'s leading man reign, 2001), *Freaky Friday* (Lindsay Lohan, 2003, unquestionably iconic) and, of course, *Mean Girls* (2004, what more is there to say?) dominating the adolescent box office and forming the core of a golden age of subversive-minded teen girl–centric cinema. (Fun fact, the tendrils of uncanny interconnectedness among the Waters brothers, Bendinger, and their movie creations extended all the way to the stage: *Mean Girls*, *Heathers*, and *Bring It On* all received the musical adaptation treatment, and even had cast in common. Barrett Wilbert Weed originated the roles of Veronica and Janis in *Heathers: The Musical* and *Mean Girls*, respectively, and Taylor Louderman made her Broadway debut as the conniving Campbell in *Bring It On: The Musical* and later received a Tony nomination for originating the role of Regina George in *Mean Girls*. Small world? The smallest.)

Daniel Waters saw teenagers as the perfect canvas for an exploration of identity and social norms, an experience as universal as it is unique. There's no getting around the fact that everyone who's grown up now had to be a teenager at some point, and so will have their own memories and past to hold up against whatever they're seeing on the screen in front of them, squint their eyes, and note the differences and similarities.

"My brother and I always believed that the reason why the high school movie is something that is kind of quintessential or just timeless: that everybody goes through it," he said. "And even though, like, yeah, there's differences now with social media, there's differences from when our parents were in school in the '50s, there's still this ripe time where you are filled with underconfidence and yearning and are going to have a hellacious time that will be funny in retrospect. The great thing about making a high school movie is you're able to go out and have the perspective of, you know, of time to realize the comedy. While you're in it, you certainly don't. That is something that is always going to be timeless, I think, and always have a connection with people."

If *The Breakfast Club* taught us to look beyond surface appearances and high school stereotypes in 1985, the family lineage of *Heathers*, *Clueless*, *Bring It On*, *Mean Girls*, and their extended family tree of female-fronted movies with a satirical edge or social message, featuring the protagonist chasing a goal that her peers have ridiculed (among them *Bend It Like Beckham*, *She's the Man*, *Easy A*, *Jennifer's Body*, and *Legally Blonde*, to name a few) have since dialed the focus in on the Princess and the complexities and contradictions she can contain beyond the polished veneer and social standing.

Tim Shary, a media scholar who teaches at Eastern Florida State College and whose work focuses on teen movies, said that though teen and young adult audiences disproportionately make up movie ticket sales, movies for and about them aren't taken seriously, by academics or, well . . . anyone, really.

"In the '90s when I started it was evident that people, for instance, took gangster movies seriously," he said. "Film noir was taken very seriously, because it had a kind of, you know, French term." Movies about adult women were worthy of study and celebration, but "pre-adult [women] are still women. What about feminist issues in movies about teenagers? And *Bring It On*, what about racial issues in movies? Whenever the field would look at one of those big topics like race, class, gender, politics, religion, it would only be movies about adults almost exclusively. They wouldn't be looking at teenagers and kids, because it's as if that that population, not to mention that market, just didn't matter."

Not to mention: teenagers are talked *at* and *about* in movies, by definition. Shary pointed out that "teen movies are the one realm of all media that the audience for [it] is essentially excluded from making and the production process," both because of how long it takes to make a studio movie and because, let's face it, the vast majority of fifteen-year-olds don't have the perspective, skills, and contacts to write and produce a screenplay about their lives.

So a movie that connects and makes the case for more of those kinds of movies, that's important, not just for aspiring filmmakers but also for the young audiences who are sponging up the content. Culture reporter Blay told me about being a Black teenager and lapping up teen movies like *Bring It On*. "I think that's why I like teen movies so much: When you're a teenager, everything is so serious, right? In a way like everything is like, *ugggghhhh*," she said. "But then, because you're young and you're not completely jaded yet—you think you're jaded, but you're actually not—there's still this level of levity and hope. Teen movies are able to capture that. The movies we grew up on, you know, the *Bring It On*s, the *Jawbreaker*s, the *Mean Girls*, even, all of these teen movies we watched informed our idea of what it means to be a teenager in a sentence. These are movies written by adults who are contemplating their own teen years, and their teen-agedom was informed by the movies they were watching, and it's just going on and on and on."

A fan of sci-fi and fantasy as well, Blay said that as a Black teen in the early aughts she "did not go to those things to feel represented or centered. . . . When I think of *Lord of the Rings*, do I need Frodo to be played by, like, Regina Hall? No."

Watching teen movies, however, was a different story. "I think that those were the times when I did feel that sort of distance between me and the characters in those worlds the most, because [stories about teens] were the most like my life," she said. "Teenagers going to high school, crushes, shit like that, it was the most like my life and there were more opportunities for me to compare and contrast and see where I fit in. The Gabrielle Union character [in movies like *10 Things I Hate About You* and *She's All That*], she was always there, always looked cute, but was always serving one-liners, the best friend. So as a fourteen-year-old girl watching this, you're like, 'OK, so I'm not Julia Stiles. I'm not Lindsay Lohan. I'm like . . . *that* girl.' And then you have to sort of reconcile: you're in high school and you feel ugly and you feel like no one likes you, and then you watch these teen movies that are giving you a sort of manual for how to be. But then you don't know how to be, because you don't see anything that you can latch onto. I also look back on these movies and have a lot of fondness for them and a lot of love for them. I fucking love all these movies. I think of these movies, and I get so fucking excited and I'm glad that they exist."

But *Bring It On* was a revelation for Blay and other young women watching, scrying for themselves in their favorite movies: Union wasn't just serving one-liners, she was in charge. She had goals.

That Isis and these other teenage girl characters had ambitions and passions was a boon to audiences, but a barrier to getting the movie made in the first place. "Hollywood always wants the last best thing, it's never the next best thing," Wong told me in 2015 of the Beacon team's difficulty in getting a green light on the project. "So because there hadn't been movies like *Bring It On* in the marketplace since, like, *Bad News Bears*, I don't think people understood how it would fit. They made this assumption that nobody would see this movie, since there hadn't been a movie like this in forever."

In a twist of irony (check me here, Alanis), after the success of *Bring It On*, it *became* the last best thing, the point of comparison for movies in the pipeline hoping to prove their case and trundle down the path to silver-screen glory. That's not necessarily a bad thing, though. If the "last best thing" is a movie with mostly progressive attitudes that takes the passions of young women seriously, respects their power and talent, and revolves around a search for excellence and self-assurance, yes, please, keep that last best thing coming. I'll take thirds and fourths, thanks, hold that door open a little longer.

That *Bring It On* slipped in as a mainstream studio release, not a limited art-house pic, is important, cultural critic and reporter Joanna Robinson, a longtime *Vanity Fair* contributor and now *Ringer* staffer, told me. "I think the way in which it was pushing the envelope at all at the time, because if this were queerer and Blacker—which it should have been—it would be more like cult status, like *But I'm a Cheerleader*," she said, "which is a fantastic movie and has its own place in the culture, but it is a cult-classic place in the culture."

Dan Waters concurred: "The good thing about *Bring It On* is that they can still say it's a movie about cheerleaders, right? It's about a cheerleading competition, so people are maybe not gonna look too close to see that it's got a subversive edge to it."

"It's a surprisingly sophisticated movie," critic and journalist Matt Jacobs said. He described his year 2000 self as "the ten-year-old who every weekend, like, wanted my mom to take me to Blockbuster" so he could cajole her into letting him rent new releases that he was too young to see on the big screen. That's how he first came to *Bring It On*, naturally, in true "Be kind, rewind" fashion. "This was an era of incredible teen movies, particularly teen comedies," he said. "I really do think that Hollywood had hit a stride with teen movies at the time. *Bring It On* was one of those movies that everybody you knew had seen within a couple years of its release. It was one of those things that saturated American teen culture at the time. Maybe the spirit stick is a real cheerleading thing outside that movie—OK, maybe it didn't invent lexicon vernacular, but it *felt* like it did. . . . It's an overgeneralization to say that that kind of stuff doesn't happen today, because now we have [for example] the Sunken Place [from *Get Out*]—there are still ways that pop culture infiltrates that way—but it just felt like such a huge deal."

He also saw it as continuing the noble work begun by the character of Cher (Alicia Silverstone) in *Clueless*: "You really do look at that wave of movies that came in between like '97 and 2004 or 2005 and it feels like so many of them are taking the model of Cher," Jacobs said. "It's like, do we have Elle Woods without Cher, do we have Torrance without Cher, that sort of lovable teen narcissist who's the beautiful but intelligent, all these different things, schemey scenarios. It just feels very of a piece with what Amy Heckerling did with *Clueless*."

Clueless is certainly the teen movie that launched a thousand ships, but it was still an outlier at the time. Sarah Karp Ward, a former high school cheerleader and current thirtysomething who piped up when I said I would be doing a deep dive on *Bring It On*, pointed out, "Look at any teen movie from that era, and it's still centered around men and stereotypes of women, like *American Pie*, a lot of those stupid movies. They were all still—women were sex objects, and to be conquered. And [*Bring It On*] really wasn't about that at all."

Moviemaking is a gamble, and the reality is that the majority of movies don't make money; maybe a third of them do turn a profit, by Shary's estimation. And that one-third, they justify the low-grossing awards contenders and prestige pieces, and make up for the cinematic bets that didn't pay off. Obviously, nobody wants to make a flop, no matter how little attention the brass seemed to be paying attention to *Bring It On* prerelease.

"*Bring It On*, the producers in the company behind it, they had to be thinking, 'Well, what's going to make this sell?' and they had a pretty reliable teenage market," Shary said, before highlighting where it broke from the reliable formula of teen movies at the time: "It is the rare film that doesn't rely on dominant male presence. There's a brother who's the basic love interest for our protagonist, but otherwise guys factor into it pretty marginally. I think they probably thought, well, not only will girls like it, guys might see it because the girls are attractive. And it's fun. It's not going to make you have to think too much."

Indeed: "I was just trying to make a movie that doesn't make anybody feel too bad and [everyone] gets it," producer Shestack told me. "The truth is *Bring It On* did a lot of things right, and it did it because people weren't trying that hard. I mean, they were all good people, but nobody was saying, like, let's break the mold. They were just trying to make a funny movie for girls when people weren't doing that. I don't think anybody knew that they were being political at the time."

That's part of the win, actually: not trying too hard actually makes the subtly subversive messages of *Bring It On*—young women's passions matter, originality is important, appropriation is bad—more lasting in audiences' minds. Scientific studies have shown that when you're laughing, you're more able to accept ideas and come up with creative solutions to problems. Comedy literally lights up your brain: MRIs show that your left brain processes the incoming joke, and then the right hemisphere interprets it. Comedy, it would seem, is serious business. Poet and writer Cathy Park Hong, in an interview with *Ssense*, called comedy "an argument," a way to convince you of a truth, a spoonful of sugar to help the medicine go down. "The punchline has this element of surprise," Hong said. "Comedy, as an argument, is trying to convince you of some unpleasant truth that you wouldn't otherwise face."

Dan Waters, too, said that he and Bendinger bonded over their love of teen movies and the power that they hold, the respect they both feel the genre deserves. "We both like the genre," he said. "We both like teen films, and so it's like we're trying to use the teen genre as a Trojan horse to do all sorts of other shit. But, still, we're not just making fun of it, we still have a love for what we're making fun of while we are making fun of it."

In short: it's that the movie respects its characters and respects its audience, while still acknowledging that both can be a little silly sometimes, that made it so sticky with viewers, and so smooth that the messages don't stand out as Trying to Tell You Something Important in the moment.

"You don't feel like you're being preached to," the *Ringer*'s Robinson said. "It's just the premise of the movie: it's just obvious that the Clovers are better, it's obvious that the Clovers deserve this and no one ever has to say it in an anvil-falls-from-the-sky-on-your-head kind of way, or even like some of the girl power messages that I find really off-putting [in movies] . . . there isn't anything here that feels like that. Just the characters take this seriously, so we have to take it seriously. Torrance does have a conversation with her mom in the beginning where she's like, cheerleading matters to me. Like, OK, I'll take advanced chem, but, like, *this* is what matters to me."

Writer Emma Gray, who was a teen in a Maryland suburb of Washington, DC, when *Bring It On* came out, wasn't a cheerleader either, but the movie resonated with her then as it does now. "There was something very special about being a teenager in that moment and feeling really seen," she said. "The story wasn't about—like, cheerleading is the backdrop. The story is about growing up and finding yourself and finding the joy in creative work, and in having relationships built in honesty and respect with your peers, and that is a story that's really universal. And cheerleading is just like a really freaking fun backdrop to explore those universal themes."

Dunst, an honest-to-god teen herself when she acted in *Bring It On*, now sees that "a lot of people identified [with the movie] and needed a movie like this.

"I don't think there had been a movie where it's like these two worlds coming together and in this way—like in a poppy way that was fun, but also proving a point too, in a way that wasn't hitting you over the head with anything either," she said. "It was natural and just telling a story, but I think it was a story that people really identified with from different cultures. I think that made it. It was a smarter movie, more subversive than we needed to be.

"I just was doing movies that I wanted to see," she said of her choice to take on the project.

Kristin Russo, an LGBTQ+ educator and consultant and author of the book *This Is a Book for Parents of Gay Kids*, was a junior in college when *Bring It On* came out and had freshly arrived in New York City, where she was waiting tables and "probably a few months out from breaking up with my first girlfriend." Though "I was not the kind of person who saw everything," she remembered seeing *Bring It On*. "This hit a lot of interests for me. I didn't know who Eliza Dushku was, I came to *Buffy* super late"—she now cohosts a podcast about *Buffy the Vampire Slayer*—"so I definitely wasn't like, 'Oh my god, Faith is in this, I have to see it!' Knowing where I was at the time and who I was at the time, it was a combination of the choreography, good music, feuding teens energy, and Kirsten Dunst that brought me to see the film in theater." On rewatching the movie, decades later, Russo said it held up for her: "I deeply understood why my gay self was so obsessed with it." Quotable one-liners? Yes. Musical theater sensibilities? Check. Queer and plausibly queer characters? In spades, honey.

Madison, the *Keep It* host, *was* the "see everything" kid growing up in Milwaukee, "before assigned seats and everything," he said, so there wasn't always a ticket involved, if you catch the drift. But the summer *Bring It On* came out, when he was between middle school and high school, he "probably saw the film six times. It's been up there as one of my favorite films." So much so that he hosted a virtual screening of the movie as part of the Toronto International Film Festival's "Loved It" screening series in November 2019, screening the movie for a sold-out crowd and hosting a talkback afterward. "It surprised me that it sold out, that people liked that film so much, even in Canada," he told me. But *Bring It On* elevated the teen movie without elbowing you in the ribs and going, "Hey, see how I'm elevating this? Get it?"

"They weren't the war drama or films from plays that people would consider what was *cinema* at the time," he said of the genre and how it was—and often still is—overlooked and underestimated. "Teen movies in the 2000s had mass-produced pop songs, and they had pretty actors in them. No one was making them thinking that they were going to win an Oscar. No one was thinking, really *thinking*, about the cultural relevance of them in terms of what it had to say about society and how we interact with each other; these are films that are going to appeal to teenagers and what they want. It just so happens that some of those end up with filmmakers who actually want to make a good product. A screenwriter who actually is telling funny jokes that actually sort of say something about how teenagers interact. And I think that this is one of those films."

So you didn't have to be a cheerleader for *Bring It On* to resonate, nor did you have to be a teenager, though both groups obviously went gaga for it, along with that surprise older, male, non-cheerleader, whatever audience. Suddenly, this "stupid girl movie," as the producers felt it was treated in early days of the project, had launched the genre to the top of the early-aughts pyramid.

Bring It On was not the first cheerleading movie, but it's undoubt-edly the most widely known and quoted, then and today. The team captain of the genre, if you will. *But I'm a Cheerleader*, a 1999 film starring Natasha Lyonne as a cheerleader sent to antigay conversion camp against her will only to realize that, yep, she's totally gay!, is a cult classic (for good reason—peep the cast featuring Clea DuVall, Michelle Williams, RuPaul, Melanie Lynskey, and more). However, as a micro-indie, it was and remains harder to discover than a more mainstream release like *Bring It On*. Rival cheerleading movie *Sugar & Spice*, of course, flopped when it was released a few months after *Bring It On*.

It's worth noting that Roger Ebert, to whom budding film critics construct their shrines, awarded *Sugar & Spice* three stars, calling it "alive and risky and saucy," while his two-star review of *Bring It On* served largely as a screed against the MPAA's ratings system and contained ample speculation about what had been cut to get a PG-13 rating instead of an R, with little about the film's actual plot. Inter-estingly, he categorized both movies as runners-up to 1999's *Election*.

"I felt scolded by Ebert in that original review," Reed said.

Despite his initial tepid review, even Ebert seemed to come around to the charms of *Bring It On* eventually. In 2009, when Screen Gems (a division of Sony) released *Fired Up!*, the tale of two high school men who decide to join the cheerleading squad in hopes of getting some tail, Ebert thumbs-downed it (one star, way harsh, Tai) and alternately praised *Bring It On* as "the *Citizen Kane* of cheerleading movies."

In 2020, Bendinger told the AP that her father, in a moment of Big Dad Energy, confronted Ebert about his initial review. "I'm from Chi-cago and Roger Ebert was a neighbor of my dad's and he would see him at the grocery store," she said. "Apparently after that review, my dad confronted Roger in the Carnival Grocery like, 'Hey, I'm Jessica's dad and I really don't like what you wrote.' People like to quote the *Citizen Kane* line, but my dad was [mad]."

And then there's *American Beauty*. Featuring Mena Suvari as the cheerleader object of fascination at the center of a man's midlife crisis, it won the Academy Award for Best Picture in January 2000. But like other films before it, *American Beauty* featured a cheerleader *character*;

its plot didn't revolve around cheerleading itself. It was a hobby, not the main feature. *Bring It On* changed that, proving interest in cheerleading and its personal rivalries and drama in a way that got studios and TV networks to perk up their ears.

In 2006, Country Music Television premiered the new show *Dallas Cowboys Cheerleaders: Making the Team*, about the high-stakes process of donning a spangled cowboy vest and kicky lil' boots as one of America's Sweethearts. As I write this, the sixteenth season of the show is airing. (In one episode, finalists for the squad participated in a photo shoot in uniform and one candidate "struggled with her hip planes" while posing, and the dancers all received hand-sewn white cowboy boots.) Lifetime created the reality series *Bring It!*, the title an obvious nod to the movie, in 2014, and aired five seasons following the members of a Jackson, Mississippi–based hip-hop majorette group. On Ryan Murphy's hit show *Glee*, members of the high school's Cheerios cheer squad were the glee club's nemeses turned members, echoing that "cheerleaders fart and curse too" mentality that *Bring It On* brought into mainstream pop culture. (They also took a page from *But I'm a Cheerleader* with a same-sex relationship between Cheerios Brittany and Santana.)

There's just something about a cheerleader on-screen that will draw viewers, though, again, no cheer movie has been quite the phenomenon *Bring It On* continues to be. Many content houses seem to be favoring quantity at the risk of quality. Take Lifetime again, and its now-annual "Fear the Cheer" made-for-TV movie event, which started in 2018. Karen Wheeler, director of acquisitions for Lifetime, told MediaVillage in 2021 that the channel had leaned into the camp of the cheerleading movie after noticing viewership trends.

"A couple of years before [this first "Fear the Cheer" programming event] we noticed that when we aired movies involving cheerleaders, even if [they were] a minor part of the story, having the word 'cheerleader' in the title, or some kind of cheer-centric storyline, popped with viewers," she said.

"One of our 2018 titles had cheerleading as a minor part of the story, and it just did bonkers. We were like, huh? Was it the cheerleader part? So we aired a couple of other cheerleader movies, and they did really well. I think there's a curiosity about cheerleaders; everyone has a feeling about them. They either were a cheerleader, they looked up to them in school, or they were the mean girls and they weren't so sure about them. Everyone has this curiosity of what would it be like to be those girls, and you want to see them do great things because it's a challenging sport."

The made-for-TV movies in the series leaned into the camp and genre factors, a veritable Mad Libs of plot summaries. In 2021, one of the films was *The Wrong Cheerleader*, a whodunit murder mystery with a cheer captain as the prime suspect and Vivica A. Fox playing a cheer mom determined to get to the bottom of the case. Does she say the movie's title in character? You bet she does.

And then, of course, there's *Cheer*. The Netflix docuseries following the travails and triumphs of the Navarro College cheer team made less of a splash and more of a tsunami in early 2020. You can't mention it without mentioning its cinematic forerunner—even the real-life Navarro squad can't. "This is not *Bring It On*," assistant coach Kapena Kea lectures the squad in the first episode of the series. "As much as we love the movie, this is not *Bring It On*." There's just no getting away from it. In fact, Bendinger had originally envisioned *Bring It On* as a documentary about high school cheerleaders, but the concept was a bridge too far, truth stranger than fiction, so she pivoted quickly to a fictionalized screenplay. The specter of *Bring It On* looms so large that *Cheer* literally couldn't go a full episode without acknowledging the pleated-skirt-wearing elephant in the room. If *Cheer* was the flashy stunter on top of the 2020 pandemic streaming entertainment pyramid ("I would die for the Navarro College cheer squad" was a common tweet early on in lockdown), *Bring It On* was certainly one of the bases holding its gleaming white tennis shoes steady, maybe that first peewee coach that inspired it to tighten that ponytail as a kid and try the stunt one more time, level up.

But the success and ripple effect of *Bring It On* wasn't just due to the cultural cachet of cheerleaders, the up-and-coming cast, the deft handling of social issues, the notable quotables, any of that—it was lightning in a bottle that occurred because it hit on that exact combination, at the exact time, while not acknowledging that anything it was doing was at all unusual.

"It's a sports comedy," producer Shestack told me. "So you don't really want to say, 'Oh, it was visionary,' but I don't think anybody set out to be visionary. But it is true that there was hardly any comedies just for girls, and not really any sports movies that were really primarily for girls. And this did a lot of weird things. There was a lot of queer people running in the background, and that wasn't treated as bad. It wasn't so snooty about it. There was Black and white tension, there was a lot of stuff that was running in the background that nobody really called a lot of attention to. Because the real goal was just to make a cheerleading comedy. And it turned out to be good!

"There was a cheerleading movie that came out around the same time, that is sort of not a good movie," he continued. "*Sugar & Spice* and *But I'm a Cheerleader*, the point of those cheerleading movies was they came to it from a place of sort of making fun of cheerleading, and I felt that *Bring It On* came to it from a place of having fun *with* cheerleading. There was no joke in it that a cheerleader wouldn't think was funny. You found everything that was funny about it, but you never made fun of it. It wasn't very mean, really. It was sort of, given that actually the writer has the potential to be a snarky person, it was a very un-snarky movie. I think that's what makes it great."

In *Bring It On*, audiences could find a rarity in mainstream releases: a sports movie that takes women seriously. The All-American analog to the cheerleader is the football player, and look at the treatment they've gotten in pop culture: James Van Der Beek spitting out "I don't want . . . your . . . life" in that drawl ("*lahhhf*") in *Varsity Blues* just a year before in 1999, Tom Cruise as the high school football star hoping to ride a scholarship out of his small town in 1983's *All the Right Moves*, basically any moment in *Rudy*. Young men's obsession with and passion for football in these movies isn't treated as silly, it's an inspiration. It's a ticket out of this place. It's what brings the small town together, their real troubles forgotten under those glaringly bright Friday Night Lights. Inspirational speeches and slow claps, that's the stuff of the typical football movie.

Cheerleaders on film, however? Well. *Debbie Does Dallas* must inspire . . . something, right?

The serious treatment of female characters who take their sport seriously was unfortunately a novelty on the big screen. It was a love letter to passion and the pursuit of athletic excellence. By high-kicking the door open, *Bring It On* made the way for other movies to do the same thing.

Take, for example, the indie *Bend It Like Beckham*, distributed by Fox Searchlight in 2002 in the States and starring Parminder Nagra and Keira Knightley as talented soccer players who fall into friendship and separately struggle for their parents' acceptance. The movie, directed by Gurinder Chadha, explores cultural expectations and differences (the main character, played by Nagra, is Sikh, and her parents deeply disapprove of her playing soccer to the point that she hides her participation as a star player on her team), gender roles, sexuality, and racism. While it didn't enjoy the same commercial success as *Bring It On*—it grossed $76.6 million worldwide—it was met with glowing reviews and international acclaim, maybe owing partially to the familiarity with soccer (you can't make me say "football") on a global scale, while cheerleading embraces its thoroughly American origin story. *Bend It Like Beckham* took home a GLAAD Media Award for Outstanding Film and the 2003 ESPY Award for Best Sports Movie. It was also adapted into a stage musical that opened in London in May 2015 and ran for nine months, with a short revival in Toronto in 2019.

Speaking of soccer, please turn your attention to 2006's *She's the Man*, another classic of the early-aughts teen-movie genre, in which Amanda Bynes's Viola poses as her twin brother Sebastian to play soccer at an elite boarding school. A retelling of Shakespeare's *Twelfth Night*, the plot is obviously more contrived than Torrance's fairly straightforward quest for the national cheer championship, but it shares the overall story of a female protagonist driven to prove herself and be recognized for her athletic excellence.

The mega-successful *Pitch Perfect* franchise, the first installment of which was released in 2012 to a monster $115.4 million box office, a number that *Pitch Perfect 2* more than doubled in 2015, is also a direct descendent and beneficiary of *Bring It On*'s trailblazing attitude.

Though it's not a traditional sports team, the disgraced all-female a cappella group the Barden Bellas, the heroes of the comedy franchise, are also on a quest to prove themselves, albeit through making guitar sounds with their mouths. Like *Bring It On*, it's a story of a group of women working together to reinvent and prove themselves in the field of their passion—a passion that many onlookers find to be totally ridiculous. *Pitch Perfect* tapped into a fairly subcultural niche and found massive popular appeal in the comedy, drama, and intensity in the details of die-hard collegiate a cappella performers, with the same group bond you might find in a fraternity, just with more young people singing Billy Joel songs, one group member inevitably relegated to standing in the back row singing *"mow-mow-mow"* for the entire number. The movie's cast of characters even mirrored that of *Bring It On*: there's the perky blonde leader of the group and an eyelinered newcomer who arrives and shakes up the group, leading to reinvention, strengthened bonds, a moral victory, and, in *Pitch Perfect*'s case, a victory that comes with a trophy. Again, the romance plot, another scruffy dude with snappy one-liners and a heart of gold, could be excised from the movie without changing the main themes. The line from *A League of Their Own* to *Bring It On* to *Pitch Perfect* is faint, with decades between the first two, but the momentum (and box office proceeds and business savvy) have picked up with each subsequent filmic argument in favor of women throwing themselves wholeheartedly into their passions and beating the odds.

Bring It On's status as an iconic sports movie can also be cemented by the hundreds of people who attended Cinespia's screening of the movie in July 2019 at the Hollywood Forever Cemetery, an event that former high school cheerleader Ward, in Los Angeles visiting a friend, found herself at.

"My friend was like, 'Oh, hey, you're a cheerleader, right?'" Ward agreed to go, but "I didn't have much expectation for it. I just thought it sounded cool. And I got there and I was like, holy shit. . . . people wore homemade cheerleading uniforms, and they're like, posing in front of graves. I knew there was nostalgia, but I just didn't know. Gabrielle Union was there and everyone was, like, losing their shit.

"I don't think in the early 2000s when I [first saw *Bring It On*], I don't think I would have been like, I'm gonna want to go see it in a cemetery in 2019."

That the masses sold out the screening and turned out that Saturday night to drink wine outside and watch a movie is a testament to its popularity. Keep in mind that 2019 wasn't a landmark anniversary year for the movie—nineteen years minus one month isn't typically cause for much fanfare—and Union's appearance before the movie was a surprise that hadn't been publicized. Enough people liked the movie enough to just . . . go.

Katie Barnes, an award-winning features writer with ESPN, knows sports, and they firmly believe that *Bring It On* is "one of the best sports movies ever made. Like, it's one of the best in the genre. And, *yes*, it is about teenage girls cheerleading. That's always been really important to me."

Barnes, who grew up in the fifteen-hundred-ish-person town of Culver, Indiana, which they describe as "middle of nowhere," caught the movie a few years after release—they were nine when it came out—and were "absolutely obsessed with it pretty much immediately," they told me. "I don't remember a time in my life when I have not loved *Bring It On* as a piece of pop culture." And when they say that, they mean it: in an essay on ESPN.com for the movie's twentieth anniversary, a date Barnes said they'd had circled for years, they estimated that they'd seen the movie over three hundred times, with multiple stretches of watching it once a morning, or playing it on loop throughout the day, a balm of a background noise as they went about their routine. They fully believe that it should be alongside *Rocky* on the top sports movies of all time lists that float around, and they are *vocal* about it, to say the least.

"I talk about it all the time," Barnes admitted to me, laughing. "I have ever since I was a kid and, yeah, you know, if you start an argument with '*Bring It On* is the best movie ever made,' well, you're starting it to be provocative and get to make your case in defense. But even on Twitter, like anytime somebody puts out a graphic about the best sports movies and *Bring It On* is not present, like, what are we even doing here? We're just having a conversation without the best one? I don't get it. Like, I don't understand why *Bull Durham* was on the list. It's trash. Get this out of my face."

A backbone to their argument, and the reason why they think the initial shocked reaction to their assertion that *Bring It On* should top the list, is that problem that keeps coming up: the ease with which culture at large dismisses women, their passions, their brilliance, the art made for them and about them.

"We devalue things that are marketed towards teenage girls," they said. "And also, of course, we culturally devalue women's sports in general. And when it comes to cheerleading, we like to pretend like it's not even a sport, right? And so, all of those things, I think, work in tandem in the way that people culturally view *Bring It On*. And especially in sports movies, as sports writ large are, largely that conversation is driven by men. You know, I find it to be really important to consistently push back against that narrative. And by taking every opportunity I have to say, no, the best three sports movies ever made were *Bring It On*, *Love & Basketball*, and *Stick It*. There's no others."

Barnes is biracial, with a Black father; they are queer and nonbinary; they love sports. *Bring It On* was on the nose in describing the contours of what would be major themes of their identity in decades to come, before they even really knew themself.

"It was important to me," they said. "With seeing a piece of myself represented in a subtextual way, we're talking about Missy being queer, which is not canon but canon. Even for me as somebody who was working through that identity and not quite understanding my attraction to her as a character and also feeling like she was a bit of a mirror for a gendered part of myself that I didn't fully quite understand. It was one of the driving reasons why I just completely fell in love with the film, and have loved it forever."

The movie not only shows respect to its characters and their passions but also allows fans to share their love for it without feeling sheepish. There are a few raunchy references, sure, but there's no nudity, nothing graphic. Not even so much as a sip of beer. You're not going to feel, when you profess your love for *Bring It On*, the way you might for fanning out over, say, *Varsity Blues*. Imagine watching that whipped cream bikini scene sitting next to your grandma on the couch, or your four-year-old cousin: Yikes. You could watch *Bring It On* on a plane. That's before you even get to the actual plot.

Jacobs, the critic, pointed out, "Nobody's ever embarrassed to say they like *Bring It On*. There are certain teen movies that you end up as an adult you have to like ironically, right? There are certain movies that just don't have the cultural cachet for you to proselytize for them in the way that you can something like *Bring It On*. I think *Legally Blonde* occupies a similar sort of status, where there's enough interesting gender politics or there's some kind of statement about higher education system or teen cheerleading politics or whatever this is. Again, it's our own fault that we think something can't 'just' be a teen movie, but nobody has to shy away from their affection for this movie. I think that's really critical to its success and legacy."

Even Bradford, who initially turned down the role of Cliff for Serious Actor Reasons, said with the benefit of hindsight that *Bring It On* ended up being much more than a silly teen movie. It shouldn't be a surprise, he said, that the little movie that could is still persisting, even now.

"The movie turned out really good," he told me. "It just really works and fires on every cylinder it can fire on and works on levels that exist above and beyond just the trope of the teen movie, or just the trope of a cheerleader thing. You know, it's not a movie for kids. It's not a movie for teens. It's a movie for anybody who likes a fun movie and can suspend their disbelief a little bit in terms of what to expect. When I think about the movie I go, well, of *course* this movie did well. It's a good movie."

NOT ANOTHER

TEEN INTERSTITIAL

They say that imitation is the sincerest form of flattery, and when it comes to teen movies, the saying can be altered to add: and satire is the surest sign of canonization.

Not Another Teen Movie, which heavily draws from tropes and plot points in *She's All That*, *Varsity Blues*, *10 Things I Hate About You*, *Can't Hardly Wait*, *Cruel Intentions*, and, of course, *Bring It On* (among nods to many other teen movies; the movie was at one point known as *Ten Things I Hate About Clueless Road Trips When I Can't Hardly Wait to Be Kissed*, according to *Variety*), was released in theaters on December 7, 2001, just over fifteen months after the release of *Bring It On*. With an estimated $15 million budget, the R-rated Sony release leaned on gross-out jokes and in-jokey references to movies largely from the handful of years before its release (*She's All That*'s Laney Boggs became Janey Briggs, for example), as well as nods to older classics of the genre intermingled with the new guard (the movie's characters are students at the fictitious John Hughes High School).

Director Joel Gallen had built a reel making short movie parodies for events like the MTV Movie Awards, the little spoofs of the year's most memorable scenes for Best Kiss, things like that. He had a hand in the original *Zoolander* short, in fact. You've seen his stuff. When Sony had a script called *Teen Movie*, a follow-up to the goofy parody *Scary Movie*, the project made its way to him.

"The script wasn't really very good, but the concept of making fun of teen movies was obviously right in my sweet spot," Gallen told me. He got three writers on board to rewrite the script with him—he said only one scene held over from the original script to the finished movie—and started in on his directorial debut. (The scene they retained, at the studio's insistence, is one that infamously ends with four teenagers and a diarrhea-spewing toilet falling through the ceiling of a classroom, shellacking several people in a mud bath–like coating of poop.)

"Obviously teen movies were exploding at the time, so it was the perfect genre to make fun of, and we also noticed that a lot of things in teen movies were sort of recycled from previous teen movies and there was sort of a pattern," he said.

He took his eye for humor and spinning existing concepts and went to work on the eighty-nine-minute spoof movie, casting a pre-Marvel Chris Evans in his first feature role. The two movies are tied together not only in plot

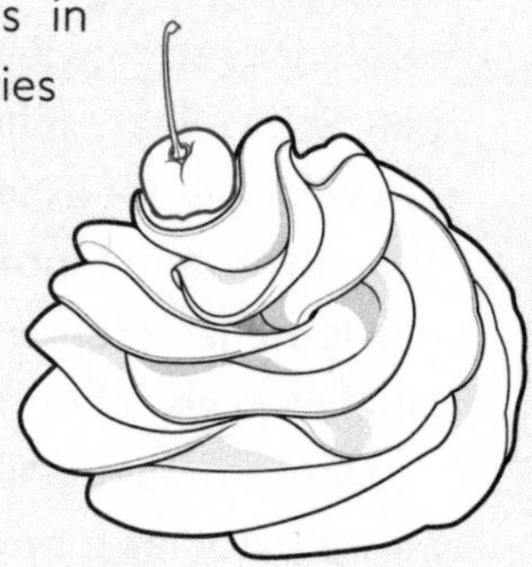

Fig. 7.1: Whipped cream. Necessary for application of certain edible body adornments.

but in a line that Gabrielle Union has said people quote at her constantly—and erroneously, since it's not a line she ever spoke: "It's already been broughten," Jaime Pressley's character's response to "Bring it." Gallen was delighted: "I love that! But 'It's already been broughten,' obviously it was our probably most famous line, absolutely, in the movie. It always got the biggest laugh in the trailer."

A closer look at the cast list reveals not only other surprising names—Samm Levine immediately off the cult success of *Freaks and Geeks*, a cameo by Mr. T, pre–*Mean Girls* Lacey Chabert—but also some meta-bombshells that tie the movie to *Bring It On* beyond just story references and tropes. For example, the films' DNAs are so linked that they share a casting director, Joseph Middleton. That could explain how Cody McMains, who played Torrance's little brother in *Bring It On* (who could forget that running-start fart directly onto Kirsten Dunst's thigh?), ended up playing Mitch in *Not Another Teen Movie*, whose personality could be a slightly more grown up, if less flatulent, version of Justin. (Ron Lester also played a spoofed version of his *Varsity Blues* role in the movie.)

"There was no question in whether or not I would do it or not," McMains said. "You don't really get solidified in history in entertainment unless someone's making fun of you. Like, if you get made fun on *South Park* you have arrived . . . Those movies . . . *She's All That*, *10 Things I Hate About You*, you know, *Bring It On*, they got to get made fun of, which I think definitely puts them in that 'live forever' category."

Not Another Teen Movie, in all its snarky glory, is also permanently etched into the personal history of another *Bring It*

On star: Nathan West auditioned for the male lead for the movie, which eventually went to Evans. His girlfriend, Chyler Leigh, was cast in the female lead of Janey. While Leigh was in California shooting, West was in Toronto shooting *Skulls II*. The two movies shared a producer, Neal Moritz (also known for producing the *Fast and the Furious* franchise), who worked out a unique way for West to have a split-second cameo in *Not Another Teen Movie* that would have a lifelong impact on the actor. In the opening scene of the movie, West appears as a Freddie Prinze Jr. look-alike in a facsimile of the *She's All That* prom scene, to which Janey is masturbating (dildo-based slapstick ensues, obviously). It was a win-win: the studio got to avoid paying to license the original scene, and West got to propose to Leigh.

"I called Neil, I'm like, hey, man. You got me up here in the cold, I'm missing my girl, and I want to get engaged, and he's like, done deal," West recalled via video chat from his home, Leigh occasionally tossing in playful side comments from across the room. "That's how I ended up, I'm in obviously in the movie for a split second as Freddie Prinze. And it was really all just for that. It was just so that I could be in a tux, it was all Neil's idea to be in a tux and everything, and then turn around and use the rehearsal to propose. He flew me down and paid me for it. Everything first class, everything. He ran it just like a normal deal, and I've got this ring made up in Toronto, and got a chance to get engaged." The proposal was filmed and is a hidden Easter egg on the movie's DVD.

Rini Bell recalled West gushing about Leigh on the set of *Bring It On* the year before. "We were teasing him so much because he'd be like, oh, she's so beautiful," she said. "Talk about her body. And we'd be like, uh, Nathan, you're not going to marry her, and he totally married her. He'd be like, ahh, her body's so hot!"

As for Reed, he took the movie as flattery, an homage. Maurer, who remembered seeing the movie with him, said, "That was so enjoyable to see: *Hey, they're taking our stuff, our visuals, our iconography, and they're having fun with it.* It was awesome. That was probably one of the highest forms of praise."

And to only deepen the alchemical bond of weirdness, Reed actually visited the set of the movie during shooting for a meeting with Moritz and saw Evans—who would appear fourteen years later as Captain America in a post-credits scene of Reed's first *Ant-Man* movie—shooting. "It was a scene where Chris Evans punches a balloon as he's in a motel room. I remember seeing him live-punch a balloon." The stuff of legends, folks.

"It was a lot of fun, but obviously again, ours was far better," West said good-naturedly of *Not Another Teen Movie*, Leigh cackling and booing loudly from elsewhere in the room. "We're iconic."

"We're gonna make you an honorary Clover for life."
—Isis

There's a game that's played at parties in certain circles of entertainment writers, both super fun and—I cannot stress this enough—super, super nerdy. Joe Reid, who writes about film and hosts podcasts like *This Had Oscar Buzz* and architects the most awe-inspiringly intricate movie trivia games I've ever encountered—all for his own sadistic pleasure—made it up. We just call it "the IMDb Game." Its premise is simple, but the resulting discoveries are often surprising. It goes like this: Take turns picking an actor or director. When it's your turn, name your subject, then look them up on IMDb. Let the games begin.

IMDb is perhaps the best-known "wait, who was in that movie again?" resource available to humankind. It's a virtually endless archive of movie cast and crew lists, user-contributed movie rankings and collections, photo galleries, movie trailers, and more, so much more. That's not to say it's without error—for example, it tried to tell me that Mark Bryan, the cheer music mixer who worked on *Bring It*

On, also had several other credits for writing "Only Wanna Be with You." He is not now, nor has he ever been to my own knowledge or his, a member of Hootie & the Blowfish—but IMDb is still truly a gold mine of movie and TV trivia. What this game focuses on, however, is the "Known For" section, four movie thumbnails on each person's page below their bio but above their complete filmography. This is an algorithmically determined list of the top four movies that you'd know this person from. Not their most recent or their most praised—but the movies most associated with their name. It's a fascinating glimpse into the most popular of pop culture and general population interests, and the game is for the other players to identify all four entries on your chosen subject's list. It's often *way* harder than it seems like it should be.

Here's a spoiler for you, should you decide to give it a try yourself (make up your own house rules; in ours you can give hints but must disclose whether an entry is animated and/or a TV show): with the exception of two—Kirsten Dunst and Holmes Osborne, who played her character's father in the movie—*Bring It On* appears on every one of the featured cast's "Known For" list, as well as Peyton Reed's. (For context, Eliza Dushku's list includes *Bring It On, Jay and Silent Bob Strike Back, Wrong Turn*, and the TV show *Dollhouse.* Surprise!) And it's not a small cast. Though it was the breakout studio film role for many, the majority of the cast are still working in the industry, with lengthy résumés. In the case of Jesse Bradford, he'd already been the lead in Steven Soderburgh's Cannes Palme d'Or–nominated *King of the Hill* in 1993, a film which does not appear on his "Known For" list (hello to *Presumed Innocent, Flags of Our Fathers*, and 2002 teen stalker flick *Swimfan*, alongside *Bring It On*, of course). Gabrielle Union, who is at the level of fame and fascination that led her to have no fewer than four very well-documented looks before, during, and after the 2021 Met Gala, is typically introduced in gossip articles as some variant on "the *Bring It On* actress." It's a signature title—everyone's seen it.

And this could just be a sign that I've been thinking about this movie too long, but *Bring It On* alums and connections are absolutely everywhere. I had to lie down for a few minutes after discovering this one: Alyson Fouse, who is credited for writing four of the movie's plentiful straight-to-home-video sequels (*All or Nothing, In It to Win It, Fight to the Finish,* and *Worldwide #Cheersmack*—yes, Virginia, there is a hashtag in the title), also has a story credit on the 2019 series finale of TV's *Being Mary Jane,* which starred none other than Gabrielle Union. The director? Adam Shankman, whose near-miss with the original movie caused some to think the project would be dead in the water. Oh, and the episode is called "Becoming Pauletta," a reference to Union's character's full legal name, yes, but also a faint dotted line to *Bring It On*'s Oprah-esque Pauletta, who funds the Clovers' trip to Nationals after they plead their case as "inspiration leaders." Is your mind blown, or have I dropped my spirit stick?

Either way, it's undeniable that *Bring It On* was the start of something good for many, even the movie's "big name" at the time, Dunst, despite the fact that she's not "Known For" it, according to IMDb.

"What would Kirsten Dunst's career have been like without *Bring It On* is an interesting alternate universe," film critic and entertainment writer Matt Jacobs told me. Jacobs and I share a passion for Dunstian works from the late '90s and early aughts, like *Drop Dead Gorgeous, The Virgin Suicides,* and *Dick* (all released in 1999), and *Get Over It* (2001). They're a quartet of somewhat strange, lower-budget comedies that didn't connect at the box office but, like *Bring It On,* elicit gasps and feverishly quoted lines when they come up in conversation with certain sets. *Drop Dead Gorgeous* was the subject of a brief 2019 *New Yorker* paean by Jia Tolentino, who called it "possibly my favorite movie of all time." And *Get Over It,* which is based on *A Midsummer Night's Dream* and sees Dunst's character participating in an original musical called *A Midsummer Night's Rockin' Eve* and also at one point accidentally shooting her love interest with a crossbow, feels like more of a shared hallucination than a theatrical release. They're beloved, Jacobs said, but they certainly fall into the cult classic category. "We agree they're all good, they're all worthy," he said, but for it to add up to mainstream career momentum for Dunst, "you need one of them to break out from the pack. *Bring It On* does that for her." She'd found—and would continue to find, still finds now—art-house and prestige success with movies like *Interview with the Vampire* and *The Virgin Suicides,* but "I don't know that you get Kirsten Dunst in *Spider-Man* without *Bring It On*, a blockbuster hit that appeals to youngish audiences."

And he's exactly right, according to none other than Dunst herself. "I did get this Gap billboard post–*Bring It On*," she told me. "It was part of the reason why I got *Spider-Man*, was because [*Spider-Man* star] Tobey [Maguire] was driving down Sunset Boulevard and he was like, 'What about her for the girl?' You know, 'What about Kirsten from *Bring It On*?' That was part of it, the success of *Bring It On*."

That ladder to mainstream recognition has now, finally, led to the ultimate critical recognition in the form of a Best Supporting Actress Oscar nomination for her role in Jane Campion's *The Power of the Dog*, released in 2021.

In a 2019 interview on SiriusXM, Dunst offered a clear-eyed reflection on being a Them for decades in a sea of Whos, the subject of many a gushing "Oh, I *love* her" but not getting the same critical acclaim and awards recognition as peers such as Scarlett Johansson or Natalie Portman, to name two. "It's interesting to me. I feel like a lot of things I do people like later," she said in the interview. "I've never been recognized in my own industry. I've never been nominated for anything. Maybe like twice for a Golden Globe when I was little and one for [TV show] *Fargo*. Maybe they just think I'm the girl from *Bring It On*."

She dared to say the quiet thing loud: If she's so beloved, so good, has worked so hard for so long, where are the statues? "I just feel like, 'What did I do?'" she said in the same interview. "I am so chill. Maybe I don't play the game enough. I mean, I do everything I'm supposed to. It's not like I'm rude or not doing publicity or anything. I know that all you have is your work at the end of the day. And that's all people really care about. I'm intelligent enough to know that and have perspective, but sometimes you're like, 'It would be nice to be recognized by your peers.'"

In a December 2021 interview with the *Cut*, a month or so ahead of the announcement of her nomination, she dropped that she and friends/frequent collaborators Kate and Laura Mulleavy, the sisters behind the fashion label Rodarte, code-worded "shrimp" in place of "awards."

"When we saw this film, we said, 'Give Kirsten some shrimps, come on,'" Kate Mulleavy said of *The Power of the Dog*.

Dunst doesn't badmouth or disown *Bring It On*, but has admitted to feeling the burn of the stigma of, you guessed it, the "girl movie" genre. The same week as that 2021 first Oscar nod, she told a story on the *Hollywood Reporter*'s *Awards Chatter* podcast of another young actress making her feel like garbage around the time of *Bring It On*'s release. "During that age I was wanting to be taken seriously too, so I think that even though it was so successful, I think there's part of me that always checks myself or checks what's around me. I remember another actress said something, actually," she said. "She was like, 'Well, I'm not in a dumb cheerleader movie' or something. Her saying that just made me feel so terrible about myself."

As a reminder, that "dumb cheerleader movie" made absolute bank and spawned a franchise that's going strong two decades later, not to mention the continuous flow of fandom for the original movie.

"It's so funny how one thing can really—it's not any of the good that sticks out; it's the one bad thing that really sticks out to you always," Dunst said.

And yet, for a movie that it was easy for so many to roll their eyes at, *Bring It On* was a springboard and a signature for so many in the cast—see the IMDb game, above. (By the way, even Reid was surprised by the answers; he guessed wrong for Bradford and Dunst among the main cast—I'll give him a pass on Osborne, who has lines in maybe two scenes in the movie.)

For Gabrielle Union, who prior to the movie had scattered guest roles in sitcoms, a short arc on *Sister, Sister*, another on *7th Heaven*, and stereotypically "sassy" best pal roles in *10 Things I Hate About You* and *She's All That*, plus a small role in *Love & Basketball*, released just a few months before *Bring It On* in April 2000, the role of Isis established her as a leading lady. Sidekick to no one, her portrayal was an inspiration to viewers and a wake-up call to Hollywood. Suddenly, she wasn't landing roles as the bestie; she was the titular Eva in 2003's *Deliver Us from Eva*, and later Mary Jane in the well-received 2013–2019 BET series *Being Mary Jane*. Now, though she still takes the occasional acting role like the Disney+ remake of *Cheaper by the Dozen*, her Google

Alert pings more frequently for her social media moguldom (she's married to former Miami Heat star point guard Dwyane Wade and as I write has nearly twenty million followers on her Instagram, avidly following her stories of glam outings and being hilariously humanized by daughter Kaavia James), fashion collaborations (she has a line with workwear fave New York & Company), and as the author of two *New York Times* bestselling memoirs, *We're Going to Need More Wine* and *You Got Anything Stronger?*

But again, her public persona is inextricably linked to *Bring It On*. She's asked about it in almost every interview, and both of her books include essays that speak in depth about her work on the movie. In the second, she dedicates an entire chapter to an open letter to Isis, reflecting on what she wishes she had done differently on-screen, and how the character has been received by both friends and fans. "People love you, Isis. When they come up to me in public—Black people especially—you are who they want to talk about. Sometimes, who they want to talk *to*," she writes in the first lines of the chapter. More than any other character, Union's personal identity and life story is linked to Isis's. She *is* Isis, owing to both her well-known contributions to the character, which she's spoken about at length, and its status as her breakthrough part in an iconic movie.

Dushku and Bradford, rounding out the more established members of the cast alongside Dunst, can't escape the *Bring It On* questions either. When I told friends I was writing this book, one texted me: "Urgent question: Are you going to talk to my husband Jesse Bradford, and does he still have that Clash shirt?" The answers: yes, as we've seen, and no, it's kind of a long story. (The short version: he unthinkingly swapped it with a wardrobe person at a publicity shoot for the movie in exchange for "some dumb junk cargo pants that I don't care about, have never worn, and never should have traded for, but here we are." In his defense: the cargo pants *did* have zippers to convert into shorts. Versatile.)

As for Dushku, who mentioned that people flip her off in public as a reference to the film ("kind of weird") or bust out into Toros cheers in the produce aisle ("they know them better than I do"), Missy and her *Buffy the Vampire Slayer* character, Faith, follow her like shadows.

Now mostly retired from the entertainment biz and focusing on academic studies, she told me, "As I'm looking at my window and one of my stepdaughters is here, it was really good street cred for my three twentysomething stepdaughters when I entered the mix and wanted to marry their dad [businessman Peter Palandjian]. I don't know if it would have gone as smoothly if I didn't have my *Bring It On* cred."

The rest of the cast, earlier in their careers then, also benefited from the shine of the movie. Bilderback, who played Whitney, is still working today, recently in the streaming hit show *Cruel Summer*. West and Ritter also continued booking roles off the movie's success, then both turned to producing. West today focuses on his music with wife Chyler Leigh as half of East of Eli, and Ritter cofounded marketing firm STFRD and is its chief creative officer. Kramer continued acting, joining Dushku in *Buffy* notoriety as villain Glory, and cofounded popular entertainment website Geek Nation. She's a big hit at Comic-Con.

That's just to name some of the cast. Equally as impressive are some of the behind-the-scenes trajectories, from Fletcher's rise from *Bring It On* being her first solo studio movie choreography gig to now directing mega-budget movies like *The Proposal* and the upcoming *Hocus Pocus 2*, or cinematographer Maurer's ability to say goodbye to his film-set documentary shooting days. None, however, are more mind-blowing than Reed's.

Peyton Reed entered *Bring It On* as a rookie director on his first studio picture, after a lifetime of dreaming of making movies, and emerged a surprise box office breadwinner. After a few follow-up studio comedies, among them *Down with Love* and *The Break-Up*, headlined by big names like Renée Zellweger, Jennifer Aniston, and Ewan McGregor, he was passed the Infinity Gauntlet and directed *Ant-Man* for Marvel. Heard of it? As I write, he's shooting the third installment of the blockbuster superhero franchise, palling around with star Paul Rudd (named *People's* Sexiest Man Alive during the shoot; "We had fun with that") and Michael Douglas. One day, running late for a call with me, he entered the video chat flustered and sheepishly told me, "I couldn't get Michelle Pfeiffer off the phone," admitting that while it sounded like a humblebrag, it was really just preproduction. He said that he's always chasing the on-set vibe of *Bring It On*, trying to foster a positive attitude where people feel free to take risks, and the people in charge, like Reed, are just as excited to be there and make stuff as the greenest actors.

"I was always such a comic book nerd growing up, that was my subculture growing up. So to be able to do that now . . . of all the movies I've done, *Ant-Man* comes closest to *Bring It On* in terms of the actual moviemaking experience and also the end results of the movie," Rudd told me in 2015. "It was just a fun experience, obviously on a much bigger scale. But the spirit of the movie reminds me a lot of that first movie. Trying to re-create that experience that I had on the first movie is just really difficult, but I think this movie comes the closest to that."

All in all, *Bring It On* identified a band of newcomers thirsty for success, just like the rival squads it portrayed. As producer Wong put it, the little-movie-that-could vibe dripping off the project attracted cast and crew willing to get their hands dirty for the cause. "Everybody was really sort of empowered to do their best, because everybody was like, I have something to prove," she said. "Just like I was down there on set like, I'm going to do this, I'm going to prove that I can do this job."

"Were the ethnic festivities to your liking today?"
—Lava

here's always been racial tension in cheerleading; *Bring It On* certainly didn't revolutionize that concept, it just highlighted it in easily accessible pop culture with a healthy dose of movie magic. In 1967, seventeen football players in Madison, Wisconsin, were kicked off the team for skipping practice in protest of only one Black cheerleader being appointed to the varsity squad. After nearly thirteen hundred Black students districtwide refused to attend school for a week in response, the school board voted to reinstate the football players and make a rule that half of the next year's cheerleading squad would be Black. Throughout the '50s and '60s, the NAACP partnered with several schools to desegregate cheerleading squads. As a student in the '60s, the future Rep. Barbara Lee of California was her high school's first Black cheerleader after working with a local chapter to challenge the school rule that stopped her from trying out.

If you think this tension changed with the times, think again. Take a look at the news stories about Osceola High School in Kissimmee,

Florida, where Black students who tried out for the squad were passed over in favor of two white students whose GPAs didn't meet the requirements for participation. The year? 1985. In 2019, in Orange County, California, fans from San Clemente High School taunted cheerleaders and players from a rival team at a football game, "repeatedly using racial slurs, including the 'n-word,'" San Diego NAACP president Clovis Honoré told a local Fox affiliate. "Furthermore, cheer squad members were racially harassed in restrooms, again including the 'n-word.' This harassment came not only from high-school-age youth but also from adult fans." The times they are . . . not really a-changin', unfortunately.

In 2000, when *Bring It On* was released, "cultural appropriation" was in no way the widely understood phrase it is now. A search on Google Ngrams, which tracks word and phrase use in publications through time, shows that the term started popping up in the '80s before plateauing in the mid-'90s, then registers a sharp upward spike between 2013 and 2019 (the last year of data analyzed in the collection), with the line showing no signs of turning downward. The concept, however, is exactly what *Bring It On* is exploring, even if the term itself is never used in the film. In fact, the word "black" is spoken only once in the movie—and it's in reference to "the red, black, and white" of the Toros uniforms when the rival squad is taunting them in cheer form (the commitment to the bit that had them preplanning spelling out "you suck" on their spankies is honestly impressive). The word "white" is spoken three times, once in the above line, once in a throwaway line at Nationals about another team's uniforms being "white trash," and once in explicit reference to race, when Isis tells a disbelieving Torrance, "I know you didn't think a white girl made that shit up." For a movie whose entire plot revolves around race, it's a remarkable illustration of "show, don't tell."

Dr. Mia Moody-Ramirez, a professor at Baylor University who teaches a course called "Gender, Race & Media," said that though the words are never spoken out loud in the movie, "[cultural appropriation is] where you're borrowing from a culture and you're not giving them credit, you're actually benefiting from borrowing from that culture. So [the scenario in the film] does fit my definition."

ESPN journalist Katie Barnes agreed. "It is a movie that is about cultural appropriation, and those words are never uttered. It is a movie that indicts white privilege, and those words are never uttered, right? It's a critique of affirmative action, there are all of these things that exist in this film without any of those words ever being said," they said. "And I think that's what makes it so good. I think that's why it has endured for so long and why it's aged well, is that it's not bogged down by any of the language that is consistently politicized and is polarizing today. It's able to escape a lot of that, simply because none of those things are ever uttered."

Mark Waters, the *Mean Girls* director and a longtime friend of Bendinger's, gave *Bring It On* kudos for highlighting the issue in a mainstream pop culture product, long before it trended on Twitter. "It was almost like *Bring It On* kind of made that part of the conversation," he said.

Even as early as the casting process, the production was committed to diversity on an integral level, something that absolutely set it apart from other films of its ilk and era. Gabrielle Union was one of the many eventual *Bring It On* cast members who also auditioned for rival cheerleading movie *Sugar & Spice*, but the filmmakers of that movie "didn't want to go Black," she told me in 2015. Years later, again discussing the Tale of Two Cheerleading Movies, I asked her whether she was explicitly told that the filmmakers didn't want to cast Black women in *Sugar & Spice*. "No, no," she said. "Do we ever? When Black folks ask questions that there are no easy answers to, we become somehow the bullies and the aggressors and the sour grapes, and it's like, no, curious [*Sugar & Spice*] had, I mean it was a gaggle of cheerleaders, they had a bigger, way bigger cast than *Bring It On*, and *Bring It On* had a big-ass cast. Not one, not one [Black cheerleader]. Why? They tell your team, and that's how it was relayed to me. How they actually worded it, I don't actually know." And those casting calls? Union says they were revealing in who had been selected to read at all, even before the final casting. "Even looking at like, oh well, out of that gaggle of cheerleaders, you know, perhaps they were all just the best? Except I was at those auditions, so I saw that I was solo dolo. . . . However they worded it, what spoke the loudest was the proof in that pudding."

When Union was instead cast as the lead Clover, Isis, *Bring It On* lore has it that she played a major hand in shaping how her character was depicted. Reed recalled: "Gabrielle was very crucial to me, because when she came in she and I worked really closely together on the Isis character to kind of move her away from—some of the stuff that was written in the original drafts was really, a little, extremely heightened with that character, and we wanted to make her a little more grounded and play her point of view. I think that came out a lot more as we were developing the script further, and certainly as we were shooting."

Union was a bit more frank when we talked about it: "I remember the table read, my character being a combination of Foxy Brown and about eight other Blaxploitation, Black film characters sort of rolled into a cheer, lawyer, defender-type person," she said. "Let's just say she did not seem too, well, *educated*." To try and make Isis feel more like a role model and someone who would be not only accepted to UC Berkeley but also vying for the captaincy of the cheerleading team (against Torrance, natch), as she was in a scrapped alternate ending that appears on the movie's DVD, Union worked with Reed and Bendinger on the character, forming her into someone who more accurately modeled Union's lived experience. In her previous teen movie roles, in *10 Things I Hate About You* and *She's All That*, Union barely had any lines or character development, serving as a token BFF to the white main characters. In *Bring It On*, though Isis doesn't have a last name in the script or credits of the movie (nor, for that matter, do any of the Clovers), something that's unfortunately shared with her earlier roles, she took an active hand in reworking her character and workshopped her dialogue even throughout shooting. Now, she says that though she's glad she had the chance to have her voice heard, it was extra labor that should never have fallen to her as a young actress.

"I mean, I'm looking at it twenty years later in the midst of a different conversation," she told me. "So I try to be fair. People have told me repeatedly that I have to be more fair to myself and what I should have done and to let myself off the hook a bit, but I want to double down. I want to say, listen, because it's still a living, breathing thing that is influencing generation after generation after generation, we have a responsibility to be more critical of the entire process. Going back and saying, yeah, you know, perhaps we screwed the pooch in who we allowed to tell the story and guide the story and to even get to the point where a character is tasked with on the spot, rejiggering the work that you're doing that day. That's wildly unfair, and not really setting me up for, or any of the marginalized folks that the story is centered on—it's not really fair and it doesn't set us up for success [and] to do our best work if we are writing the thing that we're saying. Whereas other folks just had so much more time to play and screen time. So we had to come in, make a big impact, you know, get the world to—at least some people, enough folks—to be on our side, if you will, I'm using my finger quotes. You know, that's not right, and it's not normal. And today I can say that. I would never have said it. You had to stay in and still stick in a perpetual state of gratitude that you have been thrown a crumb, and you're supposed to treat that crumb like it's a five-course meal that is being paid for and financed by someone else, and aren't you satiated and grateful forever. You're like, I'm fucking hungry, is what I am."

Producer Wong recognized Union's contributions and said she was unsurprised at the direction her career had taken over the years. "Shout out to Gabrielle Union," she said. "When I see her executive producer credit now on TV shows, I am so proud of her, because, you know, even back then I was just sort of like, this woman is going to be like a writer, director, she is really, really good at this. We had to make changes for the actors, because, you know, Gabrielle had real issues with her dialogue, and we agreed that this character needed to be totally real and totally not a caricature at any level."

Bendinger is the only credited writer on the screenplay. On virtually any movie, other uncredited writers contribute to scripts, in ways as small as suggesting a line (Reed today recalls Wong tossing off Missy's "ogling my goodies" line in the car wash scene as an idea for a way to show the squad having self-awareness about using skin to raise money) or being contracted and paid to do a pass on the full script, either for an overall touch-up or for a specific focus such as comedy, romance, or race, among others. Being uncredited is not a matter of the work going unrecognized; per Writers Guild of America rules, a writer is only credited if they contribute 50 percent or more of an original screenplay.

Judd Apatow has done uncredited script work, and his scripts have also surely benefited from uncredited contributions, for example. Bendinger has worked as an uncredited script doctor herself on several major movies, including some mentioned in this book. Per WGA rules, uncredited writers are barred from claiming authorship of scripts that they do not have official credit on, or they may face "disciplinary action" from the guild. This falls under a subheading "Publicizing of Credits" in the union's guide to credits, but as any number of clicky listicles, screenwriter bios, and other sources will show, you don't have to look hard to see that script punch-ups aren't in any way uncommon.

The script that eventually became *Bring It On* is no different: Gary Hardwick, who would eventually go on to direct Union in *Deliver Us from Eva* and *The Brothers*, both of which he also wrote, punched up a version of the script before production with a focus on Isis and the Clovers' dialogue. A 2003 *Washington Post* profile of Hardwick mentions, without directly quoting him, that he said "with a certain pride" that he wrote the "bring it" line in the confrontation scene between the Toros and Clovers that eventually became part of the movie's title, and Union has mentioned his name in association with the movie in proceeding years, as in a twentieth-anniversary panel put together by the Academy of Motion Pictures Arts and Sciences, a conversation between Bendinger, Dunst, Reed, and Union recorded over video chat and shared on YouTube.

"We were aided by Gary Hardwick," Union said in the panel (I've removed a few word repetitions and verbal stalls that come with the territory of extemporaneous speaking). "It's a conversation that we're still having now when you have interracial writing. We talk about this with animated characters and who's allowed to write from what and to, and should you be allowed to write, you know, interracially. It's a conversation that's still completely relevant and timely, but the reality is, like, we did need some help, and Gary Hardwick was kind enough to dive in and to give us a leg up and a first-person voice for a lot of our dialogue as the Clovers."

Reed replied, in part, "I remember even at the time, as a white guy, making a cheerleader movie that dealt with issues of race is so fraught and it's kind of a microcosm for America and how it's very hard."

"We're very clunkily coming of age, you know, production is a team sport, and we're always doing punch-up on movies, and it's such a collective effort," Bendinger said. "And when the actor feels comfortable, the difference is palpable, right? And so that was the case here, and it all worked out."

Bendinger uses the analogy of architecture for screenwriting, and is wary of people perceiving the script for *Bring It On* as *not* hers in some way: she planned the story, drew the blueprints, placed each window and doorway with care. "I'm very proud of the movie," she said on the panel. "I worked really hard on it. I did my best. I did my level best, and then you have to go, OK, what's the process here? And how can we make it even better?"

Reed, in the same panel, called *Bring It On* "a product of its era, twenty years ago" when it came to race, and that it "would be from an entirely different perspective" if it were made now.

Perspective is a key word here: Sangita Shresthova, a PhD working at the University of Southern California who focuses on (among other things) the concept of "civic imagination" and how pop culture can help people put societal issues in context and spur change, noted that while watching interviews with Union around the movie, "in the interview, she kind of goes back and forth between her character and her real life." *Bring It On* was a big break for Union—she's irreversibly connected with the movie, her most famous film role, and in the last few decades, the line between Union and Isis does seem to blur as she's asked over and over about the role. How couldn't it, when she helped shape the character so thoroughly?

When Union says people tell her to be more fair to herself about the movie, like she told me, she's referring largely to what she discussed in the essay titled "Dear Isis" in her second memoir, *You Got Anything Stronger?*, published in 2021. In this letter to her most-recognized character, the one who she says people talk to her about the most when they spot her out and about, she apologizes to the fictional Isis for not making her angrier, bolder. For, as she writes, letting the Toros off easy.

"I realize that what you did, Isis, confronting Kirsten Dunst's character Torrance about the thievery, is way more than most characters get to do," she wrote. "When it comes to Black characters in TV or film getting to hold white folks accountable, yeah, it was heroic. But it was just a step. It wasn't everything you could have done, and that's because *I* didn't do what I should have done."

"I made you respectable," she continues later in the essay. "And I am so, so sorry." She wrote that by not allowing Isis to be angry, by walking away from the Toros in the parking lot after their confrontation—which she writes she now feels, in retrospect, amounted to a surrender by Isis—and citing having class, she bound the character in the same chains of fear and need at all costs to be seen as respectable that she herself had lived as a Black woman navigating a white world. Art imitated life, and Union regrets it.

One of Union's points that absolutely rings true is the undeniable unfairness of Isis being labeled in the minds of many as the villain of the movie. These audience members see Isis and the Clovers as mean, antagonistic, and aggressive for calling the Toros out on stealing their cheers and their creative work, for showing up at the Rancho Carne High School home field and showing up the Toros, our POV characters and therefore by default our heroes. Anyone who inflicts discomfort on our heroes must be a villain, right? It's not so black and white in the case of *Bring It On*, pun cheesy but totally apt. While speaking with me in 2015, Union recounted the impressions that fans would do of Isis to her face, mistakenly attributing to her the over-the-top *Not Another Teen Movie* spoof line "It's already been broughten."

"I think it's also interesting that when people do reenactments of my scene, they turn me back into the caricature that we didn't want," she said. "I was like, 'What'd you get about me speaking that somehow turned into neck-rolling, finger-wagging, just awful, crazy stereotype that you imagine in your head with this young Black woman telling a white woman no and enough is enough?' That somehow turned into this over-the-top, crazy, stock-ish Black woman stereotype. It became the angry Black woman stereotype, and I never played that. It's very interesting; perception is reality, and the perception of my character was that she was an out-of-control young Black woman." The fact that Isis *was* calm and cool and together is part of what Union regrets about her portrayal of Isis—but also arguably part of what made it so impactful. Had she let that fury burn hot, would she have run the risk of playing into the stereotype after all?

Author Zeba Blay said that she was somewhat surprised to read Union's regrets about how she portrayed Isis. Union writes of a specific moment when she played Isis's reaction to Torrance congratulating the Clovers on their Nationals victory with "bashful humility," responding to Torrance's "You were better" praise with "We were, hunh?"

"Now? I would do that line so differently," Union writes. "There would be no surprised 'hunh,' and certainly no question mark. It would be, 'We were.' Period."

Blay, who first saw the movie as the Black tween that Union fears in the essay that she let down with moments like that, told me she did and does interpret that moment in a different way. "I always thought her *hunh*ing was like [Isis saying], 'You dumb bitch,' sort of sarcastic," Blay said. "It's interesting that [Union] said that. I understand the desire to correct societal bullshit by pushing up against these so-called stereotypes. Like, 'Oh, I'm not going to do the angry Black girl, I'm not going to do what they expect of me.'"

Union wrote that she chose to make Isis "make space for the white fragility you encountered." Blay agreed, but praised the realism: it sucks, but it's also what happens.

"I actually liked her choices, because I think as a young Black girl from the hood, cheerleading is the thing that is sustaining her. She takes pride in it," Blay said. "But as a young Black girl, you navigate the world in that way sometimes. You're pissed, but you have to act like you're not pissed. Because sometimes your life depends on it. Your life depends on some white girl not taking what you say the wrong way and then crying, so for me, I think that her choices were appropriate. I think that they were in line with that tightrope of trying to be respectable when you don't want to be, but you have to make that choice out of survival or out of expediency. That's really interesting, though, that the person who is closest to that character has that impression so many years later."

Cultural critic Cate Young also underlined what Union has pointed out so many times before, but somehow needs to repeat because it keeps coming up: "Isis isn't the villain," Young said. She remembered listening to Union on a podcast, "and she said, you know, it was always surprising to me that people talked about Isis like she was the villain, because like she's not the one who stole any cheers.' And I was like, you know, I never thought about it that way, because I honestly knew that I rooted for her, but I had also very much like internalized the idea that she was an antagonistic force, which is to some extent true. But I hadn't even realized until then that I had internalized both that she was right and also that she was the bad guy, when she was *not* the bad guy."

It's the presentation of white entitlement and the creeping realization that, *wait*, the Toros are the villains here, that makes *Bring It On* relevant today, Young said. "This idea that, like, 'No one knows who the Clovers are anyway, we can get away with this, it doesn't really matter,'" she said. "And that is still an attitude that people can encounter today. And to me, that is part of what makes the film so evergreen, because those attitudes can and have been applied to so many different scenarios. I think that what's exciting about this movie is the way that it forces Torrance to engage with that idea that this thing that she's so proud of and that she has worked so hard for is not only built on a lie, but it's a lie that she has the ability to perpetuate, should she choose it, but she would always know that she hadn't earned what she had. I think the fun thing about watching her in this movie is having her kind of recognize that she may not have done this harm, but she does have a responsibility to—not undo it, but to mitigate it in some way, and she does try."

The basic sketch of the steps that Torrance goes through in *Bring It On* seems to predict what white Americans would go through two decades later: realize she's been profiting off Black labor and a tradition of white supremacy, freak out, try to throw money at the problem, get uncomfortable, then shut up and do some hard work. If Torrance had had an Instagram account in the summer of 2020, she absolutely would have posted a black square to her grid in #solidarity and told her followers how she was #listeningandlearning. She likely would have leveled up in anti-racism techniques and rhetoric just as much as her aerials.

Shresthova, too, pointed out that part of the persistence of *Bring It On*'s popularity—"At this point, it's older than its protagonists, if you think about it" (raise a hand if you just let out a small gasp of horror like I did)—is the opportunity it presents to combine nostalgia with conversations around current issues and race. Parents who were teens themselves in 2000 can take a walk down memory lane and share more than an old favorite movie with their kids, actually have insightful discussions not just about race and appropriation but also about sexuality, sexism, high school, and more.

"Because the characters are complex, because there are multiple ways into the narrative. Yes, there's a linear narrative, but there's all these other sprawling narratives, some of which are actually not even fully closed off," Shresthova said. "I think it actually is a great film for intergenerational conversations and ways into having conversations around these kinds of issues. So I think that's really interesting because, you know, many, many youth-focused films are much more linear and much more straightforward in terms of like the protagonist's journey. This one's just a little bit more complicated, even to the outcome where the Toros don't win. I think that's worthy of a discussion. Why make the film and not have them win is another one."

Part of the secret sauce of *Bring It On* is that it's a movie about race that never actually talks about race outright, incorporating a bitter truth into a PG-13 package that can be easily digested by mainstream white audiences. You think you're in for an hour and a half of cattiness and aerials, and you do get plenty of both of those, to be sure, but you also get the message, softened as it may be.

Dan Waters, the *Heathers* screenwriter and another Bendinger friend, likened the progressive message of *Bring It On* to "wrapping the medicine in candy" and paraphrased George Bernard Shaw, saying, "If you're going to be serious, you better be funny."

"I think both me and Jessica take that as a model, like I could have done a much more serious movie about teen suicide. She could have done a much more serious movie about cultural appropriation. But I think the fact that we keep it fun and we keep it real, we keep it human. And we give everybody good lines. To me the most versatile thing you can do with a female character is not be a hit man or act like she's tough like a man, but give her a good line. To me, wit tops everything. Part of me is like, oh no, here comes some heavy-handed subject matter about racism, then I'm like, oh no, it's Jessica, who in a funny way is going to deal with it in a way that may get you into it more because you're not being lectured."

Many people who first saw *Bring It On* as teens and tweens have had an evolving understanding of it as the years have passed, myself included. As I recall, my first big takeaway upon seeing it as a twelve-year-old was that when you got older, sometimes sports bras counted as shirts? Like that was just . . . the whole thing? Now, clearly, I—and fellow audiences—see a loftier and more nuanced moral and ethical message while watching the film years later, with older eyes and a broader experience of the world. Suddenly, "You didn't think a white girl made that shit up" isn't just a laugh line from Isis, it's a shorthand for the pain and damage of cultural appropriation, exploitation, and abuse of privilege stretching back into history, as well as a celebration of Black creativity, terminally underappreciated.

Even Shamari DeVoe, the member of Blaque who played Lava in the movie, didn't fully take in the racial divide the movie so clearly illustrates while she was shooting it. "When we were shooting it, I really didn't see [the race content] until I watched the movie and as I got older," she said. "The white cheerleading squad stealing the Black cheerleading squad's cheer moves and trying to claim them as their own. It just kind of made me feel about how Black people were taken from Africa, stolen away, and then just thinking of how certain things like even our skin color, or our big butts, or whatever it is, it just seems like people want it. It just makes me think about stuff like that. Even our culture and our dance, and our singing and different things like that, that we hold near and dear, dancing and all of the things that we can do, just wanting to be noticed for it. I feel like at the end of the day, we just wanted to be noticed for the originality and the fact that we were all winners, we were the best, we just wanted to be looked at as what we were instead of it being, 'Oh my god, you guys, someone else is trying to take your cheers and be what you are,' instead of us just getting the recognition for how good we really were, you know, so I look back at it now and I'm like, yeah, that was definitely some sort of racial, cultural appropriation."

Movies and pop culture pointed at teens are often Trojan horses, some more obviously than others, and are worthy of examination and serious thought, Shresthova said, though they're often written off without the realization of the real-world impact they can have "You don't go to pop culture to engage politically, generally. I mean, that's entertaining! People think of entertainment as a separate realm. It never is, fully, but people think of it as a separate realm. And so to me, popular culture and pop culture fandom is really an amazing space to think about how, through the topics that are covered there and the stories that you care about, they open up spaces for political discussions or discussions around issues that may otherwise be something I say I don't really care about, right?"

Vanessa Willoughby, now a freelance pop culture writer and then, at the time of *Bring It On*'s release, a middle school cheerleader who loved seeing fellow Black girls cheer when the movie was a "go-to sleepover pick" with her squad, is the perfect example of the movie's message sliding into teenage minds: "It's not something I thought about when I was watching the movie. The phrase [cultural appropriation] obviously wasn't around when we were that age," she said. "It was obviously something I was like, This is wrong. And like, this sucks. This sucks! Based on the fact that the Clovers are a Black squad from the inner city, they're looked down upon versus the Toros that come from a privileged white background. So even though I may not have had the vocabulary or the word for it, I knew what they were trying to get at, and then put them away. And it wasn't until I was older and our culture started talking about these things that I was like, Oh, *yeah*, this movie totally does tackle cultural appropriation."

The flip side of the fictionalized portrayal of cultural appropriation and its consequences is that while it opens the door for discussions of the issues, it may be *too far* from real life. The discussion needs to extend to the real world as well, no matter how uncomfortable that may be. Union pointed out that too often, when white people talk about cultural appropriation, they're not taking the final step of acknowledging how they may have participated.

"It's also interesting who exactly is talking about what, who's taking different parts of the movie and having those conversations and who isn't," Union said. "I don't think white folks have cultural appropriation conversations in a way that centers their own complicity. It's almost like you're taking an anthropology class, you're like 'those people did terrible things,' and it's like, mmm, that's you as well. Still happening. So if it's discussed, it's discussed at arm's length, and you are absolved of any responsibility or accountability. . . . It's a different conversation when you're the one being harmed. When your culture, your race, your features are handpicked or cherry-picked to be used, not to benefit *you*, not to line *your* pockets, not to celebrate *you*, but to make someone else rich or give someone else an opportunity or give someone else shine, yeah, it's a cultural currency, and that can be used as currency-currency. And all of us are looking at it that way."

Blay told me that she basically wore out her *Bring It On* DVD as a New Jersey tween, and "had a crush on the brother." She's still into the movie now, and turned to it frequently in recent years as a sort of cinematic security blanket, though she also views it with the context of time and the keen critical eye she showcased in her essay collection *Carefree Black Girls: A Celebration of Black Women in Popular Culture*. Sometimes you look back on a piece of pop culture that you remember being a touchstone as a kid and can't suppress the full-body flinch. That's not the case for Blay and *Bring It On*, even though "you have the sassy sort of one-liner thing, that shit, that's just par for the course. But I think that the movie surprisingly holds up well. The Black girls are not—I don't see them as teachers, they're just really good at cheerleading, and they have some beef with other people who stole their shit. That's the story.

"Being a teenager in the 2000s, as all decades, it's such a specific experience," she told me. "Now that I'm this age, I can see, 'Oh, this is what it means to engage with this kind of work at this time in your life.' When you're a teenager, you're not thinking about the racial issues, you're just watching girls cheerleading. I saw a TikTok that was like, 'This is what your parents listened to in high school,' and it was Death Cab for Cutie! We're old now! It's the circle of life, dude, but that's how I try to look back. I am angry [about what I wish was different], but I'm also grateful. For better and for worse, this is the pop culture that made us. *Bring It On*, *Best Week Ever.* These are all the things that created the sensibilities that we have now.

"All you can do is take it, and for me, art is always about being in conversation. . . . That is what is supposed to happen, instead of just seeing the flaw in something and just being like 'Fuck this.' It's more fun and activating to be like, 'Well, fuck this, but also, let's talk about it.'"

I firmly agree with Blay that you can interrogate a movie while still loving and appreciating it. It's possible to point out that the Clovers are not fully fleshed out, and that their story is not centered in *Bring It On*, which it should be as the wronged party, but also to examine it in the context of the time it was released and against its peers and see that it was ·elatively progressive on racial issues. To throw out *Bring It On* or any other film with flaws would mean having . . . no movies. No art and nothing to discuss. Boring and counterproductive, to say the absolute least.

Critic Stephanie Zacharek, who originally reviewed the movie for British Film Institute's magazine *Sight and Sound* in 2000, said, "I think it actually holds up really well. You know, these are complicated issues, because, obviously, in the movie, the white girls basically stole from the Black girls, and nobody picked up on it, because—the Black girls knew about it, but if they complained about it, then they'd be complainers. Basically it takes like the one kind of cool white girl, Missy, to say, hey, look, you know your team stole from this team, not cool, and that sets the whole thing into action, which is great. But, you know, my feeling about this movie is that it's kind of like a micro version of what our culture can be at its best."

That is to say: an injustice is discovered, work is done, credit is given, and some degree of justice is served. *Bring It On* is by no means an anti-racism handbook, but the demonstration of recognizing, reckoning with, and changing behaviors is an optimistic case study. Is Torrance handing over the Toros' past championship trophies to the

Clovers? Are there reparations? No. But she does take steps to make systemic changes to stop actively benefiting from stealing their labor, a process that's been increasingly centered in the real-world spotlight over two decades later.

Ashley K. Smalls is a mass communications PhD student at Penn State whose work focuses especially on race and pop culture. (Her current research also revolves around the Marvel cinematic universe, which includes Reed's *Ant-Man* movies, a parallel she was thrilled to discover as a longtime *Bring It On* fan, noting to me that Reed has been "putting in the work" for years.) Smalls has special perspective on that idealized but necessary interplay between Isis and Torrance, the fine line that the movie walks when Isis rips up Torrance's offered check and literally throws it back in her face. The Clovers then get the money they need to go to Nationals from Oprah stand-in Pauletta. Smalls was a cheerleader on a predominantly Black squad at a Catholic school and remembered constant fundraisers to get what her team needed to compete. That moment of Isis rejecting Torrance's earnest but problematic sponsorship is a defining moment for the movie, she said.

"Oftentimes these movies, especially when they pertain to race, desperately try to [say] if we're just all really nice to each other then all these issues just go away. And that's really not the reality of it," Smalls told me. "That check would have gotten them to championships. But again, this was about proving we *can*. Would they have felt like they needed to hold back if they had taken that check? If they had taken that check, would they have still gone as hard or as diligently as they did?

"There's another iconic scene of Gabrielle Union when she's walking past the Toros and one of them says hi, and she looks at them and raises her eyebrow. It's one of my favorite GIFs that's ever been made. But it's not like, 'I hate these girls who are looking at me,' it's more, 'I'm here to win. I'm not here to be nice to you. I'm not here to be your friend. I am here after years of not being able to be here and watching you win with the things that we create, to prove we are the best at it.' And had they been given that check, would they have been able to still have that mentality? I don't think so. She probably would have felt obligated to say hi back, she probably would have felt obligated to act like these are my friends from around the block. And without that check, she was able to just like, 'Y'all do what you do. And you will see what we do.' And I'm very, very grateful for that, because we do know how a white savior movie, they are our favorite in Hollywood. Not just to be made but even to win the Oscars. So I'm grateful that they didn't do that."

The Clovers have an outsize impact on *Bring It On* and its legacy, something that Union is very aware of. "It's interesting because you would think that the movie was fifty-fifty, and it just isn't," Union pointed out. The first shot of the Clovers isn't until twenty minutes into the movie, when Missy drives Torrance 102 miles down I-5 to East Compton to see the squad in action. And Union is right: it's nowhere near equal screen time for the two squads. By my tracking, stopwatch in hand, the Clovers are on-screen for roughly 20.9 percent of the movie, not counting the blooper reel and end credits dance scene.

Barnes, the ESPN reporter, pointed to the underuse of Black characters across mainstream movies, both then and now. "Black people and Black characters are not fully fleshed out and are not given their time and their weight that they deserve," they said. "I think that's also true in *Bring It On*. The storyline between the Clovers and the Toros dominates the film, and also when you look at it there is far too little of it. I would sacrifice the car wash scene for more Isis any day of the week. And I think that that's important to say as well."

Cate Young, who grew up in Trinidad and Tobago, when asked if she found the movie good, enjoyable, or useful—which can have very different definitions for different people, and the same person may have different answers among those three qualifiers—answered yes to all three, "with caveats."

"I think your mileage may vary in terms of what counts as good and if this would fall into that category, but I definitely find it enjoyable. I think that it is a millennial classic, personally," she said. "And I do think that it is still useful as a demonstration of ideas that are still coming up for us today in different forms, whether it's TikTok dances or hairstyles. It's still dealing with the central issue of who gets to profit and benefit from the work that Black people, and specifically

Black women, are doing and what it means for white people and white consumers when they come up against the knowledge that they are complicit in theft, whether specific or, more generally, broadly cultural, and what the responsibilities are when they understand that to be true. Because like I said, all of the stuff that doesn't hold up, I think you can take out and this movie is still legible. This movie still makes sense, and it still tells the same central tale. I think that it's a story that's still relevant."

"Hate us 'cause we're beautiful, well we don't like you either."

—RCH Toros

The same question that's been asked about cheerleading ever since it shifted from a male-centric activity (student "yell leaders" like George W. Bush at Yale were typically male and highly respected in the social stratosphere) to being perceived as male-centric in a different way (short skirts and "cheering for the boys," insert eye roll here) also envelops *Bring It On* in a concentric circle on the Venn diagram: Is it feminist?

And just like the question about cheerleading, the answer to the same query about *Bring It On* is both "It's complicated" and "That's too broad a question."

Does *Bring It On* pass the Bechdel Test, the simple measure of representation in fiction that notes whether two female characters discuss something other than a man? Oh, absolutely. In fact, Cliff's character, Torrance's love interest, could be cut entirely from the plot without a loss to the overall movie. Sorry, Cliff, but it's true. *Bring It On* would still be what it was without the smooches (though "Just What I Need"

is a verified banger of a pop-punk anthem, movie or no). Even with a
bonus layer on the Bechdel Test—that the female characters in question must also be named—*Bring It On* passes with flying colors. With
a *mostly* female cast that *mostly* talks about cheerleading and their own
ambitions, whether that be the captaincy of the team or nailing the
SATs, that's an absolute gimme. But just because a movie is about
women doesn't mean we automatically get out the hot pink rubber
stamp and approve it as feminist.

But maybe we should throw that stamp in the trash, to be real.

"I don't think it's an *anti-feminist* cultural product, I'll put it that
way," Emma Gray, the cultural commentator and podcast host (the
series she cohosts, *Love to See It*, offers recaps and analysis of the *Bach-
elor* reality TV dating franchise and other pop culture phenomena
through a snarky, thoughtful, and critical feminist lens), told me. "I'm
happy it exists, and I am happy that girls our age had access to it at the
time, totally. . . . I certainly think that there are elements of this movie
that are reflective of the understanding of feminism at the time and
the understanding that teen girls are full humans worthy of having
their creative, romantic, and, like, professional, for lack of a better
word, or educational lives interrogated and treated with care."

This shouldn't be a break from the norm, but unfortunately, especially for the time, it was. In teen movies of the late '90s and early
aughts, female characters were objects, not subjects. They were there
to be wanted by a male protagonist (or, depending on the genre,
wanted and then killed—remember that this was the heyday of the
Scream franchise and the literally interpreted bloodlust its success
inspired). In beloved classics like *10 Things I Hate About You* and *She's
All That*, women who stand by their passions are seen as weird and
damaged, angry. They're something to be fixed, and once they can be
understood and unknotted, that's when they're available and appropriate objects of desire. Non-explicitly teen movies, too, are plagued
by this problem. An all-time favorite of mine, Cameron Crowe's
Almost Famous, was released in 2000, and its main female characters
are a frigid mother, a sister who ran off to chase her dreams and blew
up her family dynamic, and Penny Lane, the shiniest trophy of the
Band Aids, the groupies-but-don't-call-us-groupies who follow the

fictitious rock band Stillwater on tour. By the end of the film, through young protagonist William's eyes, we see that Penny's ultimate passion in life is the music, not the man, but it's manifested through her devotion to bassist-with-mystique Russell, who in turn treats her like garbage and trades her to another band for a case of beer. She's something to be won, swapped, and had. By the film's finale, she takes her own trip, not following any tour or whim except her own, but for the majority of the movie, she has little to no agency.

These aren't bad movies, and no art is perfect, nor should a work of art be everything to everyone. All this is to say that *Bring It On* really was doing something unusual for the era in its treatment of personal passion first, romantic passion second or even lower, for a female lead. And to wrap all that up in a little pleated skirt and a bouncy ponytail? Unheard-of, for the time.

"Teen girls have maybe never been taken seriously until the last handful of years—and that's debatable, but at least more seriously than we ever were," said Kristin Russo, the educator and writer. "They're acknowledged, right, *considered*. Like, just maybe what you're saying has validity and importance, and I think that we were figuring that out big time back in the late '90s and early 2000s. Because it seemed like if you had an opinion that felt valid, then you needed to be like listening to Bikini Kill, which I fully support, but like you had to be like on the outskirts, on the fringes. You couldn't be cheerleading."

All eyeliner must be thick, nail polish black—peppy applicants will not be considered. Take Missy's first appearance in *Bring It On*, with her drawn-on armband tattoo, low-slung pants, and whatever is happening with her hair. That sneer. Courtney and Whitney's take, immediately expressing disbelief and hurling slurs and catty comments, could not be clearer: she couldn't possibly be one of *us*. But Torrance, all sunshine and chipper cheertatorship, sees: actually, maybe I'm like *her*. All it takes is an outfit change, and Torrance and Missy see they're ideological and moral equals. They're a matched set in their Toros uniforms, just as they are in their casual school clothes or their loungewear when they have a slumber party. Once they're out of their respective armors, they're speaking the same language, and most of what they're talking about is the value of originality, hard work, and creativity, expressed through their determination to win Nationals. They're not really talking much about boys, and it isn't just because the object of Torrance's skittish affection, Cliff, is Missy's brother—gross.

Romance is such a secondary priority to Torrance that the boyfriend she has at the beginning of the movie—the late Richard Hillman as Aaron, with the iconic delivery of "I got the door, Tor" and the undying passion for "Cal. State. Dominguez. *Hills!*"—is largely forgettable, and serves only as a thorn in her side, ushering in her humiliation at the regional competition by recommending the self-plagiarizing and incredibly cheesy choreographer Sparky Polastri. Aaron stands gawking alongside former captain Big Red at the competition, a matched set of baddies, and sells Torrance out, telling her that she should step down as captain of the squad and let Courtney and Whitney quietly rehab the Toros' reputation, hoping that by fading out for the year everyone will forget what happened. "You're a great cheerleader, Tor, and you're cute as hell," he says. "Maybe you're just not captain material." Torrance refuses to step down, and, shortly after, dumps Aaron.

Cultural critic Joanna Robinson said, "I love that the number one, other than him cheating on her and being unavailable, the main sin of her current awful boyfriend is him telling her she's not captain material. That gaslight that in the guise of supporting her, telling her she doesn't have what it takes. I think that is a really strong, that's the bigger one than him cheating on her, honestly."

Contrast that with the behavior of Cliff. Scruffy, punky, rolling around on the bedroom floor with his electric guitar Cliff. He doesn't *get* the whole cheerleading thing, but—as Torrance screeches at his retreating back in an incredible record-scratch moment, "That's important to me! You believed in me!"—he supports her anyway.

And who does Torrance end up with? The one who believed in her.

"He's not telling her she's trash, and then he gets the girl," Robinson said. And honestly, the ending of the movie still would have been satisfying even had it *not* involved a Torrance/Cliff smoochfest. They could have honestly just high-fived or even made meaningful eye contact, and I would have been fine with it. The victory wasn't in the romance—it was in the effort, leadership, and originality. The romance, again, isn't this movie's priority, just as it isn't Torrance's.

As for Aaron, he's never mentioned again after Torrance dumps him, not even to point fingers for the trashy, duplicated choreography and the spiraling mess of fallout the Toros find themselves in as a result, as if scrambling to replace a routine in the first place weren't harrowing enough. When it comes to Aaron post-breakup, Torrance is Don Draper in spanky pants: "I don't think about you at all."

Self-assurance like Torrance's was to become even more atypical in female characters in years to come. *Bring It On* was one of the last gasps before the "era of the Manic Pixie Dream Girl," Gray said. The term, weirdly enough, originated to describe a character played by none other than Kirsten Dunst in 2005's Cameron Crowe–directed *Elizabethtown*. *AV Club* critic Nathan Rabin wrote of the character, a quirky flight attendant who, like, *connects* with Orlando Bloom's moody, mournful failed sneaker disruptor:

> The Manic Pixie Dream Girl exists solely in the fevered imaginations of sensitive writer-directors to teach broodingly soulful young men to embrace life and its infinite mysteries and adventures. The Manic Pixie Dream Girl is an all-or-nothing-proposition. Audiences either want to marry her instantly (despite The Manic Pixie Dream Girl being, you know, a fictional character) or they want to commit grievous bodily harm against them and their immediate family.

The archetype ran rampant through movies in the first decade or so of the twenty-first century, exemplified by characters such as Natalie Portman's quirky, tap-dancing hometown girl who wants you to hear the song that'll change your life in *Garden State* and Zoey Deschanel's male-gaze-ified greeting-card-company secretary Summer in *(500) Days of Summer*. It was then examined and surgically dismantled by Zoe Kazan as the title character in *Ruby Sparks*, about a mopey novelist who writes his fictionalized dream girl into being, then is horrified when she dares to break free of the idea that he has of her. In short: Manic Pixie Dream Girls exist for the men who desire them.

The ungettable girl who must be gotten—that's not Torrance. No way. She's the getter, going after what she wants: the championship, a clean win, and, yes, the guy. The respect of her teammates, like Missy, is important to her, but so is the respect of rival Isis. She wants a lot of things, and *wanting* is womankind's cardinal sin, all the way back to Eve.

Manic Pixie Dream Girls "were accessories," Gray told me, "and one thing that's great about *Bring It On* is that the women characters are front and center—the friendship and the dynamics between women are front and center. It employs rom-com conventions and tropes in a really wonderful way that I love, but the romance isn't the only arc of growth, for Torrance specifically. That definitely still feels special. . . . *Bring It On*, you got to have the romance, but you also got to have friendship, you got to have growth in terms of ownership over creative work, and teambuilding and all of these themes, where the worth of the characters was determined by more than romantic success. That's something that I still really appreciate."

While the Manic Pixie Dream Girl was a trope that churned out women who serve as saviors, intrigues, or objects of desire for men in those films that followed, predecessors like *Spice World*, with its winking girl-power-style empowerment, TV's *Buffy the Vampire Slayer*'s fight against the underworld and the patriarchy, and *Bring It On* took care to center their female heroes and their missions, whether they were dusting vampires or making it to the concert at Royal Albert Hall on time, frightening minimal pigeons in the process. *Bring It On* has stood the test of time in part because it dared to introduce yet another subversive idea that bubbled to the surface of mainstream consciousness decades later: Wait, what if something doesn't automatically suck just because young women care about it? Gasp! Maybe the girls are onto something?

Robinson pointed out, "There's a lot of things I could pick apart [about the movie], and I'm happy to, but another major accomplishment I think of this movie, at the time, is that it takes something that, stereotypically, young women care about, which is cheerleading, and treats it as something serious to be taken seriously. The fact that the cheerleaders are serious athletes, that they work really hard, that they win trophies, that the football team is a disaster—it just reminds me of the evolution that we've gone through where we have gone from punching down at things young women like to more and more and more taking it more seriously. So what if someone likes a pumpkin spice latte or so what if someone likes Harry Styles, like that's a bad thing? That the things that young women like, we need to make them feel small for liking it. The way in which this movie takes cheerleading seriously, I think is really, really valuable."

Especially since *Bring It On* presents so many models for the kinds of people who could be passionate about cheerleading: not just bubbly blonde Torrance, the stereotypical image that immediately comes to mind, but driven Isis and sarcastic Missy—they both care too. Even the caustic Whitney and Courtney or ditzy Kasey, they're all working toward the same goal and have the same passion. Here's a way you can be, the movie told young female audiences. What you love and work at isn't silly, no matter what they tell you. Even if cheerleading isn't your thing, *your thing* is valid.

And really, even if cheerleading isn't your thing, *Bring It On* is still an incredibly accessible story of leadership and insecurity, of doing the right thing even when it's hard, and caring a *lot*. Is there anything more relatable than Torrance literally starting the movie with an anxiety dream, waking up panting and panicked? What high schooler hasn't felt that pressure to strive for perfection during that first practice round for adulthood?

"That is such a good lesson for young women to see in a film," Robinson said. "This idea of when you're put in a leadership position, people inside the house and outside the house will come at you at all times, and believing in yourself or having someone help you believe in yourself doesn't necessarily end in the biggest trophy, but there is a moral victory there. I think that's a really interesting message in the movie."

And so we arrive again at movie as Trojan horse, delivering a palatable bundle of feminist messages and empowerment to unsuspecting audiences without ever calling it such. And, look, this is not advanced feminist theory; bell hooks, *Bring It On* is not. There are cringey moments of body shaming, and really no body diversity in the movie;

women are catty to one another; and the male gaze is not totally absent—there's plenty of ogling of goodies, as Missy puts it. But the movie does introduce some simple feminist ideals in action. There's no doubt that they're largely mainstream ideas of the girl-power flavor, but there's also a sprinkle of intersectionality at play in the movie, though it's not thoroughly explored. Consider Isis, who turns down Torrance's check and instead models her own version of power and leadership, turning to high-status members of her own community for a sponsorship to get the Clovers to Nationals. Feminism is infinitely relational, and we get a glimpse of a few of its faces in *Bring It On*.

"I think it is a film that explores feminist themes in a way that is legible to most people, and does not concern itself with like the theory of feminism so much as it does the practical applications," cultural critic Cate Young told me, pointing at Mikki Kendall's *Hood Feminism*, which in part unpacks the lived feminist actions of those who may not have the access, use the vocabulary, or have the other tools to practice modern feminism as we usually recognize it and call it by that name. "It's about how feminism shows up in practice and what living feminist principles looks like in real life. To me, that's what this movie is more about. It's less about, like, have they used all the right words, which they very clearly did not, and more about what lessons are we taking from this. How are we understanding that we have to show up for the people in our community, and what responsibility do we have to the people that we are interacting with? I think the film does a good job of asking and answering that question."

And, as Young pointed out, "being feminist" can mean a lot of different things. To her point, what goes on behind the scenes and in the production of the movie is also something to consider.

This is unfortunately a place where *Bring It On* fell prey to the male-dominated tendency of the movie industry, which was even more prevalent in the late 1990s. While Torrance, in the movie, chalks up a moral win and her determination and belief in herself is rewarded, the real world isn't always quite as impressed with women who dare to lead. The cast was mostly female, yes, but the assemblage behind the camera was a different story. Wong and Scanlon were two women who championed the project from the beginning, but Scanlon left early in production for another job, and Wong had to drive herself between Los Angeles and San Diego to get the on-set experience she felt she deserved. After Scanlon's exit, a more senior producer, Patti Wolff, was brought in above Wong to supervise the set. The cinematographer and editor were both male, along with director Reed, of course.

And then there's Bendinger, who lived and breathed the project for years of preproduction but was a scarce presence on set and didn't feel she was seriously considered to direct. Her script was hailed as genius, and has obviously been quoted and remembered in the decades that have followed, but the fact that *Bring It On* was a surprise hit and had defied the odds didn't turn Bendinger's career supernova like it did for the others. She worked, yes, racking up uncredited script doctor and writing gigs and punch-ups, a writing credit on an episode of *Sex and the City*, and a few other scattered credits, but it was 2006 before she got what has so far been her only shot at the director's chair, for gymnastics comedy *Stick It*, which she also wrote.

"I worked hard-core trying not to blow the moment, and I burned myself out," she told me of that era following *Bring It On*'s release. "It's so hard to have succeeded and be, like, excluded, I can't explain it, it's very hard," she told me. "I don't think this happens to men. I really don't. I hope I'm wrong."

She's not alone, by any means. Take a look at *My Big Fat Greek Wedding* star and writer Nia Vardalos, to name an example from the same time period. Her 2002 movie was (and remains) the highest-grossing rom-com of all time, but with the exception of a short-lived TV series, *My Big Fat Greek Life*, which lasted seven episodes, and the 2004 box office disappointment *Connie and Carla*, she had a nearly decadelong dry spell in the industry. Women are wildly underrepresented in the industry, and even when they do manage to rise to the top, the odds are stacked against them.

After all, we wouldn't need scholarships and advocacy groups and more to support gender equity in Hollywood if there was, you know . . . gender equity in Hollywood.

Reed, now a certified blockbuster director, recognized the injustice of the system that left Bendinger behind after the movie. The two remain friendly.

"If it were now, and Jessica Bendinger went to market with a cheer-leader comedy with herself attached to direct it, you probably have a hell of a lot better chance of getting it done," he said. "But in 1999, that was not the case. And then you look at *Stick It*, which she wrote and directed, and it's phenomenal. . . . The changes that are hopefully happening and that need to happen in the business, and that's one of them. I do look at that sort of alternate reality . . . in a better world, in a just world, there would have been feature sequels to [*Bring It On*] instead of straight to DVD. And even if they're straight to DVD, Jessica should have directed them or been given the option to direct."

Bendinger has been working all these years, publishing books and producing and hosting podcasts. She has script deals and development deals, and has served as a mentor in official and unofficial capacities to help other women do what she wasn't allowed to, back when she was driving around in that rusted-out Saab with no air-conditioning, pitching the idea for *Cheer Fever* over and over and over again: get a fair shot.

"I feel like I fought really hard and I did really well and then, because the industry I was working in was so entrenched in structural bias and so behind the curve in the data game and just really didn't take me seriously or what I was making seriously that, yeah, here we are," she said. "It's really hard to talk about it. All I can say is that it sucks."

"No way jumping up and down screaming 'Go, team, go' is gonna satisfy me."
—Missy

Whoever thought that teen girls wouldn't buy a ticket to *Bring It On* must not have ever met a cheerleader in real life, and/or grew up in a cave, their eyes unused to the glaring sun and the cultural practices of this alien world. Cheerleaders are the ultimate archetype of Americana and have long been held up as iconic to the American sporting experience—scratch that, to the sporting experience worldwide. Not only iconic but actually essential. Why else, in the shadow of the COVID-19 pandemic in 2021, would a Japanese baseball team have rallied a squad of one hundred humanoid cheerleader robots to rally their players? Even in an otherwise empty stadium, it's barely a game if there isn't an organized cheering section, it would seem.

Just as ubiquitous as the presence of cheerleaders at sporting events is the stereotype of cheerleaders as, well, bitches. Catty. Vapid. Airheaded. The queen bee, or maybe one of her desperate followers, the willingness to wear a matching outfit and *exert* obviously an indicator of conformity and rigidity. Natalie Adams, coauthor of *Cheerleader! An American Icon*, told me that as an academic, she was "in the closet for years that I was a cheerleader. In my world, that wasn't something you wanted to be." She dove deep on the history and culture of cheerleading in the book, and has a simple theory about the hold cheerleaders have over us.

"I say that one of the reasons we as a country are obsessed with cheerleading is because everyone has an opinion, whether you hate them, love them, want to deride them, ridicule them," she said.

Those opinions berth the stereotypes that are so persistent throughout pop culture and in the real world—on the track "You Belong with Me," Taylor Swift sings, "She's cheer captain and I'm on the bleachers," and we instantly know what she means, and that it's not something good, the narrator both scoffing and revealing her own envy at the perception of their social castes. In the X-rated 1978 film *Debbie Does Dallas*, a squad exchanges sex for money. In *She's All That*, released in early 1999, the villain is the protagonist's cheerleader ex-girlfriend, the prom queen apparent who ruthlessly cheats on him while they're together and later publicly humiliates his new flame, among other sins. In yet another example, Rory's arty bestie Lane on TV's *Gilmore Girls* hides that she joined the cheerleading squad for fear of Rory's judgment. "I want you to rest assured that I remain me: a Nico-obsessed, X-scene wannabe with forty Korean bibles under her bed. I just bounce a little more." The stigma of cheerleading is so strong that Lane genuinely feels she needs to reassure her lifelong best friend that she hasn't gotten a personality transplant via extracurricular activity.

The cheerleader contains multitudes, but typically the attributes that come to mind for the non-cheerleading public are not positive. TV Tropes, a site where users contribute to build a database of common devices in media, sums it up: "In any high school setting, no stock character is portrayed as harshly as the cheerleader."

This perception, of both the personality and activity associated with cheerleading—Lane's primary descriptor is "bouncing"—is what *Bring It On* came up against when Bendinger pitched the concept in the '90s, and part of why its box office success was such a surprise to some industry execs.

Bendinger's acid-tongued script with humanized cheerleaders whose main goals were doing the right thing and working hard to achieve excellence in their sport, not working hard to step on the necks of those lower in the social hierarchy, combined with those jaw-dropping tapes of elite competitions, was a revelation.

"When we showed the tape to people within the company, of the competition, people were like, I thought cheerleading was making a little pyramid and having little pom-poms and some bitchy girls," producer Scanlon told me in 2015. "So then you're like, oh my god, these feats of athleticism!"

We've discussed the noble lineage of Bring It On in movies and TV, the Pitch Perfects and Whip Its and Cheerios that came after, but the spotlight the movie placed on the athleticism and difficulty of cheerleading, and the film's against-the-norm depictions of the people who participated in it also had real-world implications. For what is estimated to be an industry that these days pulls in roughly the GDP of Bhutan annually—upward of $2 billion—the cheer world has always been on the receiving end of a lot of shade. Some activities carry stereotypes of personal attributes—chess players are smart, field hockey players are aggressive—but cheer is the rare activity that seems to come with a wholesale, ready-made assumption from outsiders that people who participate are, to use the scientific term, kind of sucky.

Sarah Karp Ward, who was a high school cheerleader in Connecticut when Bring It On came out, credited her heavy involvement in cheer with helping her learn to "balance things in life," gain confidence, and strengthen her sense of self. "I got into cheerleading, and I kind of came out of my shell and was like, 'Oh, I can be the person I want to be a little more unapologetically,'" she told me. "And it's great, you know? It's fun having the attention on you when you want it, when you asked for it."

At her small school, she said, nasty jokes about cheerleading were quickly shut up when it was pointed out that the squad won championships and the valedictorian was on the team. It was those culturally ingrained stereotypes that triggered the comments, but reality would quickly correct the record. When Bring It On came out, it was a squad staple and a breath of fresh air for how it portrayed the sport.

Cheerleaders, for once, were allowed to celebrate themselves in popular media.

"It wasn't male-serving," she said. "Compared to other cheerleader movies and like '80s movies, which were so misogynistic, it wasn't cheerleaders for the male gaze. It was cheerleaders for the female gaze. There's that owning of our shit and like owning our sexuality. This storyline isn't for men to ogle a girl in a cheerleading uniform, like yeah, she's hot and she looks good. But like, that's not the principal of the movie. It's not *for* men."

This one was for the girls in the skirts, but was legible as well to those who had no intention of ever laying hand on a pom-pom.

Kristin Russo, the LGBTQ+ educator and author, was one of them. "Did I have any interest in the cheerleaderness of it all? Probably not," she said of seeing *Bring It On* as a newly out college student in New York City. "I think it's really interesting when you talk about like how this movie maybe made us think more about cheerleaders, because at this point there's been documentaries and series and all these things that like have really legitimized cheerleading in a way, but I don't think that it was there in the year 2000. I definitely don't think that I went in thinking, 'Oh, these cheerleaders are probably going to be like super awesome and like make me feel like even more feminist.' I think I still at that point had a mind of like if you were a cheerleader or if you were in a sorority, then you definitely didn't share any interests with me. It took a while to unbraid what the late '90s and early 2000s did to those of us who are like, 'I'm a feminist.'"

She left the theater with a different impression of cheerleaders, a new respect—a sentiment that commentator and author Emma Gray shared.

Gray called herself "never that hot, elite, bubbly type" and "very solidly middling," and told me that *Bring It On* and its depiction of cheerleading as a subculture softened her to squads as a high schooler. "It just felt like there was a diversity of personalities and there was a quirkiness and characters in it that really genuinely felt framed as outsiders," she said. "I think really having that sort of diversity of personality and diversity of teen-movie archetypes baked into the world and cheerleading made it seem more human."

If there's a real-world embodiment of Torrance's adamant "I *am* only cheerleading" line reading, Jamie Gaskill might just be it. The Oregon native was born into a cheerleading legacy, with a mom who led a local high school squad to "about twenty" state championships in her thirty-year career with the team and continues to be active in state-level cheer organizations. Gaskill, who graduated high school in 2001, shared four state championships during her four years as a member of that same high school squad, and also ran track and played volleyball and basketball, as well as competing in gymnastics from a young age. She cheered in college at the University of Oregon, then continued her involvement coaching her old high school squad, as well as her college team. At that point, she was also carpooling weekly for a four-hour all-star squad practice a hundred miles up I-5, just for the love of it. She is still a coach at the U of O. She *knows* cheerleading, was one, makes them.

Bring It On was a staple watch for her back then, just as it is for her squads now. The beauty of its appeal for cheerleaders is its understanding of them and their humanity and work. They're seen. For non-cheerleaders, it's a glimpse into another world.

"It didn't totally sell out the cheerleaders, you know?" Gaskill said. "They poked fun at some of the stereotypes without being disrespectful. I think that was a good niche. They somehow figured out how to make light of or make fun of certain stereotypes without losing that crowd, which obviously is a big crowd that continues to follow if they're continuing to make so many sequels afterwards.

"I definitely think it had an impact [on the perception of cheerleading]. And I think that people really started to kind of understand and appreciate the sport, as opposed to just the girls on the sidelines. It was like, oh, OK, so this is what's happening behind the scenes, and although I can say things were super exaggerated [in the movie], the overall takeaway was that they are really athletic and put a ton of work into this and it's not just a pom-pom on the sideline kinda deal."

"It never talked down," casting director Joseph Middleton told me. "That movie never talked down to its audience at all." Middleton's eyes were opened when he and assistant Michelle Morris went to Orlando with Bendinger to scout the talent that would bring the script to life and saw just how true to life some of the things she'd written were.

"It's just fun and it's fluff and it's enjoyable," Morris said of the script, "but I think it took a very silly thing because again, none of us knew this language. And when we would go to the competitions and immerse ourselves in it, from the outside it looks like a very silly, silly thing. But I think what Jessica did very well is she respected the material. She respected that world. She wasn't making fun of it. We weren't trying to have a spoof or to be like, 'Oh my gosh, can you believe these people live and die for this?' And so I think honestly, it's probably the respect you know that it was given in a very real way, not a *Dance Moms* way or anything like that."

When Morris says "live or die," by the way, she's barely exaggerating. *Bring It On* acknowledged not only the emotional involvement but also the athleticism of the activity.

The sometimes literally bone-crushing reality of cheerleading's physicality was highlighted in the early sequence where a stunter, Carver, falls during an ambitious attempt at a trick in practice. Years later, millions would wince along with the Navarro cheerleaders' every fall, captured in HD surround-sound (those thuds! every time!) while binge-watching the Netflix documentary *Cheer*. The danger of concussions in football and the impact that it can have on adolescents' development rightly gets a lot of attention, but a 2019 study in the academic journal *Pediatrics* revealed that in practice situations, while football players incur the most concessions, cheerleading is in a not-so-distant second place. (As Torrance might say, feels like first.)

The participants may be wearing skirts and bows instead of pads and helmets, but there is no question about it: they are absolutely athletes.

"It was the first movie I saw that was very clear on the fact that cheerleading is a sport, and that it is extremely athletic and extremely competitive," Gray said. "So many things that are coded as feminine, we tend as a culture to devalue those things. And like, oh, cheerleaders are there to look pretty and be popular. And this movie was like, *sure sure sure*, maybe that's a little part of it, but these cheerleaders work fucking *hard*."

Blake Cavner, a twelve-year-old in Oklahoma who spoke to me from the car as her mom drove her home from a Friday-night cheer practice, said she liked the movie. She first saw it with her mom Amy, who also cheered as a kid. Blake is on her school squad as well as two all-star squads, and spends twenty hours or so a week, the equivalent of a part-time job, on her cheertivities.

"I do like it," she said of the movie, and praised the realism of "how many practices they have. We do have *a lot* of practices."

"I always loved that movie, and I think I loved it because it was the first movie I knew of that showed the athleticism of cheerleaders who go to competition," Amy Cavner added from the driver's seat. "I was glad to see that, where they actually showcase how hard it is in the competition and the grueling time and work that it takes. Watching it now, I see it a little differently, but I feel like I have more understanding now, with how much involvement I have with Blake's cheer. [Her teams are] more intense than I was ever really exposed to."

The understanding of cheerleading has evolved just as much as cheerleading itself. The younger Cavner saw *Bring It On* as a little, well, *retro*. It's fair: the industry has grown, and there are so many flavors available, from all-star to sideline cheer, itty-bitty Tiny Tots to the postcollegiate groups who gather to keep throwing each other around just a bit longer.

Blake Cavner said that those different formats can make it hard to get through to people what it means when you say, "I'm a cheerleader." "My good friends, they understand because I'll explain, and they see how hard it is," she said. "People that don't really see it, they only hear it and you really only know what sideline cheer is. They'll be like, 'What are you talking about? That's not really a sport, why are you there so much?' Sideline cheer is definitely a sport, but it's not the most competitive."

That eternal debate, whether cheerleading is a sport, is another one of those complicated and reductive questions—the definition of "sport" varies from context to context, and in some cases denotes who's funding it or where its participants compete—and Lauri Harris, executive director of USA Cheer, the relatively young governing body for cheerleading in the US, told me that it's not necessarily an important one, to be real.

"I know there's been the debate for years of whether cheerleading is a sport," she said. "We've gone back and forth on that for multiple reasons. More important than if it's labeled a sport is we've always tried to get across that cheerleaders are *athletes*. That cheerleading is athletic in nature. Let's just take the sport piece out of it. Do you think these girls and boys are athletic? Well, yeah. Do you think what they're doing takes a lot of skill? Yes. OK, so recognize them for that."

Harris is another cheerleading lifer, having cheered at Sacramento State and graduated straight into a twenty-five-year career at Varsity Spirit, the commercial powerhouse of the cheerleading industry. After that, in 2017, she became the executive director of USA Cheer and took the show on the road, helping to establish rules and regulations for cheerleading and help other countries get involved in the sport as well. "You can't just go in there and be like, 'Hi,'" she said of the need for a governing body. Harris is quite literally a cheerleader for cheerleading, and proudly shared that, yes, she still makes a point to do stunts once or twice a year at events, recruiting college cheerleaders to "throw the old lady up." "People think I'm crazy," she said. "I get really good, really strong guys. I'm getting older, so I make sure they're just better than me."

When *Bring It On* was released, Harris was out of college "but very much in the cheerleading industry" and knew many of the cheerleaders who filled in the ranks on the Toros and Clovers in the background. She and her fellow cheer pros waited with bated breath to see what non-cheerleaders thought of the movie. After all, the cheer industry has a vested interest not only in positive portrayal of cheer but also in the success of that positive cheer-centric media to keep the activity growing. She called the movie "pivotal" in the public understanding and awareness of cheer.

"The number one thing they all said was, they loved it, very entertaining, but they said, 'I didn't realize how athletic it all really was,'" she said of friends' reactions. "It was nice to get the perspective of people who aren't really involved in cheerleading. I think from the inside and the outside, that is what I think a great takeaway was, and how it really helped to shape and bring a bigger conversation. Cheerleaders are having these conversations individually and with their boyfriends or their friends. 'You're not an athlete.' 'Yes, I am!' They don't go see them cheer, it wasn't super popular. Now it's on social media, so that's how a lot of people are seeing the skills now. People are like, whoa! A week and a half ago, a friend sent me a video clip, [asking] 'Have you seen this?' It was literally one of our national teams. Like, yes, I've seen it, I know him, I was there. But those are the things that weren't available in 2000. For the masses to see the type of skills that are really being done, I do think really helped to elevate cheerleaders, how athletic and their skill and the teamwork. It's not just something you hop out there and do. It's a lot of practice. You really rely on each other more than you do in probably most other sports."

In the original outlines for *Bring It On*, back in the *Cheer Fever* days, Torrance is actually seen writing a letter to the International Olympic Committee, advocating for cheerleading as a qualifying sport in the Olympic Games. Talk about full circle: in July 2021, the IOC voted to recognize cheerleading as an eligible Olympic sport. While that doesn't mean we'll be seeing it at the next Olympics, we could someday. IOC recognition opens the doors for certain government funding and grants, potentially affecting would-be cheerleading Olympians worldwide.

It's an important designation, Harris said, "in order for us to even be considered for the Olympics." In other countries, a governmental ministry of education and sport funds athletics, so the distinction can help cheerleading happen at all. In the US, "it helps to elevate and legitimize what everyone's been working towards, and put us in the spotlight of being able to be open to more opportunities." And, of course, that cheerleader who's being sarcastically rah-rahed at in the hallway of her high school can now point to the potential of being an Olympian someday.

Through the fictionalized *Bring It On*, cheerleaders became real people.

Smalls, the race and pop culture scholar, was on a competitive and predominantly Black cheerleading team when the movie came out. "It was a movie like *Bring It On* that made me still feel like I belonged there," she told me. "I remember seeing the Clovers and watching them move, and watching them being the best team that was in the movie. Going to cheer camp every summer, usually we were one of the only predominantly Black teams there. That was when the movie took on a whole different role in my life, because that was a reminder that *you can be a cheerleader too*."

She remembered, "If we do certain moves, we'd either be told we're gonna get points taken off, or 'That's not how we do things.' But other teams were able to incorporate those same moves into their work, and I guess it looked different for them." Now that she's had decades of being "the only" in different situations—the only Black journalist in a newsroom, or the only Black person in a classroom—"this is a synopsis of life."

Vanessa Willoughby, another cheerleader turned journalist, also held the Clovers' presence near, saying "I still see myself in it," praising the movie for not turning "cheerleading into girls just standing on the sidelines and waving pom-poms; it actually does take the commitment and dedication to it seriously."

"The town that I grew up in was very white," she added. "So I do understand that aspect of being a marginalized person and trying to prove yourself and having to be better than the mediocre person next to you and having to make that double effort just to be noticed and recognized."

The actors went through cheer boot camp to learn the skills for their roles, but that doesn't mean that they connected what the movie would mean to real-world cheerleaders.

Huntley Ritter, who plays Les, "didn't know anything about this cheerleading world" when he got the role, he said. He recalled seeing the call sheet leading up to the Nationals scenes, listing an eye-popping fifteen hundred cheerleader extras on set. "Where are you going to find fifteen hundred cheerleaders?" he asked, assuming generic costumes would be provided for extras to meet what to him was an impossible number. How wrong he was.

"Those buses rolled up," he said. "You should have seen it. Just bus after bus after bus, from all over the country, I think, and they were getting off already dressed, already ready to go, cheerleading outfits, legit cheerleaders. And we're like, Damn, I can't believe this. We got talking to some of them later. They were all excited to meet the cast and stuff and that somebody was making a movie about this, and so they started telling me about it, and they were like, this is huge. This is *huge*."

Nathan West, who played Jan, recalled, "For those cheerleaders, it was such a gratifying thing. I think it gave them a sense of, like, we matter. What we do, we're not just girls, we're not dumb blondes and all those stereotypes. There's so many stereotypes. And then of course, my character, being a male cheerleader, like, 'Oh, he must be gay,' and it's like, no. I think that they just felt respected for the first time. They were just honored that someone did it and it's funny and everyone loves the movie. I know people that went and saw it, six, seven times, you know? That was really a special thing."

Now, decades later, the movie persists, as does its status as SparkNotes for what it's like to be a high school cheerleader.

Ward, long out of her cheerleading uniform, said that cheer "will forever be part of my identity.

"When I tell people I was a cheerleader, they get excited. And then I'm like, 'Yeah, we were competitive.' They're like, '*Bring It On!*' And I'm like, sure. I think twenty years later, it paints cheerleading as something that's serious, not this like rah-rah-sis-boom-bah thing like in the '70s and '80s. It continues to help add the pride to the sport, of being part of it."

That "sure" echoes among the cheer professionals and former squad members I spoke with, the knowledge that the truth of certain elements has been bent or exaggerated, a little sprinkle of movie magic. As Harris put it, "I'm sure it's like being in the air force and watching *Top Gun*. Like, 'You're not going to do that flyby,' or whatever. But it's the movies and it's fun."

One of those exaggerations, which almost every cheer person I spoke with pointed out, was the infamous spirit fingers. Contrary to the movie's undulating digits, spirit fingers are a silent applause and a tradition at cheer camps or as a crowd hype gesture on sidelines, but its outsize reputation from the movie is dismissed by those in the know. While everyone I spoke with admitted to learning the movie's cheers and still being able to recite them (and, in many cases, demonstrated that ability to me), as Gaskill laughingly said, "Not one cheerleader has ever done spirit fingers on the competitive mat. No spirit fingers allowed. Automatic loss. Everybody would be like, 'What are you doing?'"

Blake Cavner, the young all-star cheerleader, paused in seeming disbelief when I asked her about spirit fingers, before answering, "No. If you did spirit fingers on a competition floor, you would probably get deducted." She called them "a distraction" and told me that your hands should be blades on the cheer floor, fingers together, thumbs tucked.

So, the veracity of spirit fingers aside, does *Bring It On* still bring it with the cheer community, all these years later? Oh yeah. Just look at how often cheerleaders tell one another to "bring it," Gaskill said.

"Jokingly, we'll go, 'Yeah, you better bring it.' I mean, yeah. That has lived on forever. You just don't have to explain anything, everybody just knows. People just know."

THE ANATOMY OF SPIRIT FINGERS

> "These are not spirit fingers. These are spirit fingers, and these are gold."
>
> —Sparky Polastri

Have you ever wondered if Sparky Polastri continued to work with cheerleaders after his short tenure with the Toros? The answer is, yes, he did. Below is key information distilled from a recent weekend seminar Sparky offered, dedicated entirely to the mastery of spirit fingers. Sweater monkeys, take note: these pointers are the key to the crown jewel of cheerleading, the one move that can elevate the tawdry subset of dance known as cheerleading to the level of art. These are *gold*. (*Special thank you to Ian Roberts for contributing his expertise.*)

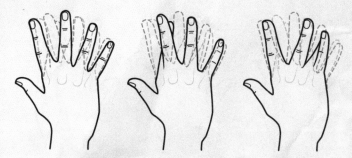

Fig. 11.1: Not spirit fingers.

In a high school gym, Sparky Polastri walks down a line of cheerleaders who are dressed in workout clothes.

Attitude: Enter into this quest for mastery with fear and trembling. Proper respect will be paid, and inadequate flanges are unwelcome.

Arm position: Elbows by your sides, upper arms parallel to the torso. Forearms at an 85-degree angle to the upper arms.

Fingers: I would sooner have you cut off your hands than "wiggle" your fingers. Spirit fingers aren't something you *do*. Spirit fingers are something that happens to *you*. They are energy, or "spirit," expressing itself through you. And during that expression, your fingers do not "wiggle," They vibrate with the spirit your body cannot contain—spirit which must be released through the fingers, lest your body explode like a supernova from the pressure of trying to contain it. Allow the spirit to build up within you and release through your fingertips.

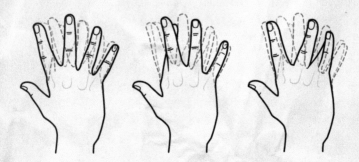

Fig. 11.2: Spirit fingers, i.e., gold.

Hey, what was the name of that woman in *Bring It On*? The cheerleader? The queer one? No, not that one. Not that one either. Ah, yes, *that* one.

So goes the (hypothetical) conversation about *Bring It On* in some circles where there are more 'ships sailing than Boston Harbor at rush hour and multiple members of the Toros scan as queer-coded.

Just as it was on the issues of cultural appropriation, the passions of young women, the absolutely *metal* nature of competitive cheerleading, and more, *Bring It On* was surprisingly progressive when it came to the sexuality of its characters. In the 1990s and 2000, it was relatively rare to see a non-straight character on the big screen, and the LGBTQ+ characters you did see were typically tragic or the

---

NOTE: *This chapter discusses sexuality and quotes offensive terms. It has been edited according to the recommendations of the GLAAD Media Reference Guide.*

245

punchline of a joke. In *Bring It On*, however, the character of Les, played by Huntley Ritter, is canonically gay and has a cute flirtatious moment with another male cheerleader at Nationals, while many of the film's other characters are, to borrow Les's descriptor, "controversial" in the minds of fans.

Universal exec Tim O'Hair, who worked on the movie, told me, "This movie is incredibly forward-looking. It wasn't a film where they said 'OK, we need to have a lesbian figure, a gay figure, a biracial figure,' where you feel you're checking boxes, it was extremely organic to Jessica's script."

Let's start with Les. Ritter booked the role and steered well clear of how people expected a gay man to behave in the late '90s—effeminate—in his acting choices, playing Les like he would any high school boy, because that's exactly what he is.

"It wasn't interesting to me to play something predictable," Ritter told me. "I thought, I'm gonna play this dude super strong. There's lines in it where they're being harassed by the football players and I stop Jan and say some of those things. And I was like, I'm gonna play this character proud and strong. High school is a vicious place for all, everybody. Even if you're in the cool crowd, it's fucked up.

"Looking back on it, after the movie came out, I didn't really think a lot about, if I'm honest, that that would have an impact on anybody. I wish I could say I did it in order to try and help people. I didn't realize there were people that were struggling with something, and also it didn't ever cross my mind that I would have an impact on anybody, to be honest, doing this little movie."

But the character, with his straightforward ownership of and lack of shame about his sexual orientation, *did* make an impact.

"I go back down to L.A. and I go to my PO box and there's that letter in there that says you have too much mail. This must be like six weeks after the movie's out, right?" Ritter remembered. And I got into the post office box, and I take it to the counter and they're like, 'Oh, you're Ritter,' and they're like, 'Who are you?' I was like, 'What are you talking about?' And they're like, 'Are you famous?' I was like, no, and they're like, 'Well, you got a shitload of mail.' They just kept wheeling them out, they were on those big baskets on wheels. It filled my trunk. I had a two-door Tahoe at the time and it filled the Tahoe. . . . I had thousands of letters, and I remember bringing these things in in bags and dumping them on my apartment floor. I didn't know where to start, and I started reading them."

The letters were from fans thanking him for his work, grateful to see an LGBTQ+ character on-screen. A positive portrayal, and a hopeful one at that. "That really opened my eyes," he said.

Kyle Menard wasn't writing those fan letters, but he told me he absolutely felt seen by the movie when it premiered. Menard is the proprietor of Totally Good Time, an online clothing store that sells designs based on and referencing beloved movies, largely from the '90s and early 2000s, *Bring It On* included. He told me that *Bring It On* was "a little bit smarter than a lot of the other movies of the same genre that were coming out," which could have been a secret to its longevity.

"The other big thing is that I'm gay. I think it really resonated with a lot of gay boys, gay men of that age and that time, because it wasn't really talked about, it was kind of taboo still," he said. "You didn't really see it on the big screen or too many people talking about being gay or anything, and here's boys on the cheer squad. And then in the car, driving around and talking about being gay in a very, like, flippant way, which was kind of nice. It wasn't like they were getting hurt or anything, so it was kind of a break from what we had seen. I think that's also another big reason why it still resonates with people, especially gay men. It's just kind of like that coming of age, where they see themselves in a character where they hadn't seen themselves before."

Les's gentle flirtation at Nationals was actually shot in reshoots, and Reed remembered having to fight to get the film time. "Huntley had come out so well in the movie, and I loved where Les, his character, was," he said. "I went to that moment where he's waiting backstage to see the kid from the other squad come out and have a moment that really was an unabashedly gay moment in the movie that wasn't cliche, just like a real, you know, a guy who has a crush on another guy thing."

He faced resistance with the studio, but he bundled it in with a few added gross-out laugh moments backstage at Nationals to cater to the *American Pie*–obsessed higher-ups.

"They're not highbrow laughs, but they're laughs of like the girl's bloody tooth, the girl vomiting, Torrance's little brother coming in there with the spanky pants, like that stuff. And the Les moment was one of those. So it really was like a bargaining chip: 'Yes, you can shoot that, *but*,' and we pitched all those other things, and it felt like a good thing to me, because we needed the laughs in there but I also wanted that moment. . . . The studio was kind of 'meh,' coming from a place of money. 'Do we really need that?' I felt we needed that, and I love that it's in the movie. It's such a small moment. For Les, it felt like the right kind of moment at that point in the movie. There's something very cool about that scene to me. I really like that scene."

That *Bring It On* resonates with queer audiences and is packed to the gills with both explicit and conjectured queer content (*Bring It On* superfan journalist Katie Barnes called it "should-have-been-gay canon" in their essay celebrating the movie, which they said they've seen more than three hundred times) is certainly no accident. "Gay men and teenage girls are part of the secret of my success," screenwriter Jessica Bendinger told me in 2015. "They just really know their stuff with boys and clothes. So I vetted a lot of my jokes and stuff with gay men and drag queens, that was really my audience when I was writing the script. That's who I was writing the movie for." Lines like "hate us because we're beautiful, well, we don't like you either" went straight from conversations between Bendinger and her friends into numbers like *Bring It On*'s iconic opening cheer. Queerness is part of the movie's DNA.

Drag queen Peaches Christ, who writes, directs, and acts in a long-running series of live movie spoof/tribute drag shows, gave the Peaches Christ treatment to *Bring It On* in 2019. The show had "queens flying through the air," Peaches told me, and featured *RuPaul's Drag Race* alums like Monét X Change and Bob the Drag Queen. Peaches only pays homage to movies she truly loves, and *Bring It On* originally made an impact on her because "at the time to be that nonchalant about having queer characters was truly progressive. Now we take it for granted, but that was a big thing twenty years ago."

The storyline, too, parallels how marginalized groups like the drag community are often co-opted and turned into currency by mainstream culture. "It could be about voguing," she said. "It could be about all these different things, you know, hip-hop, drag, this sort of commodification of drag that we see happening right now, it is all there in the movie. So I think that's why probably it speaks to queer audiences so much as well." And, of course: "It's *cheerleading.*"

Though Les is the only openly and explicitly gay named character in the movie (in an earlier cut, Torrance's trash boyfriend Aaron was depicted in bed with a body of ambiguous gender when he's cheating on her, but it was cut when test audiences didn't seem to get it), you can hardly swing a pom-pom without hitting fan discussion about where characters fall on the Kinsey scale, with some actors like Clare Kramer, who played Courtney, joining in.

In June 2021, Kramer posted a still from the movie of her and fellow cast member Nikki Bilderback in uniform as Courtney and Whitney. "Happy last day of Pride to them," the image read. "PS: Go Toros!" she added in the caption.

When I asked her if she thought Courtney and Whitney were an item, she was coy. "Courtney is just a free agent. Whatever comes her way, she likes what she likes, boy, girl, doesn't matter, you know?" she said. "I think that's a great thing about *Bring It On*, with the sexuality of the characters, nothing's like, you know, I'm gay and I'm straight . . . it's all just there, and you interpret what you want to interpret, and I like that."

Bilderback, for her part, first told me that she didn't "think they were lesbians at all. I think they were two bitchy girls who falsely validated each other in high school. It was ego, control." But Kramer's meme, she said, was "amazing.

"I mean, I embrace that if people want to think that, I really think it's up to the viewers' choice, their perception of it. I know Clare and I, we embrace it all, so we're open to all of it. Sure, why not?"

After all, you don't have to identify as a lesbian to have sex with another girl.

The film's generally positive depiction of sexuality was careful and safe, not radical by broad definition. But when there's an absolute lack of non-traumatic, non-punchline LGBTQ+ representation in mainstream teen movies, it's undeniably refreshing. That's not to say *Bring*

It On doesn't have its hurdles when it comes to sexuality. One point in particular that inevitably bubbles up when you're talking *Bring It On* and depictions of sexuality is the use of anti-LGBTQ+ slurs in the movie. How can a movie that uses epithets multiple times throughout the film be considered progressive on depicting LGBTQ+ kids? As with all tricky topics, let's again look at the context, in this case who's saying those words and how.

At various fan events, the filmmakers' feet have been held to the flames over the years for the inclusion of such language. In the case of the bro'ed-out football players who sling an F-bomb at Les and Jan, with Les holding Jan back from starting a fight in response, Reed told me, "Honestly, I wouldn't change that, because the context in which we use it, it is intended to be hate language in the movie. Those football players are the antagonists in the movie. And I think it was important to show how inclusive the cheer squads were. But for that to have any weight you had to sort of see what they were up against in terms of the other kids in school, and it felt very real to me."

He points out the inclusiveness of the cheer squad, but, hold on, the Toros are *also* using those words, both Courtney at Missy's cheer audition, and Missy later dropping a few eyebrow-raising terms. How does that hold up?

Barnes explained it perfectly while unpacking the movie with me. "To me it's really interesting, the way that that language is deployed," they said. They called a scene where Missy talks to Les, Jan, and Torrance in the car on their way to the first home football game "maybe the most pivotal scene in that film, there's so much that happens in those two minutes."

From the script:

MISSY: What *is* your sexuality?
LES: Well, Jan's straight, while I'm . . . controversial.
MISSY (to Les): Are you trying to tell me you speak fag?
LES: Oh, fluently.
MISSY: And Courtney and Whitney, dykeadelic?

"Well, you know if he was offended, he wouldn't have responded that way," Barnes said. "And to me it was interesting in the context of the film that he was not offended, because if I'm having a conversation with gay men that I am close friends with, I may use the word 'fag,' in an in-community way, just like I may use the word 'dyke' in an in-community way. So to me as a queer person, it denotes that Missy is one of us. She is allowed to use the language that way."

Courtney, however, is definitely being pejorative toward Missy. Courtney begins the movie as a B-level villain on a quiet redemption arc. Missy is merely curious whether she and Whitney are hooking up.

"That's really interesting," Barnes said. "Like, let's unpack that and talk about the ways in which language can be used in both affirming community ways, and also pejorative ways that can be the same words. I think that's fascinating. I think it speaks to the richness of this piece as a cultural artifact."

Which brings us to Missy, played by Eliza Dushku.

"There are so many, I think, queer kids my age who saw Missy, and saw parts of themselves," Barnes said. "That was wild. Like I feel like in general, we're talking about subtext representations of queer women, Missy Pantone is right at the top."

From her introductory shot of a ring of keys swaying on her hip to her be-Sharpied tattoo, Missy was the alt-girl poo, so take a big whiff. Film critic Joe Reid shared a story of an *extremely* year 2000 experience with me, of a Tori Amos message board he lurked on with a subforum discussing *Buffy the Vampire Slayer*. When *Bring It On* premiered, the admins of the board, "two girls from California, one of whom was a lesbian and one of whom was bi and they were both *so* into Eliza as a persona and as this sort of queer icon," couldn't stop talking about it.

"Eliza was also, like every gay guy, I'd still have a crush on Eliza, because I think she just put out a persona," he said. "So they were so into *Bring It On* as a queer subtext movie. A lot of the Torrance and Missy stuff was very much pored over, and the sublimated sort of vibes. The Missy character is so interesting in that way, because she's very sexual, and very brash and that kind of thing, but she has no love interest in the movie. Her only real relationship in the movie is

Torrance. Whether that was an intentional subtext that they wrote into it or not, it's definitely there. It's one of those things where sometimes you go back, and it's just like, how much were we reading into things? And it's like, no, it's definitely there."

Here is where we have to apologize to Jesse Bradford, who seems like a really nice person: the queer *Bring It On* fandom doesn't have a lot of use for Cliff. Peaches Christ admitted to writing that romance out of her tribute ("What I did find that I didn't care about, and maybe this is just because I'm a cynical bitch, was the love story. I just was kind of like, whatever."). Of fifty fan works categorized under *Bring It On* on the fan fiction site Archive of Our Own, twenty of them showcase the romantic pairing of Torrance and Missy. There are ninety results for the fandom on FanFiction.Net, and one of the first hits is for a Missy/Torrance story with "or how the movie should have gone, basically" in the summary field.

Kristin Russo, who in addition to being an LGBTQ+ activist and educator is also CEO and editor-in-chief of *Everyone Is Gay*, basically squealed with joy when I brought up the pairing. "I was dying last night [rewatching the movie], *dying* at some of the moments that they had," she said. "She's like sleeping over at Missy's house and has to have feelings so like she's standing in the doorway of [Cliff's] room, like, OK, and then she gets into bed with Missy!

"Cliff is literally a stand-in, I mean no offense to him and his beautiful self," she said. "There were some scenes where I was like, they have put this man's body here so we can digest this as a 2000 audience. They're fucking brother and fucking sister, come on! . . . Kinda the same vibe, kind of the same tone, dark hair, kind of the same attitude. It feels like he was added to simply make it so that the girls didn't have to be in love with each other. Like, I don't get those vibes, I don't get vibes they have these huge crushes on each other, though there's a couple moments. But yeah, especially at the end, Missy has her arm around his shoulders, and it's almost like handing off the male version of herself to Torrance."

For what it's worth, Russo also caught a vibe of unresolved sexual tension between Torrance and Isis in the movie. "She's like, she understands me and it's really all about leadership and power. That's pretty sexy, there's a little something there," she said, then laughingly referenced the deleted ending depicting the duo on the same college squad. "What went on there at UC Berkeley? I'm just saying. I have a question. I have a follow-up."

Dushku, for her part, told me it was "not at all surprising" to her that many viewers read Missy as queer, though it wasn't explicitly in the script or direction.

"It was very similar, I think, to my [character] Faith in *Buffy* fan fiction or people's read on those," she told me. "I'm totally cool standing by that that is a possibility for either of those characters and that I value and appreciate that my portrayal of this characters was so important for people that saw it and resonated with it or that it helped them discover their own and embrace their own queerness or nonbinary identities. And again, that's one of the things that I think makes this movie able to live on and today where people can see themselves in some way in the movie, or on the characters, which again, is just rad, it's really cool. It was never something that was talked about or intended, I guess it's just something that I brought."

Reed told me he gets asked all the time about Missy, or Courtney and Whitney, or any number of characters, and "I've learned not to comment on any dynamic of anybody in the movie.

"I feel like movies have more power when people bring what they bring to the movie," he said. "I know how I feel about them, but I'll never say. If you make a choice or you say it's going to be this or that, if somebody who loves that thing about the movie feels like, oh, that wasn't intended, it robs it of some power. It's not that choices were made. This has remained my feeling about those things now, is like everything that you need to know, if you interpret it one way, then that's great."

THE QUESTION OF CONSENT

> "Courtney adjusts her spanky pants. Jan looks
> at her. She bends over to tie her cheer-sneaks,
> knowing full-well that he's looking."
> —*Bring It On* shooting script

For a movie that had to make edits to avoid an R rating, *Bring It On* is actually remarkably chaste. The most sexual tension-laden scene involves copious amounts of saliva . . . in sinks. Try to tell me there's a scene hornier than the Torrance and Cliff toothbrushing sequence, I'll wait. It's very . . . *wet*. There's no steamy hookup, regrettable or otherwise, for our characters to agonize over, and the movie closes out with the main duo sealing things with a kiss—playful, yes. Explicit? No.

In sharp contrast to the innocence of the Cliff/Torrance courtship, a brief scene that gave the MPAA pause while screening to assign the movie a rating has modern audiences raising their eyebrows, and filmmakers rushing to add context.

From the script:

> COURTNEY AND JAN do the same lift. As
> Courtney nails her "chair," her eyes
> pop out. Jan grins wolfishly, his hand
> clearly holding her by the butt.

Courtney WHOOPS and jumps out of her
stunt early, thwacking him.

Jan admires his thumb and cheers.

It's a quick joke set up a few pages earlier in the script, when Torrance, Missy, Jan, and Les are driving to the game (a scene that's important for other reasons and resonates decades later as well) and Jan mentions Courtney's tendency to go commando under her spankies. "I can't help it if my digits slip occasionally!" he exclaims.

In fact, it can be helped, and two decades later, that "slip" is glaring for a viewership that has a heightened awareness of the importance of explicit consent and bodily autonomy.

"That's the thing I would change," Reed told me. "I hate that. I hate it. I mean, again, it was always in Jessica's script and it was based on an actual thing that she heard from a cheerleader, it was an anecdotal thing from a cheerleader. And it is, and we at least I think set it up as, whatever how weird that relationship is, it's a consensual one between them and weird, but it's still just like *bleh*. She throws him a look before, like it's this weird perverse thing that they have, which does have its footing in that story that Jessica heard originally as it was in the script, but it's still like, that's the one thing, if we were doing a director's cut [today] I would snip that out."

However, Kramer, whose character Courtney was on the receiving end of said digit, told me: "That doesn't bug me."

"It was a moment in time," she said. "As a society we evolve and some things, you know, change, and we've become more aware of what's appropriate or inappropriate and perception changes. At the time it wasn't viewed as inappropriate and Courtney wasn't against it. So, you know."

According to her, off the page, she understood the relationship between Courtney and Jan, played by Nathan West, as consensual and Courtney's swat as faux outrage, playacting that she wasn't interested while really she thrived on the risqué attention.

West told me he felt that "obviously, there was a relationship going on behind the scenes with those characters, obviously that's what it's insinuating and stuff too. And it played to who the character was, but yeah, it makes me cringe a bit, especially now, having two daughters and stuff. Even though it was supposed to be lighthearted, and it is, at the same time it's still something that nowadays it's like, no. A little bit of an eek."

Bendinger agreed, telling me back in 2015 that she'd had a lightning-bolt moment about that gag in particular, which was indeed based on a story she'd heard in her research.

"I went to a screening of *Bring It On* last summer, and I brought a bunch of friends and I was like holy shit, this is bad. I was even shocked. You couldn't get away with it now, the whole thing where he's lifting her, lifting Courtney and he shoves his finger up her butt, wherever he's shoving it, that's so *Porky's*," she said. "You can't do that now! I guess [there was] *American Pie*. And the whole 'Do you speak fag' and he says 'Oh, I speak it fluently,' even though it was positive."

I'll say it again: no art is perfect. Not the year it comes out, not two decades after it's made, never. That doesn't excuse those moments that the filmmakers have themselves said that they'd cut now, like that one, but that doesn't mean the

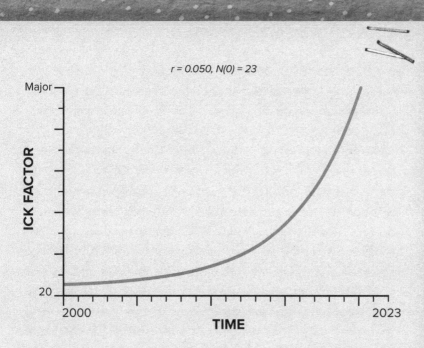

$r = 0.050, N(0) = 23$

Major —

ICK FACTOR

20 —

2000   2023

TIME

Fig. 12.1: Perception over time—not that it was ever really OK.

movie isn't worth engaging with. As commentator Gray put it to me: "Inevitably any cultural product is going to reflect the time that it was made in. I think it is worth both being able to enjoy the thing for what it is and what it does really well, and also healthy to be like, 'Yes, my perception of the world has grown and changed for the better and so my understanding of this cultural product that I still love is also going to change, and my thoughts are going to be more critical on it.' And that doesn't mean we should throw it away. I'm just gonna have a more complicated understanding of it, and that is healthy."

In other words, as she said, "there totally are some movies that you're like, what the absolute fuck is happening." *Bring It On*, for the most part, isn't one of them. Overall, the movie is well intentioned and holds up. We can watch it and not give it a pass but still understand the context of the time it was made. Enjoying a movie that has a moment that doesn't stand up to our understanding of sexual consent doesn't mean you don't understand or believe in consent.

As journalist Katie Barnes, who counts the movie as a favorite, said, "It's a cultural artifact, right? That's not something that is unique to *Bring It On*. You can pick any film at any point in time and rewatch it, and with today's eyes, it doesn't read the same. And you could also make an argument that such things were never appropriate, right? And I'm not gonna say, like, 'Oh, well, that was fine in 2000 and it's not now,' but I think we have moved considerably in how we think about consent, how we think about bodily autonomy. And there are multiple perspectives, I think, especially in the scene between Jan and Courtney and sort of the joking around and what some people read as assault, because there is no verbal consent given. I think it also embodies the messiness of relationships and of the ways that we interact with one another and how the standards for those interactions and parameters around what's appropriate have changed and are changing in terms of what consent looks like and what it should be."

But we can still acknowledge that "that doesn't mean that that particular scene did not perpetuate harm for survivors and that's, you know, perhaps more important to consider. I think it means something that Jessica says that she would take it out if she was writing it today, but I don't think that that means that we can't talk about those things. Like for me, what makes *Bring It On* really powerful is that it's a conversation starter in so many ways. So we can talk about how where we've moved in discussions about what is considered to be sexual assault has changed considerably, and here's an example of where we were, and what perhaps didn't really sit well with some folks then, and what definitely doesn't sit well with a lot of people now."

Author Blay agreed, pointing out, "everything is going to be problematic at some point.

"It very much speaks to that time," she said. "Those are the ways in which you can have that conversation. Let the movie be what it is, let it be what 2000 is. I promise you in twenty years we're gonna fucking watch, I don't know, *Squid Game* or whatever is popular now, and be like, yikes. That's just the nature of humanity and time."

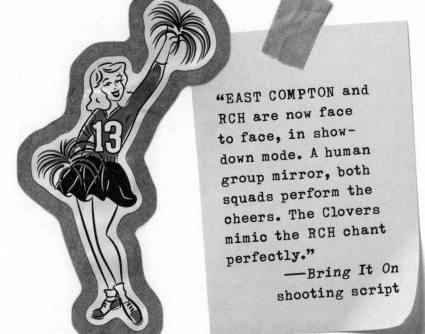

"EAST COMPTON and RCH are now face to face, in showdown mode. A human group mirror, both squads perform the cheers. The Clovers mimic the RCH chant perfectly."

—*Bring It On* shooting script

Want to go viral? It's simple: just invoke the holy name of *Bring It On*.

When British evolutionary biologist Richard Dawkins coined the term "meme" in his landmark 1976 book *The Selfish Gene*, he probably didn't have cheerleaders on his mind. He originally defined a meme as a cultural unit passed down through generations and time, as with a gene. It's a shared trait and reference point, an underlying commonality that is understood, even between two people who may have never met before. The meaning of the word has evolved through the years to often reference a cultural touchstone, an idea that is often tweaked slightly before being passed on.

Bring It On has become the ultimate meme, two-plus decades after its release.

In the same way that dead languages die because nobody is speaking them anymore, so go movies. If a movie is released in a theatrical forest and nobody quotes it, did it even make a sound? (My grandmother had that old chestnut cross-stitched onto a throw pillow, didn't yours?) According to Box Office Mojo, a division of the Internet Movie Database (IMDb) that tracks historical box office data, the highest-grossing film of the year 2000 was *How the Grinch Stole Christmas*, raking in $251.6 million. (A Universal release like *Bring It On*, for what it's worth.) *Bring It On*, according to the same data, ranks thirty-second on the list for the year. Nothing to sneeze at, higher ranking than any movie I've ever released (read: none), but its $68.3 million gross for the year isn't mind-blowing in the grand scheme of things.

What do the movies *Dinosaur*, *What Lies Beneath*, *U-571*, and *Rugrats in Paris* all have in common? At first glance, not a lot, but I can spot at least two: they all had higher grosses than *Bring It On* in 2000, and if you say the beginning of one of their lines, I challenge anyone to complete it. On the other hand, fill in the blanks: "Brr, it's _____." "We're sexy, we're cute, we're _____." And on and on and on. Box office is not the only marker of success, nor is it a sign of cultural relevance and longevity.

Of course, neither is quotability, though *Bring It On* has that in spades, obviously. So what is it?

"This is literally the plot of *Bring It On*," Ashley K. Smalls, the mass communications PhD student, tweeted on March 29, 2021. The tweet, which racked up nearly half a million likes in less than six months, shows a side-by-side video of fifteen-year-old Mya Johnson and twenty-year-old Addison Rae in split screen, performing the same choreography to Cardi B's "Up." Or at least, kind of the same. Johnson, dressed in hot pink high-top sneakers and baggy white joggers paired with a white crop top, moves with her whole body—the tips of her fingers seem to be engaged in the dance; she may be actively involving the vellus on her earlobes. Next to her, Rae, in baggy acid-wash jeans with prefab rips across the knees, black cropped tank top, and pristine white sneakers, is a paint-by-numbers kit displayed in a place of pride next to the Mona Lisa. If enthusiasm were the same as skill, sure the videos would match—but it's not. As someone who is a certifiably Bad Dancer, I can't tell you exactly how it looks different when Johnson and Rae both shimmy their hips and put their arms above their heads, ostensibly the same move, but I can definitely tell you it looks different.

Oh, and another difference between Johnson and Rae? Rae's dance was filmed as a segment on the *Tonight Show,* with host Jimmy Fallon cheering her on through a series of dances made famous through viral social media video app TikTok. Johnson's video is lifted directly from her own TikTok account, where she debuted her original choreography. Yet another contrast between the two: Rae is white. Johnson is Black, as is her fellow creative who appears in the video with her, Chris Cotter. Rae was named on the segment, a boldface promoted guest, star on the dressing-room door, the whole shebang, while the work of Johnson and other mostly Black creatives who created the choreography that Rae was running through went uncredited, Johnson and her fellow dancers unnamed and unseen, the side-by-side video only surfacing after social media outcry and subsequent investigation. Rae's net worth is estimated by Forbes to be in the ballpark of an eye-popping $5 million, a fortune built in less than two years via her TikTok popularity and parlayed into endorsements, sponsorships, and even a lead role in a movie.

"This isn't the first time this has happened and I don't want it to continue," Johnson told *PopSugar* in an interview after the segment and its resultant controversy. "I feel like it is very important for us to get our credit because we are very good creators that are very overlooked in what we do." (For her part, Rae offered *TMZ* the bland statement that "they all know that I love them so much and I support them so much and hopefully one day we can all meet up and dance together.")

Smalls, who was a high school cheerleader herself, immediately spotted the parallel with the movie. "All I could think about was the epic scene when the Toros are doing their cheer during the game and here come the Clovers, from the stands, doing it with them," she told me. "And of course, doing it twelve times better, because they are the originators. And you know, that scene is iconic, that scene goes viral on Twitter, like, at least once a year, if not every couple of months, as it should. But seeing the side by side of the original choreographer next to Addison Rae doing it, seeing that, it was just literally like that bleacher scene of the Clovers doing their choreography in front of the award-winning Toros."

Smalls spends more time thinking about this stuff than you or me; her dissertation in progress examines the intersection of Black feminism with nerd culture with a particular focus on the films of the Marvel Cinematic Universe. All she could see in the dawning controversy was Big Red lurking in the shadows with her video camera and Isis saying "I know you didn't think a white girl made that shit up" to a disbelieving Torrance. Two decades later. In real life.

"It's a reflection of a larger thing in society," Smalls said. "It's definitely about race, but it's also about resources as well, when you have less of a means to get on a platform like Jimmy Fallon or the followers for people to know it's yours immediately. Thankfully, people were calling out that the choreographers weren't getting credit without even knowing who the choreographers were, but, like, this wasn't something where we knew who to call or who to tag—we didn't know because the national platform chose not to tell us, and I can only think about the days before social media, when something like that couldn't get called out. . . . So just imagine this being ten years ago, and someone going on TV doing something they didn't create, the whole world will look at you as the choreographer, and there's really nothing that can be done about it."

Bring It On has become our pop cultural shorthand for cultural appropriation and plagiarism, the film's popularity sticky enough that if you invoke its themes—putting some blonde hair on it and calling it something different—it's immediately understood what you meant.

In another case of life imitating art (which imitated life in the first place), see the Republican National Convention in July 2016, when Melania Trump, wife of then presidential candidate Donald Trump, delivered several lines almost verbatim from former First Lady Michelle Obama's 2008 speech at the Democratic National Convention. They both, it would seem, share a belief that the only limit to your achievements is the reach of your dreams and your willingness to work for them. Trump campaign speechwriter Meredith McIver took responsibility for the oopsie, and her resignation was reportedly rejected. "No harm was meant," she said in a statement of what she described as a misunderstanding while underlining Trump's admiration for the former First Lady.

Predictably, social media had a field day. GIFs flooded social media, mostly reaction shots of Isis and the Clovers, often the scene of the Clovers outclassing the Toros on their own home field, performing the same cheer but multitudes better because it's theirs. In July 2016, the title of the movie saw a 33 percent spike in searches, according to Google Trends. The phrase it was most commonly searched alongside? "Michelle Obama."

Union sees the memes circulating every time there's a headline about cultural appropriation, her twenty-seven-year-old self in a cheerleading uniform breaking it down for the world over and over again as Isis: "I know you didn't think a white girl made that shit up."

"I would say it's the biggest" example of cultural appropriation and theft in po culture, she told me. "I'm trying to think of others that are as commonly used as *Bring It On*, and I can't think of any others. It's just the one that is always used."

Of course, Isis's iconic quips and glares aren't the only *Bring It On* memes lighting up the Internet. Catch Torrance blowing a kiss or delivering her *buh-bye* kiss-off to Aaron, Missy's dorky-happy door-frame dance the first time she dons her Toros uniform, or any of many other instantly recognizable frames from the film, or notice someone reciting a line from one of the movie's cheers in casual conversation. A well-placed reference to the movie, something that happens more often than you think, is a little exclamation point of nostalgia in the day of whoever comes across it, and does even more to fan the flame of *Bring It On*'s legacy all these years later.

Take Gabrielle Union dressing up with her toddler daughter in matching replica Clovers uniforms (she said in an interview with *Vogue* that Universal wouldn't loan her the original costume, and that "it should be in the fucking Smithsonian") and posting it to Instagram with the caption "brought it" or sharing a homemade GIF in 2017 captioned "THESE are spirit fingers," Clare Kramer sharing that on-set snapshot of her and Nikki Bilderback in character as Courtney and Whitney wishing them a happy Pride month, or even Eliza Dushku sharing a black-and-white snap of her throwing up hook 'em horns in front of a cow with the caption "#gotoros." Anytime an original cast member makes a nod toward picking up a pom-pom, it's a Moment. Fun fact: when Union and her daughter (a meme in and of herself, to be real) donned their green uniforms to attend Union's birthday/ Halloween party in 2019, they weren't the only Clovers in the atmosphere. Rapper Saweetie—who happens to be Union's cousin; "she's my first stop if I ever needed a kidney," Union told *Vogue*—was *also* rocking a Clovers uniform at the same party in an unplanned twinning moment. She performed, and the photos are epic.

Toros and Clovers costumes are evergreen hits among all kinds even now, from big sister / little sister sorority reveal schticks to drag shows to Halloween costumes. Even Vanessa Hudgens, who made it big as the star of the *High School Musical* movies, donned a gothed-out cheerleading uniform in a Halloween 2021 Instagram post and recorded herself with a friend performing *Bring It On*'s opening cheer, to the tune of close to one million likes. Ahead of Halloween 2019, social media influencer Rickey Thompson, who has over five million followers on Instagram, posted a video of himself and two friends in Clovers uniforms, twerking to Meghan Thee Stallion's "Ride or Die."

Big Red herself, Lindsay Sloane, called the annual influx of Drag Reds "the honor of my lifetime, honestly."

"Halloween is my favorite time of year," she added. "I'm not really active on social media, but I do have an Instagram account and I will say every time, like, a man in drag dresses as Big Red and tags me it makes my night. The fact that it is still like a huge costume, and it's a very recognizable choice, it just is the coolest."

Beyond its messages about race, sexuality, and, like, acceptance, *Bring It On* is, to use the parlance of my childhood, hella fun to its core. It's one of the reasons why it was so popular upon its release and remains endlessly rewatchable today, introducing it to younger generations through not only the movie itself but also instantly identifiable references to it that renew interest, drive nostalgia and comfort rewatching, and pique the curiosity of those who may never have seen it.

"I thought we made like a fun little cheerleader movie," Dunst told me. "But all these other movies were influenced by it! You know it's big when another movie has characters watching or talking about your movie. That's really how you know, like, you made a classic: watching your movie in a movie."

And there's been no shortage of references to *Bring It On* through the years in pop culture. Summer and Marissa perform the opening cheer in an episode of *The O.C.* (greatest show of our time), the movie is thrown out as a rental option on *Ugly Betty*, and a *Joan of Arcadia* character calls it *"The Matrix* of cheer films," to name a few small-screen examples.

Over in the real world, in 2008, celebrity chef (and doctoral thesis–worthy person) Guy Fieri, he of the frosted tips and classic cars and Mayor of Flavortown himself, partnered with the National Pork Board for the "Bring It t-ON-g! Pork Grilling Challenge," a celebration of the Other White Meat. The winners received a cash prize, a trip to New York City, and of course, a new grill. "I can't wait to see what people throw at me," Fieri said in a press release about the contest. "I'm one tough judge—bold is in my blood so if it doesn't get my taste buds tingling, you're going home!" The vehicle in which Fieri traveled for his tour was called the "pork mobile," naturally.

In less meaty references, the much-hyped music video for Ariana Grande's "Thank U, Next" single drove the masses to revisit Torrance and company in November 2018. In the days leading up to the release of the video for the number one single, which stayed atop the Billboard Hot 100 for seven weeks following its debut, Grande teased several images of herself paying homage to early 2000s movies on Twitter, namely *Mean Girls, Legally Blonde, 13 Going On 30*, and, of course, *Bring It On*. When she shared a photo of herself dressed in a Toros uniform (garnering nearly four hundred thousand likes) and another of a group of women in Clovers uniforms, Union replied, "Why yes, I am an East Compton Clover!" in a tweet of her own. Grande's all-lowercase fangirling reply stirred Internet onlookers into a further frenzy: "i'm gonna pass out."

When the video premiered, Grande not only donned a Toros uniform but also paid homage to fan favorite moments like the infamous toothbrushing scene and Torrance dancing on her bed to the mixtape. Viewers took notice—the video set a YouTube record for most views of a music video within twenty-four hours after racking up more than fifty-five million watches—and got nostalgic for the flicks Grande paid tribute to. According to Amazon Prime video data, in just the three days from the video's Friday premiere to Sunday, rentals of all four featured movies were up an average of 33 percent on the platform week over week, showing that the nostalgia button was being pushed, and hard. Adding to that, these weren't idle background streams: all of the rentals were $3.99 each. People were really committing to watching. "I approve," Reed tweeted with a picture of Grande in her Toros finery.

From a tumbling pass in a cheerleading audition scene in the 2007 *Bratz* movie that looks suspiciously close to some front handspring, step out, round off, back handspring, step out, round off, back handspring, full-twisted layout action to my untrained eye, to a cheerleading-themed episode of *RuPaul's Drag Race* titled "She Done Already Done Brought It On" (Lisa Kudrow makes an appearance, and the B-52s are guest judges for the episode, why not), there's no shortage of newer pop culture keeping the candle burning for *Bring It On*. It's got the door, Tor.

Even the straight-to-video sequels in the franchise have inspired art: on indie musician darling Sufjan Stevens's 2021 record with Angelo De Augustine, *A Beginner's Mind*, all the tracks are inspired by movies. Track 12, "Fictional California," is inspired by *Bring It On Again*, the second and not-so-critically-acclaimed film in the series, which Stevens claimed to be a personal top ten favorite movie of his. (He also has said he thinks it's better than the original, which is a *take*.) With lyrics like "Now Whittier arrived in fictional California /

We're gonna bring it on again / Bring it on to you hard." the song both has direct references to the movie (the main character is named Whittier, and in fact the first lines of the Wikipedia plot summary read "Whittier arrives at the fictional California State College," lending strong credence to this being a super-meta reference) and pushes the idea of being a cheerleader in your own life, one that Stevens had espoused for over half a decade before releasing the song.

In an April 2015 speech transcribed by a Reddit user, Stevens spoke onstage in Chicago of his love for the movie and its message, which he interpreted as cheerleading not being just for the popular kids, and everyone deserving encouragement. "That's really awesome that there's this idea of a cheerleading squad at every corner of every game," he said. "It doesn't matter if it's table tennis or croquet—and we need that, you know—at our jobs, at our cubicles. We need the deadbeat cheerleading squad to just pop out of nowhere and be like: 'look alive.'" Though in 2021, Stevens also told *Entertainment Weekly* of the song, "There's nothing substantially philosophical about *Bring It On Again*." When a celebrated indie folk icon like Stevens is talking about a movie, you know it's reaching more than just teenage girls.

Even the show *Ted Lasso*, a breakout hit in 2020 and 2021 while most people were cooped up at home with only their streaming services to keep them company in the midst of the ongoing COVID-19 pandemic, referenced *Bring It On*, with the titular character telling a journalist after a loss that opponents should "make like Dunst and Union and bring it on."

As Peyton Reed himself complained, and unfortunately for fans of the "take a shot every time they say the title of the movie you're watching" drinking game (they're out there, it's a thing), the words "bring it on" are never actually spoken in *Bring It On*. The closest we get is that moment when Isis tells Torrance to "bring it" ahead of Nationals. "Don't slack off because you feel sorry for us. That way, when we beat you, we'll know it's because we're better." "I'll bring it," Torrance replies.

The first cited use of the phrase "bring it on" in the *Oxford English Dictionary* (*OED*), which tends to be pretty good at these things, is in 1980, in a *Washington Post* article about the director of the Corcoran art gallery in Washington, DC. The article reads: "'I could save Chrysler if I had to,' he says, his half-smile becoming a playful taunt. Bring it on, he seems to say—then laughs at his own response: 'That's how arrogant I am.'"

The phrase, as a stand-alone challenge, might be an update to the late nineteenth-century slang "bring on your bears," a reference to the outdated practice of bearbaiting, in which spectators watched dogs harass and attack chained bears in an arena. It goes way back—Shakespeare referenced the gruesome blood sport in his works in the sixteenth century, and there were multiple arenas where it was practiced near the Globe Theatre—but is also much more recent than you would hope: "bear baying," a relative of the act, was only outlawed in South Carolina in 2013. Still, the phrase: in Louisa May Alcott's *Little Women*, published in 1869, Laurie says to the sisters, "Shall I sew, read, cone, draw, or do all at once? Bring on your bears. I'm ready." Jo orders him to read to them while she knits the heel of a sock. Isis vibes, right?

The wonderful—and sometimes infuriating, to be real—thing about language is that in most cases, there's still another place to look, the possibility that usage goes back further, meaning evolves, or there's a different origin story. Fiona McPherson, who is Scottish by birth, lives in Germany, and works at the *OED*, the most English of English-speaking institutions, proving that even lexicographers can be international (wo)men of mystery, literally thinks about and researches this type of thing all day for work. (Did you know that the word "ghostbuster" wasn't originated by the movie? You can thank a 1930 *TIME* magazine article about Harry Houdini's widow for that.) She's a senior editor at the *OED*, which is updated four times a year. Four times! In 2021 alone, an excess of five thousand entries were either added or revised in the tome. She raised another theory about the origin of the phrase as an imperative: the ding-dang Bible.

In 2 Kings 2:23–25, the prophet Elisha is mocked by youths who call him "bald-head." He turns around and "cursed them in the name of the Lord," resulting in two female bears showing up and mauling forty-two of the young men. Elisha continues on to Mount Carmel.

"I'm not saying that's where it comes from, but I don't know," she told me. "Sometimes things can sound quite plausible, and then you realize it's sort of a folk etymology."

In some breaking dictionary news, the entry for "bring it on" *was* one slated for investigation and revision in the near future when McPherson and I spoke, and we may have back handspringed our way into English-language glory.

"In all honesty, that might be something which when we come to revise the entry, we might, I imagine we'd look into it more to see if there's any connection with that," McPherson said of the "bring on your bears" theories both biblical and baiting. "Because it is kind of interesting: Why bears when you could bring on a lion? I suppose it's anything which could put up some kind of challenge, isn't it? So it's unlikely to be something which wouldn't be a challenge to somebody."

Though the movie certainly didn't invent the phrase "bring it on," there's no denying that, post-2000, its utterance is almost unavoidably paired with a mental picture of a pom-pom. It's punchy and it's memorable, and I spent an inordinate amount of time trying to figure out which former presidents have seen the movie.

Let me explain: according to a search of the online archives of UC Santa Barbara's American Presidency Project, which catalogs remarks, addresses, and writings of US presidents, a handful of commanders in chief have used the phrase in their official capacity. My guy Teddy Roosevelt said, in his annual address to Congress on December 6, 1904, "This will continue to be the case as long as they strive to make the Filipinos independent, and stop all industrial development of the islands by crying out against the laws which would *bring it on* the ground that capitalists must not 'exploit' the islands." (Italics mine.) But that's not what I mean. No, I mean a contextual, aggro "Bring it on!" in the same spirit as the movie. A stand-alone phrase of challenge, not any of this workaday midsentence transitive verb/object stuff.

In 2003, President George W. Bush famously said in a much-discussed press conference about the rising casualties in the Iraq War, "There are some who feel like—that the conditions are such that they can attack us there. My answer is, bring 'em on. We've got the force necessary to deal with the security situation." But wait, that's not bring *it* on, you say. Please hold.

Let's tune back in a few years later, in 2006. In a joint press conference with UK prime minister Tony Blair, Bush was asked about his regrets around the Iraq War. Wait for it . . .

"Sounds like kind of a familiar refrain here—saying 'bring it on,' kind of tough talk, you know, that sent the wrong signal to people. I learned some lessons about expressing myself maybe in a little more sophisticated manner—you know, 'wanted dead or alive,' that kind of talk." Ding-ding, there it is!

He's not the only one to drop the phrase: then presidential candidate Hillary Clinton, a month before the 2016 election, the day after debating Donald Trump, said it in Ohio on October 10, 2016: "On the day that I was in the Situation Room watching the raid that brought Osama bin Laden to justice, he was hosting *Celebrity Apprentice*. So if he wants to talk about what we have been doing the last thirty years, bring it on." On February 2, 2010, President Barack Obama also picked up the spirit stick at a town hall event in Nashua, New Hampshire, saying of Republicans, "Here's my thing: 'You got a better idea? Bring it on. But what I will not do is stop working on this issue.'" Even Michelle Obama got in on it, laughingly telling Barbara Walters in a 2010 Thanksgiving interview, "If it's a positive compliment, I am a woman, just, like, bring it on. I'm, I'm cool with it," she said when asked if she was tired of people commenting on her toned arms.

It's not uncommon for presidents to screen movies at the White House; it's one of the perks of the job. Unfortunately for my purposes, only official screenings and events are entered in White House records, so Freedom of Information Act requests made by Matt Novak as part of his intriguing "All the Presidents' Movies" project chronicling movies presidents watched while in office don't hold the answer to whether Bush or Obama could toss off an "I'm sexy, I'm cute, I'm popular to boot" on command. Nor has Obama's postpresidential office returned my burning inquiry about whether he's seen the movie and whether he identifies more as a Courtney or a Whitney. But considering that both the Bush and Obama families had teenaged daughters while they were in residence at the White House, it's not at all a stretch to think that they both probably have.

It's telling that all the political call-outs I identified, with the exception of Clinton's campaign stop, were off-the-cuff, unscripted remarks, showing the permeation of the phrase into our post-2000 vernacular. Presidential speechwriters are hyperaware of the fact that their choices will essentially be etched in the stone of history, and would avoid references that may date speeches or make the oratory seem more lowbrow, which I assume would include the mental image of GWB saying "I'm still. Big. Red." Probably.

"If somebody says 'bring it on,' that immediately will pop into your head," McPherson said. "So if someone said 'ghostbuster,' that's immediately going to pop into most people's heads. And I think that's the thing about popular culture. In some cases, the word might have been originated [by the pop culture product], but in so many ways, it's not really about that being the place where that came from. It's about that immediate recognition that you have. Somebody says a particular word or a particular phrase, and the first thing you think of is that film. I think it's a really, really powerful tool for that reason, because, again, it's also something which, without getting all spiritual about it, it can kind of unite people as well [through] that point of reference, which is just so strong and so immediate."

And indeed, a quick look at Google Ngrams shows an abrupt and dramatic leap in the use of the phrase beginning in 2000, when the movie was released, remaining elevated, if not totally plateaued, since then.

Of course high-profile uses of the phrase haven't escaped the notice of Reed, who said he knows he and Bendinger didn't coin the term, but that for very obvious reasons he still feels connected to it whenever he hears it.

"It always grabs my attention," Reed told me. "And I do always find myself being a little proprietary about who's using it and in what context."

In November 2017, when Alabama GOP Senate hopeful Roy Moore made headlines for allegedly propositioning teenage girls and was called on by Republican leadership to drop out of the race, he tweeted, "Dear Mitch McConnell: Bring. It. On."

Reed's ears burned: You talkin' to me?

"Dear @MooreSenate," read the since-deleted tweet on his own timeline, "You're not allowed to use the name of my cheerleader movie, you f—king pedophile."

Reed's never been shy about voicing his political opinions, but admitted that there were some mitigating circumstances. "When I wrote that tweet, I was at the *Ant-Man and the Wasp* wrap party and I had a couple of rum drinks. It's the only the only time I've ever tweeted buzzed, but it held up in the light of day."

As for political figures he's pleased to see echoing the name of the movie, Obama gets a big thumbs-up. Does he think Obama's seen it? "I think he has," he said. "Yeah, I would hope so. I mean, [Bill] Clinton saw it. I think they just get film prints at the White House, part of the job."

So next time you drop a "bring it," know you're joined by some former leaders of this cheerocracy.

All hail the cheer.

THE MUSICAL: SING IT ON

If the measure of success for a TV show is six seasons and a movie, then surely the *Bring It On* franchise must be in some kind of oddball hall of fame with six . . . sequels and a Broadway musical?

Bring It On: The Musical began previews at Broadway's St. James Theatre in July 2012, with an official opening on August 1 of that year. It closed December 20, 2012, after 21 previews, 1 extension, and 173 performances.

Even more surprising than the musical existing at all is who made it: the music was written by Amanda Green (2004's winner of the prestigious Jonathan Larson Grant for early career talent in musical theater) and Lin-Manuel Miranda. This was Miranda's project between the Best Musical and Best Original Score Tony-winning *In the Heights*, which, by the way, was also a Pulitzer Prize finalist, and *Hamilton*, for which Miranda won Tonys for Best Musical and Best Original Score, among the show's eleven Tonys overall, Grammy and Billboard Awards for best cast album, a Kennedy Center Honor, and Drama League Awards for Distinguished Performance for Miranda and Outstanding Production of a Broadway or Off-Broadway Musical. Oh, and the Pulitzer. Can't forget the Pulitzer. As if that weren't enough, *Bring It On: The Musical* teamed Miranda with Tom Kitt (Pulitzer for *Next to Normal* and

Tonys for Best Original Score and Best Orchestrations for the same show) for the music, and Jeff Whitty (Best Book Tony for *Avenue Q*, which also took Best Musical that year) wrote the book. That's a *lot* of hardware for one Playbill, and it's not even counting the serious résumés of director/choreographer Andy Blankenbuehler (a *Heights* alum and Tony winner) and orchestrator Alex Lacamoire (ditto, plus a Grammy for good luck).

The musical's plot follows the same basic beats as the franchise's straight-to-video sequels: open with a dream sequence, meet your peppy blonde hero, watch her face adversity and become a better person, with a bonus of Like, Realizing Stuff during a climactic final competition sequence. Campbell is the new captain of the elite Truman High School squad, until she's redistricted to inner-city Jackson High, which *doesn't even have a squad.* She makes new nonwhite friends (including the first transgender high school character on Broadway, La Cienega) and wins their trust, then together they form a squad of spirited misfits and face Campbell's villainous former team at Nationals. The teams' uniforms are even red for the rich kids and green for the inner-city squad.

On the *Broadway Backstory* podcast in 2017, Blankenbuehler, who made his directorial

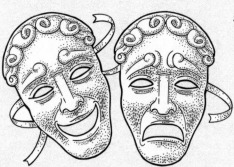

Fig. 13.1: Drama and comedy, two essential aspects of both theater and cheerleading. (And adolescence.)

debut for the show, said that he was approached and told that he could have carte blanche with the property, except that he would not be allowed to use the original film's storyline. He described his solution as *All About Eve* meets *Showgirls*, starring high school cheerleaders. He recruited his friends in the biz to fill out the creative roster.

"Andy took me out for drinks while I was still doing *Heights*, and he said *Bring It On: The Musical* and I laughed in his face," Miranda said on the same podcast. But when Blankenbuehler pitched his idea—Miranda writing the more hip-hop inflected songs for the Jackson team, Kitt handling the poppier Truman team—and the talent already signed on, "it was just sort of like, at worst, I'm going to learn so much from working with these people, and I couldn't see the downside of any of it."

The show followed franchise tradition in another way: it didn't share any creative team with the original movie, just like the home video sequels. In a lawsuit settled out of court before the musical's pre-Broadway national tour, the Writers Guild of America sued the producers of the musical on behalf of original *Bring It On* screenwriter Bendinger. "Imitation is not the sincerest form of flattery," Bendinger told the *Hollywood Reporter* in a story about the suit in 2011. "Compensation is."

She now has a story credit on the musical.

Apart from the familiar story beats, the musical retained the subversive and positive spirit of the original movie, especially notably in the character of La Cienega, played by Gregory Haney. The musical employed the original movie's show-don't-tell technique with the character. "The goal for me from the very beginning was, I'm going to put a trans character onstage, and then I'm never going to talk about it," Whitty said in the

Broadway Backstory podcast. "There's never going to be a discussion. There will never be that moment of after-school-special tears. You know what I mean, none of that shit, and just really, really make her absolutely the queen bee."

Haney does not publicly identify as trans himself. A planned UK tour beginning late 2021 announced that former *The X Factor Australia* contestant Jal Joshua would play the role, the first trans actor to do so in a professional production of the show.

The show opened to mixed-to-positive reviews, like this from the *New York Times'* Charles Isherwood: "The cast of this alternately snarky and sentimental show about rival high school cheer squads often seems to be in constant motion, tumbling and flipping across the stage in elaborate routines that culminate in towering formations of human pyramids. Such high-energy gymnastics are the animating force—and the primary distinguishing element—in this peppy teen-angst musical aimed squarely at the *Glee* demographic: adolescents, their chaperones and the nostalgically adolescent. (Not that there's anything wrong with that.) This would obviously include the devoted fans of the movie on which the new musical—like almost every new musical, I'm tempted to add—is based."

Variety called the show "pert and refreshing" in its review. "Neither roses nor brickbats are likely to be thrown at *Bring It On*, the new musical at the St. James, but you'll see plenty of cheerleaders tossed up high."

Entertainment Weekly, years after the show closed, called it, "half a musical and half the most intense (and well-lit) episode of *America's Got Talent* you've ever seen" in a retrospective ode claiming that Miranda's career-best lyrics are in the act 2 opener, "It's All Happening," not his more celebrated shows.

The show was nominated for Tonys for Best Musical and Best Choreography, as well as five Drama Desk Awards.

However critics received the musical, what Haney remembers is his Broadway dreams coming true, the full *Bring It On* effect, from the final dress rehearsal in front of all of his friends before the first preview performance in New York. "I open the show, and it's just me on the center stage with a spotlight on me," he said on the podcast. "And I remember feeling like Beyoncé. I've said that before, but that's true. I literally, as the show is starting, I'm going, This must be what Beyoncé feels like. And that for me was the first moment I really, really took it all in."

"Changing the routine now would be total murder-suicide."

—Whitney

Besides being the cheerleading movie of record and persisting for decades after its unlikely success story, *Bring It On* also holds the unusual distinction of being a franchise—six sequels that didn't receive a theatrical release and counting, not to mention a Broadway musical spin-off—whose original installment feels almost totally divorced from its progeny.

It was kind of an odd duck: After the triumph of the release and largely ecstatic fan reception, what was next for *Bring It On*?

Reed remembered having a get-together at his house to celebrate the release of the DVD. "The movie had come out theatrically, it was a hit, and the DVD was coming out, and that ended up being a hit," he said. "I remember a lot of positivity in the fact that we made this movie for $11 million and it did as well as it did. There was a lot of love in the studio for the movie, and at Beacon."

So why didn't we get a *Bring It On 2* in theaters? In short, as Dr. Seuss says, business is business, and business must grow. Hollywood is an expensive experiment, a gamble. After decades of being kind and rewinding and VHS domination as the physical media format of choice, DVDs were released in the US in 1997, with fifteen Warner Bros. titles released at once for the debut (including *Interview with the Vampire*; Dunst is a DVD original), priced around $25. DVD players, the only way to play the brand-new format, cost upward of $799.

Studios were invested in the success of the new format, because selling a DVD would essentially double their profit margin over VHS rentals, avoiding handing as much of the pie over to rental giants like Blockbuster. They didn't want another disaster like LaserDisc, the expensive serving-platter-sized format that ultimately faded into the background in the mid-'90s.

It worked: by offering extras like director commentaries and deleted scenes made possible by the format, allowing users to navigate through a menu and explore instead of being stuck on the linear track of a VHS tape, suddenly movies were a thing worth owning instead of just renting. (With a few exceptions, VHS home sales had been the purview of kid-centric movies, a tape you could pop in and play over and over to distract your kid who couldn't get enough of *The Lion King*, which is the bestselling VHS tape of all time.) More titles became available on DVD, and prices for DVD players dropped to as low as $100 for some models. By 2002, the DVD player was ubiquitous, the fastest-adopted consumer electronic ever, with an estimated eighty million players sold. The home entertainment game had officially been changed.

Meanwhile, the cast was raring to go.

"If you had left that group together long enough back then, we probably would have started shooting another movie, to be honest," Ritter told me. "We were actually gonna film something funny at the hotel as a joke."

West, too: "I remember coming out of *Bring It On* and we all thought, like, because we have this hit movie and everything, and it grew over time even more into this icon, I think we were always sitting there going, 'Oh, we're gonna do *Bring It On 2*!' You know, *American Pie*, of course they got number two, and a lot of those movies got that second and third and even fourth."

Universal's O'Hair remembered that "little *Bring It On* house party" at Reed's place. (Kramer told me about oohing and aching over Reed's new hybrid car that day.) There was talk about doing a sequel, and the cast was excited. O'Hair, excited, brought the news back to a staff meeting at the studio.

"I said, 'Good news, I saw so-and-so and so-and-so and so-and-so, and they all want to come back! We can get the original cast of the whole thing!' They obviously had options with all the actors [in their contracts] to do a sequel deal," he told me. "And the studio's like, 'Nah, we're going to just go straight to video.' As an executive, you can imagine it was very disheartening, because we're at the studio that they're making *Fast and Furious 47*. And everything was being sequelized, yet *Bring It On* got put over to the straight-to-video division."

Despite the verbal willingness of the cast to participate in a sequel, or ideas that Bendinger had bandied around with Reed and others, business, as it so often does in Hollywood, took precedence over creative desire. Abraham, one of the executive producers on the Beacon side, said, "I wasn't really keen on making them, I never liked making sequels or wanted to make sequels. But it was clear that people wanted to do to it."

Behind the scenes, things were changing at Beacon, necessitating a renegotiation of terms with Universal and a crossroads for *Bring It On*. Part of the shine of the original movie had been its low price tag and low risk; the bonkers box office was an incredibly welcome supersized cherry on top. To make a theatrical sequel using the same characters and universe would be a costly endeavor, necessitating pay hikes for the cast, as well as right of first refusal to participate for Reed and Bendinger, on top of royalties to Bendinger as creator, whether she wrote the next film or not.

A deal was struck to move the franchise to Universal's young home entertainment division and treat subsequent films as an anthology rather than a continuation of the adventures of the Toros or the Clovers. Such a deal was financially beneficial to the studio, which would be able to produce the movies at a lower budget and also save on the distribution and marketing costs associated with theatrical releases. Because the title *Bring It On* wasn't

Bendinger's creation, it could continue to be used, even if she wasn't involved.

"Some individuals get paid, everyone else gets left out," O'Hair said.

Some cast members, like Kramer and Bilderback, told me they'd been approached to appear in one of the later films, but without a theatrical release or the rest of the cast, they weren't interested. Ian Roberts, too, declined to reprise Sparky Polastri in the later movies. Lindsay Sloane called it "so upsetting" to see the franchise move on, and "a bummer."

For Bendinger, the deal was more than a heartbreak. "It's so hard to have succeeded and have been excluded," Bendinger said. "I can't explain it. It's very hard. I'm trying to get over it, and maybe I'm just perpetuating it by thinking about it."

In 2004, *Bring It On Again* was released straight to video, following hotshot cheerleader Whittier (Anne Judson-Yager) as she begins college and finds her place on the uber-competitive cheer squad alongside her cheer camp pal Monica (Faune A. Chambers), butting heads with controlling captain Tina (Bree Turner) and her jealous bestie Marni (Bethany Joy Lenz). She meets a boy she likes (Richard Lee Jackson), who is deemed "unsuitable" by the alpha cheerleaders. Whittier and Monica quit the squad to escape the tyranny, and start a rival troupe filled in with kids from the dance team, chess club, and more, a band of outcasts with a soundtrack provided by her DJ boyfriend. They compete with the sanctioned squad for a place at Nationals and win, with Tina eventually begging Whittier for a spot on the squad. The movie doesn't reference or feature any of the characters from the original, and only Abraham and Bliss remained among the original producers, a position they did not continue in subsequent films in the franchise.

It's a move that somewhat predicted the trend of anthologized media like *American Horror Story*, variations on a theme sharing the same title but following different stories. The entries in the franchise all begin with a dream sequence and the plots feature a protagonist, usually blonde, facing a cheerleading-related moral dilemma and overcoming adversity, ending with an all-cast dance sequence over the credits. Themes of teamwork and the triumph of cheer abound.

The home video sequels do feature some notable names, among them Rihanna and Solange Knowles in 2006's *Bring It On: All or Nothing* (working title: *Bring It On Yet Again*), and Hayden Panetierre in the same movie, the same year she played another pivotal cheerleader character in TV's sci-fi hit *Heroes*. ("Save the cheerleader, save the world," that's her.) Future breakouts Felicia Day (a nerd-core fave and star/creator of the web series *The Guild*), Bethany Joy Lenz (*One Tree Hill*), and Joshua Gomez (*Chuck*) all appeared in the first installment. Ashley Benson shook her poms in 2007's *Bring It On: In It to Win It*, which featured two squads called the Sharks and the Jets, and Jennifer Tisdale costarred, with her sister, Disney Channel star singer Ashley Tisdale, also making a cameo. Christina Milian and Holland Roden took up the mantle in 2009's *Bring It On: Fight to the Finish*, and Vivica A. Fox played the intriguingly named "Cheer Goddess" in 2017's *Bring It On: Worldwide #Cheersmack*. It's a scattered sorority, the network of names who have been part of the *Bring It On* cinematic universe.

The films have continued to evolve, with the 2021 announcement of a TV movie titled *Bring It On: Cheer or Die*. It's a Halloween-themed slasher movie to air on SYFY, featuring a team locked in a gym overnight who find they must cheer or, well . . . die. The installment features the franchise's first female director, Karen Lam, and was cowritten by two Extremely Online scribes, Dana Schwartz and Rebekah McKendry. As I write, the movie is yet to be released, but the premise and personnel have a whiff of "so weird it just might work."

Schwartz told me she's been "a *Bring It On* fan my entire life, obviously." Growing up in Chicago, "that original movie with Kirsten Dunst just informed so many fundamental ideas about what being cool was and what California was." She was seven years old when the original film was released, but over the years, "it just really defined what being a teenager would be like for me in my brain."

Schwartz, who is a writer on the upcoming *She-Hulk* streaming series and says she has "the flexibility of a geriatric pencil," wasn't the cheerleading type but had written a spec comedy slasher script that got her agent's attention and an offer to cowrite a Halloween-themed *Bring It On* movie. "Of course, immediately I said yes," she said. "It's a question with the easiest answer in the world."

The movie is a potential pivot point for the franchise, though it still doesn't feature any of the original creatives from the first installment. Schwartz told me that she rewatched the original film "just to get in the vibe," and that she hopes to honor the spirit of *Bring It On* and how smart and subversive and funny it is. Just with, you know. More murder.

"It's a horror movie, it's a slasher movie, but the fundamental things that we wanted to be true to is to respect teenage girls and their intelligence and their friendships," she said. "And point out that being a teenage girl is interesting and worthwhile and being interested in things that teenage girls are interested in doesn't make you shallow or flippant. We wanted to respect the friendships of the group and make all the girls on the team and boys on the team seem like fully fleshed dynamic characters, and we wanted also to respect cheerleading as a sport. It's incredibly athletic, and that was very important to us that we celebrated that.

"I hope to have honored the spirit of *Bring It On*, but the tone of this movie is so wildly different," she said. "The spirit is the same, maybe the spirit fingers, you know, the very esoteric energy. All cheerleaders have spirit fingers."

All this is not to say interest in a true sequel—a return to the halls of Rancho Carne and East Compton, some familiar faces—isn't there. The word "rampant" comes to mind. Every time Union, Reed, or any original collaborator (though it most often seems to be Union and Reed) is asked a throwback question about *Bring It On* or a milestone anniversary rolls around (anything ending in a 0 or a 5), the headlines come fast and furious: Gabrielle Union Reveals She's "Actively Working on" a "Bring It On" Sequel; Gabrielle Union, Kirsten Dunst in Talks for "Bring It On" Sequel, but Union Has One Caveat; "Bring It On 2" with Original Cast Is Happening. It's everywhere. Though the franchise now has a half-dozen entries and a musical, there's still a thirst for an update on Torrance, Isis, and their respective squads, all these years later. The interest is there from fans, and attitudes from original participants run the gamut from "sure, why not?" to "absolutely"—but what would it look like?

Reed, who said that he "would have loved to have been involved creatively in figuring out the thing," even if he hadn't directed, told me he and Bendinger talk about "trying to get the keys to the car back and take the franchise in new and interesting ways, and also create opportunities for younger voices," with Bendinger in the driver's seat, steering the world she created. "It feels like sort of a natural what you would want from a years-later thing if you were gonna reboot this franchise."

"Just as any movie you would approach differently in the year 2021 than you did in the year 2000, you would do it entirely differently," he said.

The question of reboots is a tricky one to begin with, in an entertainment landscape where original scripts are increasingly crowded out by retreads and sequels to existing IP, a hurdle *Bring It On* faced in the '90s that's only become more of an issue today. There are already so many entries in the franchise, is there really room for another take?

Yes, fans say, but it would have to walk a fine line to deliver a satisfying outcome.

Culture journalist Ira Madison III compared the idea to the recent *Saved by the Bell* reboot, which he said "recognizes that the show was sort of a morality play for white teenagers of the late '80s, early '90s, and that it put the vision of what teenage Americanness was on television. Now the new series pokes fun at that and reexamines that in a cultural context."

There's room, he said, for "a real sequel to a film like this that understands its cultural relevance, and sort of what it had to say about culture then. I think there's room for a film that honors that and then also says something else about society."

A firm requirement: "You definitely need the original cast."

Academic and culture reporter Ashley K. Smalls has been burned too many times by reboots. "Nowadays Hollywood goes in one of two ways: either it's amazing, or you see a sequel or a spin-off and you're like, this was unnecessary, you're ruining my childhood. Please just leave it alone. We didn't need this." She, too, wanted the return of the original cast, maybe an update for the TikTok age. Would Big Red have been found out through Instagram stories? "I would love to see Kirsten Dunst and Gabrielle Union being the coaches there. To see if that lesson that Kirsten Dunst's character learned twenty years ago, how would she apply it to a team who found themselves in a situation that she kinda was in herself?"

That we're still grappling with some of the major themes in the movie, like cultural appropriation, is an unfortunate truth. If we'd evolved more, maybe the movie wouldn't be so relevant today. Kristin Russo, the LGBTQ+ advocate, said, "I think a lot of the core of it holds up, I really do. Which is nuts, because twenty years is a long time.

"I think some things wouldn't look different at all, or only very slightly different," she said of a potential reboot.

Besides featuring characters and cast from the original, the two resounding pleas I heard from fans were to make the movie queerer and Blacker. With the groundwork that *Bring It On* and *Cheer* after it have laid, Russo said that a continuation could ease up on the insistence that cheerleading be taken seriously, and make more room for queer characters, even a romance outside of the main boy-girl matchup, if there was a main romance at all. "If there was a love story, maybe there was more than one and there would be some queer love happening. I think, ideally, in my universe, it would be that Missy and Torrance were falling in love as they were figuring out what to do with the squad," she said.

Katie Barnes, too, said, "I want the gay *Bring It On* that I've always dreamed of, that I deserve. I've put in my time, I want the gay *Bring It On* movie that I deserve!"

Beyond that, "people love the Clovers," they said. "But also there wasn't enough of it." That fifty-fifty poster versus 20 percent screen-time contrast comes to mind, that some of the stars of the show are relatively scarce in the movie itself, so popular with test audiences that additional footage was shot for the trailers. This time, Isis would get a last name and a home life. The Clovers would be fleshed out.

That's been Union's take on a return as well. She envisions more people of color in front of and behind the camera, she told me. "If it was going to be done well, it would center the people that were harmed and it would be told from the Clover perspective, versus how to redeem folks who have gotten away with stealing for years," she said. "To center that narrative today, I think, would be a mistake. Cringe for all the wrong reasons. I think it would be more equally told . . . The cast would look very different."

Dunst agreed: "Gabrielle should probably be the lead, and I think that my part should be secondary. I think it could be, like, she's the head of a cheer camp. I mean, I think it's totally possible."

Union also sardonically added, "If I had anything to do with it, Isis, listen, we know this story, and you're going to be called a villain anyway. Go out guns blazing. Go out full Django, you know what I mean? Like full Django."

For their part, many of the original cast have ideas about what their characters would be up to (Kramer said of Courtney, "I could see her just being like, 'Fuck you all, I'm moving to Hawaii and I'll be a writer or whatever.' She'd definitely be happy") and were receptive to the idea of a new project.

"I do think that this is a world that would be fascinating to revisit so many years later," Sloane said.

Bradford said, "I just see it as such a fun win for everybody."

There's also a question of whether that lightning in a bottle could once again be captured, even with many of the same elements in place, or if the decades of discussion and analysis and fandom would make for a self-conscious end product, the difference in vibe between a candid photo where someone looks like the most naturally gorgeous and carefree version of themselves and a portrait rendered in oils, static and staid, safe and posed, grimly staring out of a gilt frame. It's expensive, but do you need it? If Bring It On came in trying to address all the criticisms that have been lobbed at it over the years, or to please all audiences—the enduring fans of yesteryear and today's Gen Z fans and beyond—and correct all wrongs, it would run that risk. In being so self-conscious about trying to get it right, it would be too easy to get it wrong.

"I think one of the reasons that it's such a great film is how messy it is, and how it was allowed to be problematic in different ways, and it's subversive in other ways," Barnes said. "If it was a true sequel, I would want those things to stay intact. I want it to still be playful. I'd want it to still feel of the moment. I would want it to still be subversive in so many respects, but not like a very on-the-nose, 'We're going to a Black Lives Matter rally' kind of a deal. You know what I'm saying? *Bring It On* wasn't on the nose. That's, like, the best thing about it. If there was a true sequel made today, I think there will be some real temptation to be a little bit more on the nose."

Reed agreed. "I think it's also not being precious about the movie," he said. "One of the things from the beginning about Jessica's script is just the irreverence of it, and kind of like, you don't take this too seriously, and then slipping in some serious things in the midst of that tone. Not being too reverential about the original thing, because it's a low-budget cheerleader comedy that used the lightness of that platform to kind of get some cool ideas in there. I don't know. The future of *Bring It On* excites me."

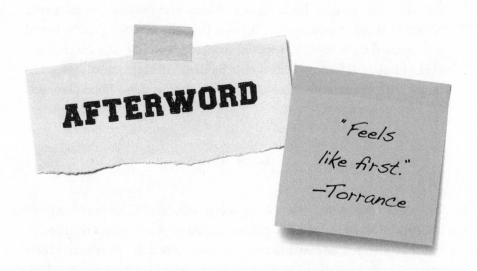

AFTERWORD

"Feels like first."
—Torrance

You can start cueing up "Mickey" soon: the credits are just about to roll on our exploration of the legacy of *Bring It On*, the greatest cheerleading movie almost never made.

From Jessica Bendinger visiting a psychic deep in the Valley, hearing his verdict about the movie she needed to write, *Cheer Virus*, to now, some thirty years later, when everyone can present their spirit fingers at the ready, *Cheer* dominates streaming platforms, and cheerleading has been sanctioned as an Olympics-eligible sport, we've come a long way.

Bring It On launched careers, set a new standard for the portrayal of teen girls in movies, changed the perception of cheerleading, heartened kids who just wanted to be taken seriously, inspired a franchise, provided a breath of fresh air to the teen-movie genre, entertained presidents, and more. It spawned marriages, friendships, and lifelong memories for those involved. It brought us spirit fingers!

The movie defied the odds to get made, dragging an industry kicking and screaming behind it to become a surprise smash, one that some involved were shocked to hear had endured for decades, finding a new generation of fans. Many longtime fans, like entertainment reporter and former high school cheerleader Jessica Derschowitz, return to it again and again: "If I was flipping through channels and it happened to be on TV, I would stop and watch it, absolutely," she said. "I one hundred percent would be like, 'All right, this is what I'm doing with my afternoon now, sorry to whatever else I had planned.' It's definitely adored."

The calls I had with cast, filmmakers, and fans alike while reporting this book were long. People were generous with their time, sure, but they also just seemed to enjoy talking about the movie and their memories. It had been more than twenty years since cameras rolled, but the impression and impact that the experience left was lasting, even in crowded careers.

Choreographer Anne Fletcher told me, "You don't ever know what's gonna take, what's gonna catch fire, what's gonna succeed or fail. But there is a feeling on certain sets that you go, 'Oh, this is magical. There's something very special about what's happening here.' So it's not surprising to me in the slightest bit. Some movies, you feel like it was great on paper but something's missing, and the audience feels that, the audience sees that. So it truly doesn't surprise me [that the film persisted], because the spirit was so good. I hate using that word, but that's what it was."

Dushku called it "one of the films and projects in my career that I truly look back with like pretty much all fond memories. It's such a bright spot in the whole, my twenty-five-, thirty-year career that I look back on. It's a joy."

It wasn't all sweeping sepia-toned memories, there were the little things too, goofy stories that don't make headlines, but little snapshots, the "You just had to have been there" stuff. Bell mused on what might have been in the Chu Surprise, the graveyard drink Lohmann would make her. Dunst remembered going to Kramer's hotel room to see her cats, and Bilderback recalled making up goofy gas-pump hand gestures that ended up in the movie as choreography for the "That's all right, that's OK" cheer. Kramer told me about Dushku going to live with Kramer's sister in New York, whom Dushku had never met, because she needed a place to crash during a shoot after Bring It On; the sister ended up officiating Dushku's wedding. West bragged to me about learning to do a back handspring on set, but "I don't have my abs anymore," so he hasn't tried in a few years. He did literally run while we were talking to grab his beat-up Toros duffel bag, emblazoned with the character name JAN. He still uses it at the gym. He flips past the movie on TV nearly every week, and "I always pause on it for a moment. Just watch a few moments. It's a great little big part of my life, and it brings back memories and stuff too. It's something I'm proud of being part of."

Ritter, who told me he answered as many of those fan letters he got back then as he could, wanting those people who had written in to make sure they were seen, said that he's still stopped by people, even though he's behind the scenes of media now. A favorite: a "tough guy, tattoos" at LAX who asked for a picture, saying, "My daughter and I watch that movie all the time."

Producer Scanlon, long out of the moviemaking business, said that the movie came up at a yoga retreat she attended in Italy a few years back with attendees from all over the world, that she mentioned Bring It On as "the best thing I ever worked on.

"Everybody was freaking out, and that was the first time I realized that it—not only the reach it had internationally but also just in terms of age. That all these kids had watched it over and over and over again on television. That was pretty cool."

Lohmann said she has "a lot of kids now," and will get stares in the school pickup line with people trying to figure out why she looks so familiar. Sometimes it clicks, and "they might bring up like the butt thing, that's a big one, and they probably look at my butt now and go like, 'Was it padded?' It's too many kids and too much time sitting watching kids do schoolwork."

Dunst knows a facialist whose little daughter, "all she watches is *Bring It On*. Like, that's her comfort." She doesn't have any idea how she found the film, but she signed a birthday card to her as Torrance once.

The tendrils extend everywhere, and the fondness remains, even as its message and legacy are examined, conversations started.

"I can be more critical of it now, and it doesn't have to be all glowing, because there's been twenty years of just, you know, joy, and I think more recently, a deeper dive into maybe, you know certain things that are a bit more problematic," Union told me. "But great art, you know, to stand the test of time is to also withstand criticism and not feel above it. Especially when we talk sequels and what could possibly come next, I think it is our duty to go back and dig a little deeper into some of the criticisms. I think that makes it better moving forward."

It feels like something of a bygone era, when a low-budget genre movie could eke through the studio system for a feature release. In the age of streaming, there's so much content, and it's rare for something to stick in the way *Bring It On* did. We have countless hours of content at our fingertips at home, but somehow it feels difficult to get a movie in front of an audience. Call it attention span, call it the industry, call it probably both those things and a little something else too, but the "sticky fun" of *Bring It On*, as journalist Robinson called it, is rare now. "I really wish that stuff like this still existed in that same way," she said. "I just really wish our culture still absorbed stories this way. I don't think we do."

If a movie is going to endure over the years and have such a ripple effect, it's lucky that it's one like this that has a good heart.

When I asked Union what the message of the movie was, in her opinion, she was thoughtful. She paused for a moment before saying, "I hope it is: You shouldn't be defined by your worst mistake. And once you acknowledge those mistakes or wrongdoing, it's OK if you don't win. The win is acknowledging the harm caused. Also: don't steal from Black girls."

Dushku, now studying psychology and raising a family, has heard "Your school has no gymnastics team, this is a last resort" chanted at her more times than you can understand over the years. She sees the Halloween costumes and hears about the college courses and theses and all of it.

"I think it did so many things right. And also even for the things that maybe we did, maybe it did wrong, it was thought-provoking and started important conversations," she said of the movie. "And again, it's not common that those two things can live in symbiosis. Where it's like, it's fun and awesome and uncomfortable and important and, like, deeply human. The cultural, social commentary, the ways that makes people feel. I just think it's extremely rare to pack all of that into a ninety-minute anything. And here we did it. We brought it."

Reed said it was "exciting that people still talk about it," but box office and all-time lists are kind of icing. "The critical assessment of pop culture stuff to me, I like it, but I honestly don't pay that much into it in a way, because none of it ever trumps how I feel about the thing that I made, the positives and the negatives. That's sort of set in stone about, like, I know how I feel about it. I know things I would change. I know the things I love about it. But in this case with this movie, it's really nice that it still speaks to people."

The lists and think pieces and accolades are great—everybody wants to hear that their movie is one of the greatest sports movies of all time, or meet the teen who can't wait to breathlessly recite *every line* to you. It's awesome to recognize the movie-biz and real-world implications of the movie, the cheerleader who felt like she was in on the joke for once when she saw herself on-screen. But none of that could have happened without the determination of those involved, not just during the shoot but also Wong and Scanlon crawling on their knees to their bosses for the green light, Demme hyping the script, Bendinger carting herself to all twenty-eight of those pitch meetings, and before that, the friends and community who helped her believe that there was something worthwhile there with her cheerleading/ hip-hop mashup, the "girl movie" that it felt like no one wanted, but it turned out everyone kind of needed.

"I think that helped me go, 'You know what? Cheerleading: I love it. I think it's really fucking rad,'" Bendinger told me. "'What if I can do that?' All these people, that whole swirl conspired to give me the confidence . . . we cannot overstate this, the kindness that artists need from others, to just live."

One thing is clear, after all these years: it's *Bring It On*'s cheerocracy, we're all just living in it.

ACKNOWLEDGMENTS

I've put off writing my acknowledgments until the last second not only because I'm a procrastinator but also because I'm so grateful to so many people for their help, advice, time, enthusiasm, and ears while writing this book that I'm inevitably going to leave someone out or not use enough exclamation points to express the hugeness of my gratitude. So if you're reading this, please consider yourself part of a blanket THANK YOU. Thank you for humoring me, thank you for talking to me, thank you for helping me, thank you for reading this book, thank you for maybe just picking it up and flipping to the back to see if I thanked you—that's cool too! And here it is, you're being thanked! But really: thank you.

And now to name some names.

Thank you to everyone associated with *Bring It On* who spoke with me for this book and your incredible gifts of time, stories, photos, documents, listening to my thoughts on the week's episode of *Succession*, complimenting my pandemic-inspired home decor projects—all of it. Thank you especially to Jessica Bendinger and Peyton Reed, who made themselves so incredibly available to me, both in reporting this book and back in 2015, when I reported the oral history that started this whole thing. To the cast, crew, producers, and associated Bringers-On who spoke with me, many of you more than once, I'm forever grateful.

To the experts, analysts, fans, and colleagues I called on to talk about, as the thesis for part 2 of this book eloquently came to be known, "Why in the heckity are we still talking about this movie?"—thank you. You are smart, excellent, and delightful people, and this book is infinitely better because of you. Any unsmart stuff, that's all me.

To the team at Chicago Review Press, and most especially my tireless editor Kara Rota: Where can I pick up nomination forms for sainthood? Is it a Google Form nowadays, or . . . ? Kara, you are a star of a human and editor and advocate, and you've made this ~journey~ a lovely one. Thank you for keeping comments on certain draft passages to "Hmm," for entertaining my (many) collages and mood boards, and so much more. Devon Freeny, thank you for your sharp eye and endless well of patience. Thank you as well to the superlative publicity, marketing, and design teams, especially Sarah Olson.

My agent, Myrsini Stephanides, is a mythical and benevolent fairy tale creature, and she has put up with a lot from me. She's always been patient in talking me through process and expectations and did not complain about me asking her to read e-mails I'm nervous about before I send them. Thank you, thank you, thank you, and big ups to the Arc Literary crew.

In so many ways, none of this would have been possible without Elizabeth Mehren, my professor turned journo-mom, who keeps telling me to call her "Elizabeth." I don't think that can ever happen, I'm *sorry*. Your narrative nonfiction class changed my life, but your belief in me has changed it even more. To the Carol Mann team, where I met Lydia Shamah, a human delight and one of the first people to believe in this book, another essential thank-you!

Thanks are also due to my very tolerant and supportive past colleagues: Eric, Monty, Alex, Crystal, Shaunna, Victoria, Colleen, and Lindsay, to name a few.

Maggie Coughlan, a hero and queen. One of the best things I've ever done is trick you into being my friend.

My husband says I have a "rich online life" and that he has no idea what I do when I'm shut up in my pink office upstairs all day. Big, big thanks to all my friends who live inside the computer, whether I've met you in person or not: the Snug, for listening to me panic and moan, and for affirming that at least one of my first-draft jokes was funny. Viv, Katey, Cheryl: what a relief to have you. The additional writers and friends who encouraged me, listened to me, asked me how I was doing at their own peril: thank you.

Thank you to my book club—I adore all of you.

Michelle Said Patches, the best compliment I ever got was when someone mistook us as sisters. It's not *not* true. Big love to the rest of the Patches fam. Spo, Angela, Daniela, Lindsey: earth angels.

Thanks to my parents and brother, who all watched this movie secondhand a *lot* when I was a kid. No regrets; my brain hasn't rotted! (Much.) Thanks to the Rosens.

Which brings us to, of course, Chris and Luna. Lu, I hope you think I'm a cool mom and that I wasn't too *too* cranky or absent while working on this project. I, for one, consider your deep emotional bond with a plastic unicorn skeleton a positive outcome. I love you. Chris, I've been working on that sainthood app for you too. Dad of dads, husband of husbands, ever patient, my first reader for life. I'm sorry for all the times I've wept at you over commas and other less important things. I couldn't have dreamed up a better partner for myself if I'd tried. Thank you for all of it. I love you.

NOTES

CHAPTER 1

"It's a mixed feeling": Jessica Bendinger, *The Bring It On Book* (Los Angeles: Verve Ball, 2020), 63.

She is five eleven without heels: Jessica Bendinger official website, http://www .jessicabendinger.com/.

"never really worked": "Low Memorial Library, Columbia University," National Park Service official website, accessed June 3, 2022, https:// www.nps.gov/places/low-memorial-library.htm.

"godmother of alternative comedy": "Bio," Beth Lapides official website, accessed June 3, 2022, https://www.bethlapides.com/bio.

"I don't know if I": Ernest Hardy, "Dancing in Serious Moonlight," *Written By*, February/March 2017, https://www.mydigitalpublication.com /publication/?i=383020&article_id=2709126.

"I think the first draft of": Bendinger, *Bring It On Book*, 53.

"unstoppable cheerleader for anyone creative": Alex Stedman, "Jodie Foster Pays Tribute to Jonathan Demme, 'A Champion of the Soul,'"

Variety, April 26, 2017, https://variety.com/2017/film/news/jonathan -demme-jodie-foster-tribute-silence-of-the-lambs-1202399502/.

CHAPTER 2

only 10.7 percent of the directors: Annenberg Inclusion Initiative, "Inequality in 1,300 Popular Films: Examining Portrayals of Gender, Race/Ethnicity, LGBTQ and Disability from 2007 to 2019," Annenberg Foundation, September 2020, https://assets.uscannenberg.org/docs/aii-inequality_1300 _popular_films_09-08-2020.pdf.

roughly $5.9 million opening weekend: "Sugar & Spice," Box Office Mojo, accessed June 3, 2022, https://www.boxofficemojo.com/release/rl2960295425 /weekend/.

CHAPTER 3

"Everyone was horny": Gabrielle Union, *We're Going to Need More Wine* (New York: HarperCollins, 2017), 132.

CHAPTER 4

an $85 million movie: "Air Force One," Box Office Mojo, accessed June 3, 2022, https://www.boxofficemojo.com/title/tt0118571/.

UST: UNRESOLVED SEXUAL TOOTHBRUSHING

"In one scene, when Torrance": A. O. Scott, *Bring It On* review, *New York Times*, August 25, 2000, https://www.nytimes.com/2000/08/25/movies/film -review-strong-modest-and-sincere-behind-all-the-giddy-cheer.html.

"Truly this scene in Bring It On": Lane Moore (@hellolanemoore), Twitter post, November 12, 2021, 12:26 PM, (post deleted), via Wayback Machine, https://web.archive.org/web/20211112174454/https:/twitter.com /hellolanemoore/status/1459211133869510656.

CHAPTER 5

"a single use of one": "Classification and Rating Rules," Motion Picture Association Inc., July 24, 2020, via FilmRatings.com, https://www.filmratings .com/Content/Downloads/rating_rules.pdf.

"In the original script": Gabrielle Union, interview with Ira Madison III, Louis Virtel, and Aida Osman, in *Keep It* (podcast), October 21, 2020, https:// crooked.com/podcast/strokes-of-dunces-with-gabrielle-union/.

"We ran a full scam": Union, interview, *Keep It*.

Roger Ebert gave the movie: Roger Ebert, *Bring It On* review, RogerEbert.com, August 25, 2000, https://www.rogerebert.com/reviews/bring-it-on-2000.

"Underneath this movie's tight acrylic": Scott, *Bring It On* review.

"If Mr. Reed's camera": Scott, *Bring It On* review.

he was "obsessive" about checking reviews: Lindsey Bahr, "20 Years Later, 'Bring It On' Still Gets the Cheers," Associated Press, August 25, 2020, https://apnews.com/article/ca-state-wire-entertainment-il-state-wire-us-news-47e79396a71d7668cd18038a2056a47c.

"earnest and arch": Lisa Alspector, *Bring It On* review, *Chicago Reader*, August 25, 2000, https://chicagoreader.com/film/bring-it-on/.

"The newest, and probably first": Kim Morgan, *Bring It On* review, *Oregonian*, August 25, 2000, via MetaCritic, https://www.metacritic.com/movie/bring-it-on.

"An army of rolled abs": Wesley Morris, "'Bring It On' Holds the (Racial) Line," *San Francisco Examiner*, August 25, 2000.

"Unexpected": Charles Taylor, *Bring It On* review, *Salon*, August 25, 2000, https://www.salon.com/2000/08/25/bring_it_on/.

"could be worse": Susan Wloszczyna, *Bring It On* review, *USA Today*, August 25, 2000, via MetaCritic, https://www.metacritic.com/movie/bring-it-on.

"the most exuberantly funny": Sean Means, "Something to Cheer About," Film.com, August 25, 2000 (site discontinued), via Wayback Machine, https://web.archive.org/web/20010215015943/http://www.film.com/film-review/2000/10013228/27/default-review.html.

"Who would have thought": Kevin Courrier, "Rah-Rah Tale Swims Against the Tide," *Globe & Mail*, August 25, 2000, https://www.theglobeandmail.com/arts/rah-rah-tale-swims-against-the-tide/article769509/.

"Conscious perhaps that the world": Stephanie Zacharek, *Bring It On* review, *Sight and Sound*, November 2000, 45–46.

CHAPTER 6

In fact, a 2013 study: Shu Zhang, James F. M. Cornwell, and E. Tory Higgins, "Repeating the Past: Prevention Focus Motivates Repetition, Even for Unethical Decisions," *Psychological Science* 25, no. 1 (2014): 179–187, https://www.ncbi.nlm.nih.gov/pmc/articles/PMC3899102/.

a Nielsen study in 2020: Bill Keveney, "Exclusive: Nielsen Finds Nostalgia Fuels Interest in Classic TV Comedies During Pandemic," *USA Today*, March

19, 2021, https://www.usatoday.com/story/entertainment/tv/2021/03/19 /nielsen-finds-covid-19-tv-viewing-spikes-classic-sitcoms/4754533001/.

this one by MRC Data: "COVID-19: Tracking the Impact on the Entertainment Landscape," MRC Data, accessed June 3, 2022, https://static .billboard.com/files/2020/04/COVID-19-Entertainment-Tracker -Release-1-1586793733.pdf.

That same Nielsen study: Keveney, "Exclusive: Nielsen Finds."

"an antidote to boredom,": Wijan A. P. van Tilburg, Eric Igou, and Constantine Sedikides, "In Search of Meaningfulness: Nostalgia as an Antidote to Boredom," *Emotion* 13, no. 3 (2013): 450–461, https://doi.org/10.1037 /a0030442.

"helps people find meaning": Constantine Sedikides and Tim Wildschut, "Finding Meaning in Nostalgia," *Review of General Psychology*, March 2018, https://journals.sagepub.com/doi/abs/10.1037/gpr0000109.

A look at Google Trends data: Google Trends, accessed 2021, http://trends .google.com/trends.

CHAPTER 7

literally lights up your brain: Moses Ma, "The Power of Humor in Ideation and Creativity," *Psychology Today*, June 17, 2014, https:// www.psychologytoday.com/us/blog/the-tao-innovation/201406 /the-power-humor-in-ideation-and-creativity.

called comedy "an argument": Thessaly La Force, "Cathy Park Hong and the Complexities of Asian American Consciousness," *Ssense*, March 11, 2020, https://www.ssense.com/en-ca/editorial/culture/cathy-park-hong -and-the-complexities-of-asian-american-consciousness.

"alive and risky and saucy": Roger Ebert, *Sugar & Spice* review," RogerEbert .com, January 26, 2001, http://www.rogerebert.com/reviews/sugar-and -spice-2001.

screed against the MPAA's ratings system: Ebert, *Bring It On* review.

"the Citizen Kane of cheerleading movies": Roger Ebert, "2-4-6-8! Who Do We Eviscerate? Fired Up! Fired Up! Yaaaaaaaay!," RogerEbert.com, February 18, 2009, https://www.rogerebert.com/reviews/fired-up-2009.

confronted Ebert about his initial: Bahr, "20 Years Later."

channel had leaned into the camp: Steve Gidlow, "'Fear the Cheer': Why Viewers Flock to This Annual Lifetime Event," MediaVillage, August 26, 2021, https://www.mediavillage.com/article/fear-the-cheer-why -viewers-flock-to-this-annual-lifetime-event/.

didn't enjoy the same commercial success : "Bend It Like Beckham," Box Office Mojo, accessed June 3, 2022, https://www.boxofficemojo.com/title /tt0286499/.

monster $115.4 million box office: "Pitch Perfect," Box Office Mojo, accessed June 3, 2022, https://www.boxofficemojo.com/releasegroup/gr3764539 909/.

In an essay on ESPN.com: Katie Barnes, "'Bring It On': From Spirit Fingers to Appropriation, the Cult Sports Film Is Much More than a Teen Rom-Com," ESPN, August 25, 2020, https://www.espn.com/espn/story /_/id/29731506/bring-spirit-fingers-appropriation-cult-sports-film -much-more-teen-rom-com.

NOT ANOTHER TEEN INTERSTITIAL

Ten Things I Hate About Clueless: Charles Lyons, "Strike Threat Greases Summer of the Scribe," *Variety*, August 9, 2000, https://variety.com/2000 /film/news/strike-threat-greases-summer-of-the-scribe-1117784813/.

CHAPTER 8

"possibly my favorite movie of all time": Jia Tolentino, "'Drop Dead Gorgeous,' Which Is Finally Streaming, Is Possibly My Favorite Movie of All Time," *New Yorker*, July 5, 2019, https://www.newyorker.com/culture/cultural -comment/drop-dead-gorgeous-which-is-finally-streaming-is-possibly -my-favorite-movie-of-all-time.

Dunst offered a clear-eyed reflection: Kirsten Dunst, interview with Larry Flick, in *SiriusXM in Depth with Larry Flick* (podcast), August 27, 2019, https:// twitter.com/SIRIUSXM/status/1166429260741009408?s=20.

code-worded "shrimp": Lindsay Peoples Wagner, "Kirsten Dunst Doesn't Need Your Oscars," *Cut*, December 2, 2021, https://www .thecut.com/2021/12/december-cut-cover-kirsten-dunst-the-power-of -the-dog.html.

"During that age I was": Kirsten Dunst, interview with Scott Feinberg, in *Awards Chatter* (podcast), February 7, 2021, https://www.hollywood reporter.com/movies/movie-news/awards-chatter-podcast-kirsten -dunst-the-power-of-the-dog-1235088295/.

"People love you, Isis": Gabrielle Union, *You Got Anything Stronger?* (New York: HarperCollins, 2021), 163.

CHAPTER 9

In 1967, seventeen football players: Amira Rose Davis, "Black Cheerleaders and a Long History of Protest," *Black Perspectives* (AAIHS blog), January 3, 2019, https://www.aaihs.org/black-cheerleaders-and-a-long-history -of-protest/.

"repeatedly using racial slurs": Malik Earnest, "Lincoln High Cheerleaders Taunted with Racial Slurs," Fox 5 San Diego News, September 16, 2019, https://fox5sandiego.com/news/lincoln-high-cheerleaders-taunted -with-racial-slurs/.

A search on Google Ngrams: Google Books Ngram Viewer, s.v. "cultural appropriation," accessed June 3, 2022, https://books.google.com/ngrams /graph?content=%22cultural+appropriation%22.

per Writers Guild of America rules: "Screen Credits Manual," Writers Guild of America, November 12, 2018, https://www.wga.org/contracts/credits /manuals/screen-credits-manual.

he said "with a certain pride": Neely Tucker, "A Bring-It-On Director Who Is His Own Profit Center," *Washington Post*, August 19, 2003, https:// www.washingtonpost.com/archive/lifestyle/2003/08/19/a-bring-it-on -director-who-is-his-own-profit-center/d348f3c9-b38c-4259-b6a8-b057 de5420c0/.

Union has mentioned his name: Oscars, "Bring It On: 20th Anniversary Vir- tual Reunion," August 25, 2020, via YouTube, https://www.youtube .com/watch?v=PB-hmSaogpw.

"I remember even at the time": Oscars, "Bring It On."

essay titled "Dear Isis": Union, *You Got Anything Stronger?*, 164.

"I realize that what you did": Union, 164.

"I made you respectable": Union, 165.

"Now? I would do that line so differently": Union, 173.

"make space for the white fragility": Union, 172.

CHAPTER 10

originated to describe a character: Nathan Rabin, "The Bataan Death March of Whimsy Case File #1: Elizabethtown," *AV Club*, January 25, 2007, https://www.avclub.com/the-bataan-death-march-of-whimsy-case -file-1-elizabet-1798210595.

CHAPTER 11

one hundred humanoid cheerleader robots: Buzz Staff, "No More Empty Stadiums? Cheerleaders at a Baseball Game in Japan Were Humanoid Robots," News18.com, October 4, 2021, https://www.news18.com/news/buzz/no-more-empty-stadiums-cheerleaders-at-a-baseball-game-in-japan-were-humanoid-robots-4281083.html.

"In any high school setting": "The Cheerleader," TV Tropes, accessed June 3, 2022, https://tvtropes.org/pmwiki/pmwiki.php/Main/TheCheerleader.

revealed that in practice situations: Zachary Y. Kerr et al., "Concussion Incidence and Trends in 20 High School Sports," *Pediatrics* 144, no. 5 (2019), https://publications.aap.org/pediatrics/article/144/5/e20192180/38225/Concussion-Incidence-and-Trends-in-20-High-School.

THE ANATOMY OF SPIRIT FINGERS

Thank you to Ian Roberts for lending some of Sparky's unpublished words!

CHAPTER 12

GLAAD Media Reference Guide: "Glossary of Terms: LGBTQ," GLAAD Media Reference Guide, 11th ed., accessed August 23, 2022, https://www.glaad.org/reference/terms.

Kramer posted a still: Clare Kramer (@clarekramerofficial), "Happy #PrideMonth2021!," Instagram post, June 30, 2021, https://www.instagram.com/p/CQw18tIrx9o/.

"Missy: What is your sexuality?": Bendinger, *Bring It On Book*, 109.

THE QUESTION OF CONSENT

COURTNEY AND JAN do the same: Bendinger, *Bring It On Book*, 109.

CHAPTER 13

originally defined a meme: Adam Lonberg et al., "The Growth, Spread, and Mutation of Internet Phenomena: A Study of Memes," *Applied Mathematics* 6 (2020), https://www.sciencedirect.com/science/article/pii/S2590037420300029.

According to Box Office Mojo: "Domestic Box Office for 2000," Box Office Mojo, accessed June 3, 2022, https://www.boxofficemojo.com/year/2000/.

"This is literally the plot": Ashley K. Smalls (@AshleyKSmalls), Twitter post, March 29, 2021, 10:44 AM, https://twitter.com/AshleyKSmalls /status/1376545774100738048.

Rae's dance was filmed: The Tonight Show Starring Jimmy Fallon, "Addison Rae Teaches Jimmy 8 TikTok Dances," March 27, 2021, talk show clip, via Facebook, https://www.facebook.com/watch/?v=1861250594025773.

Johnson's video is lifted directly: Mya Johnson (@theemayanicole), "new challenge ft @cchrvs 🔥🐐 #upwmyaxchris @iamcardib," TikTok post, February 8, 2021, https://www.tiktok.com/@theemyanicole/video /6927035476452855045.

Rae's net worth is estimated: Abram Brown, "TikTok's 7 Highest-Earning Stars: New Forbes List Led by Teen Queens Addison Rae and Charli D'Amelio," Forbes, August 6, 2020, https://www.forbes.com/sites /abrambrown/2020/08/06/tiktoks-highest-earning-stars-teen-queens -addison-rae-and-charli-damelio-rule/?sh=51b4e3705087.

"This isn't the first": Karenna Meredith, "TikTok Dancer Reacts to Addison Rae Using Her Work: 'That Should've Been My Time,'" Pop-Sugar, March 30, 2021, https://www.popsugar.com/entertainment /tiktok-mya-johnson-addison-rae-tonight-show-interview-48245258.

"they all know that I love them": "ADDISON RAE GIVES PROPS TO BLACK CREATORS FOR FALLON BIT . . . Let's Collab!!!," TMZ, March 29, 2021, https://www.tmz.com/2021/03/29/addison-rae-jimmy-fallon-tiktok -dance-controversy-black-creators-collab/.

Republican National Convention in July 2016: Kristin Oakley, "The Sudden Resurgence of 'Bring It On' Memes This Week, Explained," Quartz, July 21, 2016, https://qz.com/737539/the-sudden-resurgence-of-bring-it-on -memes-this-week-explained/.

Trump campaign speechwriter Meredith McIver: Brett Neely, "Trump Speech-writer Accepts Responsibility for Using Michelle Obama's Words," NPR, July 20, 2016, https://www.npr.org/2016/07/20/486758596/trump-speech writer-accepts-responsibility-for-using-michelle-obamas-words.

33 percent spike in searches: Google Trends, accessed 2021, http://trends .google.com/trends.

Gabrielle Union dressing up: Keaton Bell, "'I Didn't Want to Be Saved': Gabrielle Union Talks Bring It On, 20 Years Later," Vogue, August 25, 2020, https://www.vogue.com/article/gabrielle-union-bring-it-on-interview.

Kramer sharing that on-set snapshot: Kramer, "Happy #PrideMonth2021!"

Dushku sharing a black-and-white snap: Eliza Dushku (@elizadushku), "#GoToros #Buffalo #fam #ranch #UT 🐎❄️🏔️⛰️ #winteriscoming #BuffaloRunRanch," Instagram post, September 25, 2017, https://www .instagram.com/p/BZeGlF6j4Ir/.

"she's my first stop": Bell, "'I Didn't Want to Be Saved.'"

video of himself and two friends: Brea Cubit, "Rickey Thompson, Denzel Dion, and Dolce Telmah Twerking in Bring It On Costumes Is Art," *PopSugar*, October 27, 2019, https://www.popsugar.com/celebrity/rickey -thompson-bring-it-on-halloween-costume-dance-video-46812448.

"Bring It t-ON-g!": "Guy Fieri Headlines Pork Grilling Challenge," Food Channel, May 20, 2008, https://foodchannel.com/2008/guy-fieri -headlines-pork-grilling-challenge.

Grande teased several images: "Ariana Grande Got Shout Outs from 'Bring It On' Stars Eliza Dushku and Gabrielle Union," *Billboard*, November 22, 2018, https://www.billboard.com/music/music-news/ariana-grande-bring-it -on-stars-eliza-dushku-gabrielle-union-twitter-thank-u-next-8486295/.

According to Amazon Prime: Kayla Cobb, "Ariana Grande's 'Thank U, Next' Boosted the Sales of All the Movies It Referenced," *Decider*, December 5, 2018, https://decider.com/2018/12/05/ariana-grande-thank -u-next-amazon/.

"I approve," Reed tweeted: Peyton Reed (@MrPeytonReed), Twitter post, November 21, 2018, 1:41 PM, https://twitter.com/mrpeytonreed/status /1065314203198607360.

"That's really awesome": Chudaroo, "Sufjan Stevens—Bring It On 2 Speech April 25th @ The Chicago Theater," Reddit, April 26, 2015, https://www.reddit.com/r/sufjanstevens/comments/33wb1p/sufjan _stevens_bring_it_on_2_speech_april_25th/.

"There's nothing substantially philosophical": Devan Coggan, "Sufjan Stevens and Angelo De Augustine on Binging Horror Movies and Their New Film-Inspired Album," *Entertainment Weekly*, September 27, 2021, https://ew.com/music/sufjan-stevens-angelo-de-augustine-a-beginners -mind-interview/.

"I could save Chrysler": Carla Hall, "The Corcoran's Confident Captain," *Washington Post*, March 16, 1980, https://www.washingtonpost.com/archive /lifestyle/1980/03/16/the-corcorans-confident-captain/7608b2ed-5481 -43d8-8da8-202b9f72c41d/.

"Shall I sew, read, cone, draw": Louisa May Alcott, *Little Women* (New York: Scholastic, 2000), 160.

"ghostbuster" wasn't originated: "Science: Houdini, Doyle," *TIME*, March 31, 1930, https://content.time.com/time/subscriber/article /0,33009,738978,00.html.

youths who call him "bald-head": 2 Kings 2:23–25.

"This will continue to be": Theodore Roosevelt, "Fourth Annual Message," transcript of speech delivered to Congress, Washington, DC, December 6, 1904, via American Presidency Project, https://www.presidency.ucsb .edu/documents/fourth-annual-message-15.

"There are some who feel like": "'Bring 'Em On' Fetches Trouble," CBS News, July 3, 2003, https://www.cbsnews.com/news/bring-em-on-fetches-trouble/.

"Sounds like kind of a familiar": George W. Bush, "The President's News Conference with Prime Minister Tony Blair of the United Kingdom," transcript of press conference, Washington, DC, May 25, 2006, via American Presidency Project, https://www.presidency.ucsb.edu/documents /the-presidents-news-conference-with-prime-minister-tony-blair-the -united-kingdom-1.

"On the day that I was in": Hillary Clinton, "Remarks at Ohio State University in Columbus," transcript of speech, Columbus, OH, October 10, 2016, via American Presidency Project, https://www.presidency.ucsb .edu/documents/remarks-ohio-state-university-columbus.

"Here's my thing": Nia-Malika Henderson, "Obama to GOP: 'Bring It On,'" *Politico*, February 3, 2010, https://www.politico.com/story/2010/02 /obama-to-gop-bring-it-on-032426.

"If it's a positive compliment": Michelle Obama, "Interview with the First Lady and Barbara Walters on ABC's 'A Barbara Walters Special: A Thanksgiving Visit with President and Mrs. Obama,'" transcript of ABC News interview, Washington, DC, November 23, 2010, via American Presidency Project, https://www.presidency.ucsb.edu/documents/interview -with-the-first-lady-and-barbara-walters-abcs-barbara-walters-special.

a quick look at Google Ngrams: Google Books Ngram Viewer, s.v. "Bring It On," accessed June 3, 2022, https://books.google.com/ngrams /graph?content=%22bring+it+on%22.

Senate hopeful Roy Moore: Kate Feldman, "'Bring It On' Director Pushes Back at Roy Moore After Sexual Misconduct Allegations," *NY Daily News*, November 15, 2017, https://www.nydailynews.com/entertainment /movies/bring-director-pushes-back-roy-moore-article-1.3636151.

THE MUSICAL: SING IT ON

said that he was approached: *Bring It On: The Musical* team, interview with Patrick Hinds, in *Broadway Backstory* (podcast), November 7, 2017, https://broadwaybackstory.libsyn.com/episode-14-bring-it-on-the-musical.

"it was just sort of like": *Bring It On: The Musical* team, *Broadway Backstory*.

"Imitation is not the sincerest": Jonathan Handel, "Writers Guild Trying to Shut Down 'Bring It On: The Musical' (Exclusive)," *Hollywood Reporter*, August 15, 2011, https://www.hollywoodreporter.com/business/business-news/writers-guild-trying-shut-down-222926/.

"The goal for me": *Bring It On: The Musical* team, *Broadway Backstory*.

Jal Joshua would play the role: Logan Culwell-Block, "Trans Actor Jal Joshua Joins U.K. and Ireland Tour Cast of *Bring It On: The Musical*," *Playbill*, July 23, 2021, https://playbill.com/article/trans-actor-jal-joshua-joins-uk-and-ireland-tour-cast-of-bring-it-on-the-musical/.

"The cast of this alternately snarky": Charles Isherwood, "High School Rivalry, with a Leg Up," *New York Times*, August 1, 2012, https://www.nytimes.com/2012/08/02/theater/reviews/bring-it-on-the-musical-at-st-james-theater.html.

"pert and refreshing": Steven Suskin, *Bring It On: The Musical* review, *Variety*, August 1, 2012, https://variety.com/2012/legit/reviews/bring-it-on-the-musical-2-1117947983/.

"half a musical": Marc Snetiker, "Lin-Manuel Miranda's Best Lyric Wasn't in *Hamilton*," *Entertainment Weekly*, August 1, 2017 (page discontinued), via Wayback Machine, https://web.archive.org/web/20180720154849/http://ew.com/theater/2017/08/01/lin-manuel-miranda-hamilton-bring-it-on-musical/.

"I open the show": *Bring It On: The Musical* team, *Broadway Backstory*.

CHAPTER 14

DVDs were released in the US in 1997: Scott Kirsner, "How DVDs Became a Success," *Variety*, April 23, 2007, https://variety.com/2007/digital/features/how-dvds-became-a-success-1117963617/.

More titles became available: Kirsner, "How DVDs Became a Success."

PHOTO INSERT CREDITS

p. 1: Film strips and shoot schedule courtesy of Larry Bock

p. 2: Calendar and photo courtesy of Larry Bock

p. 3: Top photo by Shawn Maurer, courtesy of Peyton Reed; center photo courtesy of Nicole Bilderback; bottom photo courtesy of Huntley Ritter

p. 4: Top photo by *National Lampoon*; bottom photo courtesy of Nicole Bilderback

p. 5: Title list and top and center photos courtesy of Larry Bock; bottom photo by Shawn Maurer, courtesy of Peyton Reed

p. 6: Bottom photo by Shawn Maurer, courtesy of Peyton Reed

p. 7: Top photo courtesy of Peyton Reed; center and bottom photos by Shawn Maurer, courtesy of Peyton Reed

p. 8: Bottom photo courtesy of Nicole Bilderback

p. 10: One liner courtesy of Larry Bock; both photos by Shawn Maurer, courtesy of Peyton Reed

p. 11: Bottom photo by Shawn Maurer, courtesy of Peyton Reed

p. 12: Rental chart by the *Hollywood Reporter*; top photo by Shawn Maurer, courtesy of Peyton Reed; bottom photo courtesy of Peyton Reed

p. 13: Top photo by Jesse Bradford, courtesy of MTV News; center and bottom photos courtesy of Max Wong

p. 14: Box office charts courtesy of Larry Bock; top photo by Shawn Maurer, courtesy of Peyton Reed; bottom photo courtesy of Jessica Bendinger

p. 15: Home video charts by the *Hollywood Reporter*

p. 16: Wrap party flyer courtesy of Larry Bock